A Biography of Ordinary

François Laruelle

A Biography of Ordinary Man

On Authorities and Minorities

Translated by Jessie Hock and Alex Dubilet

polity

First published in French as *Une biographie de l'homme ordinaire. Des Autorités et des Minorités* © Flammarion, Paris, 1985

This English edition © Polity Press, 2018

Polity Press
65 Bridge Street
Cambridge CB2 1UR, UK

Polity Press
101 Station Landing
Suite 300
Medford, MA 02155, USA

ISBN-13: 978-1-5095-0995-9 (hardback)
ISBN-13: 978-1-5095-0996-6 (paperback)

A catalogue record for this book is available from the British Library.

Library of Congress Cataloging-in-Publication Data

Names: Laruelle, Francois, author.
Title: A biography of ordinary man : on authorities and minorities / Francois Laruelle.
Other titles: Biographie de l'homme ordinaire. English
Description: Malden, MA : Polity, 2017. | Includes bibliographical references and index.
Identifiers: LCCN 2017026398 (print) | LCCN 2017032929 (ebook) | ISBN 9781509509980 (Mobi) | ISBN 9781509509997 (Epub) | ISBN 9781509509959 (hardback) | ISBN 9781509509966 (pbk.)
Subjects: LCSH: Human beings. | Philosophy. | Pragmatism.
Classification: LCC BD450 (ebook) | LCC BD450 .L33413 2017 (print) | DDC 128--dc23
LC record available at https://lccn.loc.gov/2017026398

Typeset in 10.5 on 12 pt Sabon by Servis Filmsetting Ltd, Stockport, Cheshire
Printed and bound in the United Kingdom by Clays Ltd, St Ives PLC

The publisher has used its best endeavors to ensure that the URLs for external websites referred to in this book are correct and active at the time of going to press. However, the publisher has no responsibility for the websites and can make no guarantee that a site will remain live or that the content is or will remain appropriate.

Every effort has been made to trace all copyright holders, but if any have been inadvertently overlooked the publisher will be pleased to include any necessary credits in any subsequent reprint or edition.

For further information on Polity, visit our website: politybooks.com

CONTENTS[1]

[1] *(For a full analytical table of contents, see pp. 229–36.)*

CHAPTER III Ordinary Mysticism

CHAPTER IV Ordinary Pragmatics

TRANSLATORS' INTRODUCTION

At present, there are a number of sophisticated theoretical introductions to the works of François Laruelle available in English, so here we will limit ourselves to questions of translation.[1]

In the French original, three of the text's key terms are brought into even closer dialogue by their parallel, rhyming forms: *mystique*, *pragmatique*, *topique*. Unfortunately, the structure of English means we have not been able to preserve these echoes consistently. When *mystique* is an adjective we have rendered it as "mystical," when it is the noun *le mystique* as "the mystical," and when it is the noun *la mystique* as "mysticism." When *pragmatique* is an adjective, it is "pragmatic," when it is the noun *le pragmatique*, "the pragmatic," and when the noun *la pragmatique*, "pragmatics." When *topique* is an adjective, we have rendered it as "topical," when the noun *le topique*, "the topic" and when the noun *la topique*, "topics." What is thereby obscured in English is the parallelism between *la pragmatique* (pragmatics) and *la topique* (topics), on the one hand, and *la mystique* (mysticism), on the other. Although others have translated *la mystique* as "mystics" (in the works of Michel de Certeau, for example), "mysticism" remains closer to the meaning that *la mystique* normally carries in French. For example, *la mystique rhénane*, the thirteenth and fourteenth-century mystical movement that includes Meister Eckhart, Henry Suso, and Johannes Tauler, among others, is usually referred to in English as "German Mysticism." The one time in the text that Laruelle uses the term *mysticisme* it is polemical, along the

[1] See especially Anthony Paul Smith, *Laruelle: A Stranger Thought* (Cambridge: Polity, 2016); John Ó Maoilearca, *All Thoughts Are Equal: Laruelle and Nonhuman Philosophy* (Minneapolis: University of Minnesota, 2015); Alexander R. Galloway, *Laruelle: Against the Digital* (Minneapolis: University of Minnesota, 2014).

lines of the term "obscurantism"; we have made this different usage clear in the text.

In another case, the differences between French and English grammar and the precision of Laruelle's terms have forced us to stretch English conventions. Laruelle uses three different French terms – *individu*, *individuel(le)*, and *individual(le)* – for which the English "individual" is the appropriate translation. However, because each of the three terms does different theoretical work, we have found it necessary to distinguish between them in our translation, in one case using a neologism that echoes Laruelle's French and evokes what we take to be his debt to Heideggerian terminology. Our terms are as follows: First, we translate the standard French noun for "individual," *individu*, as "individual." Second, we translate the standard French adjective for "individual," *individuel(le)*, as "individuel," preserving the –el of the French. Third, Laruelle coins the peculiar adjective *individual(le)*, a term we suspect is modeled after Heidegger's distinction between *existenziell* and *existenzial*. Like the noun *individu*, we translate this form as "individual." Context will make clear which is the noun and which the adjective. Of primary importance for the reader is the fact that the awkward English "individuel" is in fact a translation of the common French adjective *individuel(le)*, whereas the deceptively familiar adjective "individual" translates the neologism *individual(le)*. This counter-intuitive distribution of familiar and unfamiliar is necessitated, at least in part, by the stress Laruelle puts on the "a" in individuality when he writes it as *individu-a-lity*. Moreover, by translating Laruelle's term *individual(le)* as "individual," we avoid what Laruelle himself is trying to avoid, namely, leaving the *duel*, or "duel" – the contest between two adversaries so central to philosophy – in the individual.

Laruelle's particular use in French – and thus our distinctive translations in English – of a group of terms related to thought and reflection also deserve explanation. While *irréfléchi* has a standard meaning of "thoughtless" or "unconsidered," we have rendered it as "unreflective" so as to capture the critique of the specular found throughout the text, and also to retain some of the strangeness of Laruelle's usage. Whenever "unthought" appears it translates *impensé(e)*, while *réfléchi* usually becomes "reflected" or "reflective" rather than its more common definitions.

A number of terms that are likely to stand out to the reader are indebted to Heideggerian thought and the way it has been translated from German into both French and English. Indeed, translating this book has made us realize that the responsible translator of contemporary French philosophy really ought to have read at least Heidegger and Kant in French translation. We outline some of the most important Heideggerianisms here so that the reader understands their philosophical baggage.

- Although the standard meaning of the French *éloignement* is "remoteness," when Laruelle uses the hyphenated term *é-loigne-ment* he is referencing a Heideggerian terminology that has its own highly particular meaning and translation history: *é-loignement* is the standard French translation of Heidegger's *Ent-fernung* (§23 of *Being and Time*) which we have, following Joan Stambaugh's English translation of the same text, rendered as "de-distancing." For the same reasons, we translate *é-loigné* as "de-distanced."
- Laruelle draws a distinction between things *comme tel* and *tel quel*. The former is the standard French translation of Heidegger's *als solche*, which is usually given in English as "as such." (For example, Chapter V of Division I of *Being and Time*, "Das In-Sein als solches," is translated into English by Stambaugh as "Being-in As Such," and by Emmanuel Martineau into French as "L'Être-À Comme Tel".) We have respected this, rendering *comme tel* as "as such," in contrast to *tel quel* and its variants, which we translate as "as it is" ("as they are," "as he is," etc.). A similar term, which appears less frequently in the text, *en tant que tel,* we translate as "as is."
- We have rendered *originaire* as originary, but it should be noted that in Martineau's translation of Heidegger, *originaire* often translates *ursprünglich*, which is usually given in English translations of Heidegger as "primordial."
- The French *sens* can be translated into English as both "sense" and "meaning." Thus, for example, the phrase *logique du sens* is most commonly known to English audiences as the title of Deleuze's *The Logic of Sense*, while *le sens de l'être* is the standard translation of Heidegger's *Sinn von Sein*, which in English is usually rendered as "meaning of being." (Both of these are obliquely referenced in the exposition of Theorem 113 below.) Unfortunately, in English there is no way to capture in one word the divergent denotations "sense" and "meaning," so we have rendered *sens* as "sense" when it is used in colloquial expressions ("in the sense that," etc.), but when *sens* is used technically (as in Chapter IV) we translate it as "meaning."

As is clear from the mention of Deleuze in the final bullet point, Laruellian terms are also frequently related to the terminology of

French thinkers. While "Other" is almost always a rendering of the French *Autre*, the several times *Autrui* ("other person" or "other people") appears in the French original it is either in implicit or explicit reference to Levinas's ethical thought. When necessary, we have drawn attention to the distinction between *Autre* and *Autrui*. And for the verb *survoler*, which has the standard meanings of "to fly over" and "to skim through," we have followed the precedent of other translators (for example Hugh Tomlinson and Graham Burchell's in their translation of Deleuze and Guattari's *What is Philosophy?*) and rendered it as "survey" throughout. The other meanings of the term should, however, be kept in mind. More generally, we have translated the prefix *sur-*, which appears throughout the text, sometimes as "sur-" and sometimes as "over-," depending on readability.

A few final translation decisions should be noted: We have rendered *scission* throughout as scission for consistency, but readers should keep in mind the more common meanings "division," "separation," "split." We have rendered *occidental(e)* as "western," but compounds such as *gréco-occidental* have retained their original inflection and have become "Greco-occidental." Additionally, we have rendered the French *mixte* in two different ways: in the adjectival form as "mixed" and in the substantive form (*le mixte*) as "mixture" rather than as "the mixed," for readability. Finally, readers will encounter both "apriori" and "a priori" in the text. Both forms appear in the French original, and while their usage is not consistent throughout, it is clear that *apriori* functions predominantly as a noun and *a priori* as an adjective or adverb. In our translation, we have altered spellings when needed to regularize the pattern.

After this lengthy explanation of complex terminology, we offer one very simple word to those who helped us with this translation: thanks. Daniel Hoffmann, Anthony Paul Smith, Andrea Gadberry, Sanders Creasy, Dario Rudy, Kelsey Lepperd, and Ben Tran all generously shared their time and expertise with us as we translated. Their help was invaluable.

FOREWORD

This book attempts a systematic foundation for a discipline that has, needless to say, already been signaled and hinted at in the history of thought: a rigorous science of man, but one different – this is its interest and its risk – from both Philosophy and the "Sciences of Man," which derive from it. It is also a sort of manual or compendium of arguments for this discipline, whose principal domains and essential modes of description it will strive to cover, at times too briefly. It can be read in two ways: either following only the series of its "theorems," or following also the explications or the commentaries that accompany each of them. Either way, its reading should be "linear" and follow the order of the parts as well as the order of the theorems in each part. We could not avoid certain preemptions intended to give a view of the whole and demonstrate, as it is said nowadays, the "stakes" of the project, but they do not undermine the necessary order of experiences, described here as those of the life of every man.

From this point of view, this essay, unlike *The Minority Principle* by the same author, finally unfolds in the rigorous order required by the transcendental science of individuals as such. *The Minority Principle* is a transitional book, a mixed attempt in the sprit of traditional philosophy to break with that philosophy, and in particular with the author's earlier books. That book was a "breakthrough" that still proceeded pedagogically and philosophically, that is to say, by means of transcendence, starting from philosophical problematics (Kant, Husserl, Nietzsche, Contemporary Thinkers) towards a thought of the One or of individuals. The current attempt, by contrast, abandons this process and begins with the One or Minorities and draws its conclusions from them. It systematically describes the essence of the domain that still remained something of a promised land or a distant reality in the previous work. Finally, it attempts to reconcile a certain theoretical rigor, which is absent, for reasons that will be explained, from even the most rationalist forms of philosophy with a certain love of human truth that is no less absent from philosophy. The wager is obviously that the two absences share a reason. This reconciliation is a thought that will appear difficult to those who separate theory and affect into two different worlds.

The flaws inherent in this sort of enterprise are, regrettably, well known, and it is pointless to pretend to lament them. Naivety and naive statements, empty agendas, aggressive declarations, successive refusals designed to cordon off a territory, the deliberate omission of all citations, or putatively idle discussions, etc., not to mention what contemporary thinkers suspect to be the unconscious of a work, a suspicion that is treated here as merely a cunning joy that has nothing to do with the seriousness of the project: there is "much to critique" in this, but hopefully it does not mask the *reality* of the enterprise. By contrast, perhaps offense will be taken at the anti-philosophical vivacity of this wager, behind which will be imagined to be some disappointed passion or institutional disgrace. It will be said that this in fact is the human, the all-too-human, side of the researcher. Perhaps a certain Cartesian deception will also be memorable enough that the intimacy of the drama will be respected rather than overcome by either the weapons of philosophy or those of the institution.

INTRODUCTION

A RIGOROUS SCIENCE OF MAN

1. From the Sciences of Man to the Science of People

It is reasonable to revolt against philosophers. But why? Is revolt its own reason, one more reason? But is it not philosophers who, dispensing reason, and particularly reasons for revolt, dispense with revolt? Is it not time to finally stop revolting and to base existence in a strong but tolerant indifference to philosophy? "Ordinary man," the finite individual whom we also call *Minorities*, is located in this indifference, which he draws from himself rather than from philosophy. We present here five "theses," really five "theorems" – human theorems:

1. Man really exists and he is really distinct from the World: this thesis contradicts almost all of philosophy;
2. Man is a mystical living being [*un vivant mystique*] condemned to action, a contemplative being doomed to practice, though he does not know why this is the case;
3. As a practical living being, man is condemned a second time, and for the same reasons, to philosophy;
4. This double condemnation organizes his destiny, and this destiny is called "World," "History," "Language," "Sexuality," "Power," which we refer to as *Authorities* in general;
5. A rigorous science of ordinary man, that is, of man, is possible: a biography of the individual as Minorities and as Authorities; a theoretically justified description of the life he leads between these two poles, which are sufficient to define him.

1

Such a description is the objective of this treatise. The description may be facilitated but not replaced by the sketch, by way of an introduction, of the most general program of a *rigorous science of man* intended to replace philosophy and its avatars, the "Sciences of Man." A *transcendental science*, which is to say a non-empirical science, but also not a "philosophical" one. . .

In the form in which they exist and triumph, the Sciences of Man are not sciences and have nothing to do with man – for the same reason. In question here is not their conflict with philosophy or the fact that they lack precise empirical procedures – two debates we will not enter. Instead, we attack the globally non-scientific character of these second-hand sciences, which do not form *a* science, and the complementary fact that they do not relate to any real object. This is not the same old fight: defending philosophy against the human sciences. Should the father be defended against his children or should he be left to die? Instead, we defend man against this authoritarian family in league against him, and attempt to constitute him (and this is not at all contradictory) as an object of a rigorous science.

Man has never been the object of the Sciences of Man. He does not recognize himself in this authoritarian and all-consuming activity, and for their part, the Sciences of Man are concerned with something other than man. The Sciences of Man combine the plural and the singular in a strange way: we have to understand, on the one hand, that man, in himself and inexhaustible, exists, man whom multiple sciences, powerless and unreal, attempt to circumscribe; on the other hand, that man does not really exist, that only sciences or methods exist, that play of universal predicates whose accumulation is expected to coincide with the essence of man. But this essence hides and flees like infinity. This indeterminate being, vanishing under the growing weight of universal determinations, which are used to exhaust him in the frustrated hope of "fixing" him, is what we are asked to consider as "man." But man is definitively absent from the gathering of the Sciences of Man because he is first of all absent from the gathering of philosophy. In both scenarios, one of the terms, science or man, must be unreal so that the other is real.

Perhaps the arrangement should be inverted: if science is to cease to be a techno-political fantasy and become a real science, it must be unique and specific; and it is man who must be irreducible in his multiplicity if he is no longer to be this anthropological fetish, this spineless phantom that is nothing but a shadow of the Sciences of Man, that is, of the sun and Reason mutually obstructing each other.

A double poverty of the Sciences of Man: as concerns "science," they admit either to an indeterminate plurality or else to the mineral unity of a nebula. Either way, they reveal that they are nothing but an artifact, the foam that the wave of other sciences left on the *terra incognita* of man.

Even combined, they still do not form a science, with an object and autonomous and theoretically justified methods. For now, these are merely imaginary phenomena deriving from the intersection of other disciplines – a theoretical *ersatz* or a "science" of synthesis. We do not recognize them according to their own existence, because it is a simple, blurred institutional network, nourished by its own plasticity, surviving only from compromise. Having not yet found their foundation or essence, they settle for being the caricature of contemporary philosophical powerlessness and nihilism: playing with the most diverse theoretical processes by targeting a fantastical and mythical figure of man, with no necessity other than the context.

Every science that comes into being strains to capture all of reality, and is animated by the old mytho-philosophical ambition of identifying the Whole with the real, Totality with the absolute. Like the others, the most recent – ethnology, linguistics, biology, and the science of history (in the Marxist sense) – do not emerge without attempting to moor man, considered as a remainder, to their continent or their raft. A series of deferred actions or anthropological artifacts results from this, and each time man is declared fully accounted for. But all these universals, even gathered together by the State in the nebula of the Social Sciences, do not in the least form a beginning for a specific science of man distinct from the science of the *historical* man, of the *speaking* man, of the *social* man, of the *psychic* man, etc. These are fake sciences of man, just like there are fake chemical or life sciences, but they have succeeded in establishing themselves and prospering because of flagrant opportunism. They lack both specific theoretical foundations – distinct from those that apply to the sciences of the living being, the historical being, the speaking being, the sexuated being, etc. – and a sufficiently determined experience of their object.

A genealogy of the Sciences of Man would show that they stem from the same archaic, metaphysical presuppositions as *rational psychology*, from which the *cogito* has not been eradicated: ontological presuppositions in general (simplicity, atomicity, substantiality, causality, etc., which are simply pluralized), combined with others that are necessary for their mathematization. Smatterings of ancient philosophy, of politics, of "rational" psychology and sociology are externally re-united by the process and security of a cheap mathematization. This generalized intersection creates the techno-political

3

wealth, that is to say, the real vacuity of this bric-a-brac, equally devoid of theoretical rigor and humanity, and for the same reasons. Because the essence of the science of man remains unthought, its rigorous phenomenal content having been forgotten, it is reconstructed from practical and theoretical elements, which are effective elsewhere but here are taken without necessity, under the sole arbitrary authority of the psychologist, the political scientist, the sociologist, the historian, etc. There is still no necessary connection between the sciences of man and their object, no theoretical foundation to assure this connection and render it necessary.

How to set up a rigorous science of man, established in the rigor specific to theory as such, that is, in the experience of the full and phenomenally positive sense of *Theoria*? A science that would no longer borrow its means of investigation, demonstration, and validation from existing sciences? It must be based in the specific essence of its object, in the truth of its object: the discovery of the science of man and the discovery of the real essence of man are the same thing.

As concerns "man," the concept these sciences have of him is doubly indeterminate. Initially, "man" is a concept indeterminate in its origin and in the Greco-unitary philosophical presuppositions that serve as its foundation. His essence – whether despite or because of the *cogito* and *rational psychology*, but since long before them – has not been clarified as a matter of principle. One cannot take the anthropological forms of philosophy for a science or a rigorous theory of man, because anthropology is only a phantasmatic projection of Greco-Christian ontological prejudices onto real man. Man has never been the real object of philosophy, which dreams and thinks of something else, of Being for example, and as a result hallucinates the individual. As a matter of principle to which we will return, Greco-ontological thought, with the related, bastard sciences that make up its entourage like so many shameful cadavers, was never able to radically determine any object whatsoever or test what the finite individual is. It is not only the *cogito*, the foundational text of its psychology and anthropology, that it leaves indeterminate in its meaning and truth, but also – and more profoundly – *the non-anthropological essence of man*. Precisely because it can be an anthropology, philosophy such as it is does not know man. Philosophy knows the inhuman, the sub-human, the all-too-human, the over-human, but philosophy does not know the human. It only knows man by encircling him in prefixes or quotation marks, in precautions or relations (with itself, with others, with the World): never as a "term." This is because it conflates ordinary man with any given man, with the universal individual whose

4

guiding pattern and excellent essence is the philosopher, the human par excellence in speech, in knowledge, in acting. Philosophy identifies man with generalities or attributes, with a knowledge, an activity, a race, a desire, an existence, a writing, a society, a language, a sex, and it is once again the philosopher who comes to the fore under the guise of these generalities, the philosopher who requisitions man for his own goals and his own values, which are very specific and need the cover of the universal. The essence of the individual has remained unthought by philosophy, which merely *posits* it and puts forward a possible presumed-man, while denying the conditions of his real experience through the multiplicity of authoritarian universals that it uses to filter him. Man remains indeterminate a second time, because the Sciences of Man, unable to reach the height of traditional philosophy, only bring out its originary *theoretical carelessness* and that with which in reality it is interconnected: its lack of humanity.

The *cogito* as well all the other unitary figures of the subject and of man remain unclarified in their essence because they are all, without exception, based in *anthropo-logical parallelism*, in the more or less distorted but never invalidated mixture or parallelity of man and logos, in this ruined cradle of the Sciences of Man that is anthropological philosophical difference.

Beginning with man and drawing conclusions from him about the State, about Power, about Language – about the World? Anthropological difference prohibits beginning with man and his solitude. Anthropo-logical difference begins from a mixture or a universal: man as language, as desire, as society, as power, as sex, etc. It cannot be satisfied with ordinary man: it does not even see him. Thus, man will already be doubled, both exceeded and devalued by these philosophical puppets: the gregarious, the common, the everyday, the exoteric, the healthy understanding, or the communal consciousness; and by their symmetrical or complementary elements: the overman, the philosopher, the authentic man, the reflexive subject, Spirit, etc. More generally, anthropo-logical difference is the scission of the indivisible essence of man; it separates or thinks it separates what man is capable of. Without a doubt, it is a hallucination that affects unitary thought – that is, the essential part of the Greco-occidental tradition – more than the essence of man. But it explains why philosophy has not known man and has given rise only to a mere anthropology. In place of man, of his real and absolutely singular essence, it employs anthropological, even andrological, images, quasi-transcendental androids (the Cogito, ens creatum, Spirit, the I think, the Worker, the Unconscious, etc.). These are fictional beings responsible for populating the desert

5

of anthropological screens, shadows projected on the steep walls of Ideas, inhabitants of ideal caves.

In this way, anthropo-logical difference is the positing and the forgetting of the real or "finite" essence of man. It is identical to its own history, an auto-destruction or auto-inhibition of the mixture of man *and* logos. It is more profound than the "humanism" attacked by contemporary philosophy, restricting and drawing closer to the target so as to be all the more certain of reaching it. It reigns even in unitary deconstructions of humanism. From now on, it is at issue as difference, and not as it speaks of man. Anthropo-logy as parallelism or as difference (the slight distinction no longer matters here) is *the* Greco-unitary myth that must be excluded by a theoretically justified science of man, but on the following three conditions: that this exclusion be not the cause but rather the effect of this science of man and of its positive essence; that this essence not take the vacant place of unitary anthropology, but on the contrary that it be the instance capable of radically determining it; finally, that the rigorously described phenomenal content of man be at once and *in an original identity – to whose non circular essence we will return* – the principal "object" and the unique "subject" of this science.

The human insufficiency of the Sciences of Man is a theoretical insufficiency. We have spoken, against common sense, about the theoretical carelessness of philosophy. The deficit in *theoria* is not actually specific to these weak and inconsistent sciences. It comes first of all from Greek ontological prejudices, which prohibited the simultaneous unfolding of the essence of theory and the essence of man, and which produced a mere counter-mythology or a counter-sophistry, "philosophy," instead of a phenomenally rigorous and positive science of man. Furthermore, in its prudence, it established an "anthropology," which became, under the assumed name of "Sciences of Man," a zone for cutting-edge activities.

Is it still a question of a final philosophical gesture? Or does this radicality no longer belong to the order of philosophy? It is at least necessary here to make a tabula rasa of the unitary prejudices of the Sciences of Man in order to be able to establish the rigorous science that philosophy will have failed to be.

2. Man as Finite or Ordinary Individual

It is no more a question of reviving the interminable combat between philosophy and the Sciences of Man than it is of making man "exit"

6

from the enclosure they form together through their very conflict. It is rather a question of showing that man never entered this enclosure, that this conflict is none of his business, save through a unitary hallucination whose mechanism will have to be analyzed; that he is determined and completed straightaway and absolutely precedes the phantasms of anthropo-logical parallelism. If philosophy is an anthropo- or an andro- eidetic, we must systematically contrast what we call "ordinary man," who draws an inalienable essence from himself (which above all does not mean that he is a *causa sui*), to the philosophical android or anthropoid, that is to say, to *homo ex machina*, a part of the philosophical machine, a part of Being, of Desire, of the State, of Language, etc. *Man, through his real essence, is not visible within the horizon of these presuppositions, which are those of the Sciences of Man as well.* Anthropology simulates him, magically gives rise to him – it is not yet the science of man; anthropological difference is not man – it is his transcendent avatar in the World. If the essence of man is not a *difference*, something like an *undecidable decision*, it is the radical subject of an ordeal that, far from alienating him, is finite, or holds him in himself and prevents him from ever leaving himself. Ordinary man is inalienable, and this distinguishes him from his projections on the anthropo-logical screen, which are inconsistent, un-real, and doomed to history.

Man is the real object of a science as soon as he is recognized in his specificity, irreducible to the objects of other sciences, and in his reality rather than in the mere possibility of his "figures." This is a single twofold requirement, which can be nuanced later, though it does not suffer from this in its principles and its foundations are undivided. Each science has its own way of sending the old unitary ideal of totality into retreat, and the rigorous science of individuals has its own: it requires, in an ultimately radical way, that the Whole and its modes, the universal or authoritarian predicates, not be "all," that man be straightaway outside-whole or that he introduce into the World, or rather outside of the World, a duality of which the World, the Whole, and their attributes are only one of the sides. For the science of man to become a reality, man must stop being unitarily enclosed in totalities or unities, and the real relations among the sciences must cease to be confused with Greco-philosophical forms of unity, which are utterly mythological. To see the reality rather than the mere possibility of man, it is necessary to abandon the unitary or Greco-occidental paradigm, which pervades almost all of philosophy up to its contemporary deconstructions, along with all of its prejudices. Man is not and has never been an object visible in

7

the Greco-unitary horizon, even in the anthropological territory of this horizon. It is useless to renew or deconstruct metaphysics. What is necessary is to change the paradigm of thinking; to move from a philosophical paradigm (from Being to Difference, from the Same to the Other) to a paradigm we call *minoritarian* or *individual,* which is based on *a transcendental but finite experience of the One as distinct from Being, the World, and their attributes.* The distinction of the individuel and the individual is the foundation of a non-empirical (non-worldly, non-historical, non-linguistic, non-sexual, etc.) but transcendental science of individuals or of ordinary man.[1] Whereas the individuel is always also universal, the individual [*l'individual*] is the individual [*l'individu*] without remainder or excess, the nothing-but-individual who a priori precedes all forms of universality. The individual problematic is thus based in a thought of the One rather than a thought of Being. Being, but also Difference and the games of the Same and the Other, are always unitary and, in addition to their own difficulties, are incapable of doing man justice. Instead of rendering him visible, they are satisfied with the substitute of an anthropology or – which is not all that different – of a unitary critique of anthropology.

We propose to break the alliance of man and the authoritarian predicates (Desire, Language, Sex, Power, the State, History, etc.) that lead to sciences that are not those of man, to break the alliance of man and philosopher, master of predicates. The hypothesis and even the paradigm must be changed: break the mixtures, base philosophy on man rather than the inverse; attempt a history of the human existent that would no longer owe anything to unitary prejudices; a biography of the solitary man, bachelor of the World, of Faith, of Technics, of Language, and even of Philosophy.

But this man, it will be objected, does he exist? Does he exist in any form that is not residual and epiphenomenal? *Is there a proper and primitive essence of man, one that would not be an attribute of something else?* The human in man is not reducible to the sum of his predicates: the living, the speaking, the acting, the historical, the sexuated, the economic, the juridical, etc. – the philosophizing, however these predicates are calculated. This is possible man, not real man. Real man is subject, nothing-but-subject. But the subject here also is not a special predicate; it is a subject that has never been a predicate and that no longer needs predicates in general, that is straightaway inherent (to) itself or a sufficiently determined essence. The essence of man remains in the One, that is, in the inherence that is non-positional (of) itself, in a nothing-but-subject or an absolute-as-subject, that

8

is, a *finitude*. As a matter of principle, which will be explained later, we identify the absolute with finitude rather than with an infinite totality. Individuals are "real" prior to totality; they are not modes of a substance and they are not even understandable starting from infinite and universal attributes (Language, Life, History, Sexuality, Economy, etc.). It is useless to wonder if these predicates are included analytically or synthetically in the subject "man," or if "man" is the difference of himself and language (anthropo-linguistic/logical difference), of himself and sexuality, etc. As we understand it, man is "ordinary" in a positive sense: he is not a residual and shifting figure of philosophy or of the Greek episteme, but rather is determined before these and absolutely precedes the philosophical calculation of predicates inasmuch as they are taken one by one.

Ordinary man is devoid of qualities or attributes through a completely positive sufficiency. He lacks nothing, not even philosophy. But being devoid of predicates does not mean that he is devoid of essence: to the contrary, this is man as he takes his essence from himself, or more precisely, immediately from his essence, without it having been an attribute beforehand. He does not take his essence from History, from Biology, from the State, from Philosophy. There is no pejorative or minorative note in this "ordinary" or this "minoritarian." I am a sufficient Solitude, too far below "solipsism" to have to extricate myself from it. I am not a Cogito, a relation to a Site or to an Other. I am out-(of)-the-question: no question of man, no ontic or ontological primacy of the question of man. I do not find my essence in my existence or in my questions; I experience my subjective essence before these questions. I am the beginning of my life and my thought. And if in this way I exclude the question and the mise en abyme from my essence, that is because my essence (and essence in general) is defined by characteristics that are absolutely original, primitive, internal, and without equivalents in the World: through the One or the unreflective. There is a question (of) Being, but the One is out-(of)-the-question.

It is the structures of this ordinary man that we will describe here. Individual structures, invisible to the light of Reason or Intelligence. They are not ideal essences, but finite, inalienable, and thus indisputable, lived experiences. Individual structures of the essence of man are describable outside of all anthropological prejudice, that is, outside of all Greek philosophical rationality. Only these individual or finite determinations grant man something other than a mere possibility: a specific and determined reality. They render possible a science of his relations to the World, to History, to Language, relations that are not

9

at all those hallucinated by the Social Sciences. This is the meaning of this "biography of ordinary man": a rigorous description of the most general experiences that govern the relation of individuals as such to History, to the State, to Economy, to Language, etc.

The text of this science is thus no longer the *cogito* and its *membra disjecta*, which the Human Sciences divide among themselves. It is the irreducible individual kernel that must be extracted from the *cogito* in which it is still enclosed and concealed. But we no longer conceive of this extraction as a philosophical operation because it is actually an immediate given, which we here merely "render percepti- ble" [*"sensibiliser"*]. The foundation of a science of man entails first of all creating a non-philosophical affect: rendering perceptible the immediate givens, the non-hallucinatory reality, *the finite transcen- dental experience* in man; it requires taking this step, without which unitary anthropology will continue to enthrall us with its tricks. Though the immediate givens of man undoubtedly do not make up the entirety of his relations to his predicates and their unity, the World or Philosophy, they nevertheless are the rock that allows the scientific description of his relations. The immediate givens of man are first, but they do not of course exhaust this science of people and of their relations. The phenomenal givens of this science and its only text is the One: but precisely because it is the One, it is not unique. The One is not – above all is not – Unity or the Unitary Ideal that still reigns in the *cogito* and leaves its essence indeterminate. The complete text of the science of man is double or dual – *dual* rather than duel, just as it is individual rather than individuel: the One and the World, minorities and Authorities, individuals and History, the State, Language, etc.

This is not strictly speaking a *Humanity Principle* whose statue we would try to erect beside or beyond the Power Principle, the Language Principle, the Pleasure Principe . . . Under the name of ordinary man, we refrain from flattering the slaves of the Cave or, for example, pro- viding a defense of the sheep against the eagles. Instead, we describe a real essence of man *before* the animal difference of eagles and sheep, which the philosophers want us to believe belongs to man and to his becoming. And ordinary man is likewise not the antidote to "superior man," that is, to the overman; he is neither the hero of the future nor the latest archaeological find. Rather, it is against this heroic and agonistic conception of man passed down to us by the Greeks, which casts a new light under the names of difference, différance, and differ- end, that we attempt to make visible man without a face and without qualities. This is a treatise of the Solitudes.

3. From Philosophy to Theory: The Science of Ordinary Man

The science of real people is therefore no longer a philosophy or a mixture of anthropological prejudices and mathematization. It draws its essential characteristics from its object: it is itself "individual" and "minoritarian." It differs from a philosophy in several ways: it is a thought that is (1) rigorously naive rather than reflexive; (2) real or absolute rather than hypothetical; (3) in essence theoretical rather than practical or technical; (4) descriptive rather than constructive; (5) human rather than anthropological.

(1) It is not philosophy that must become a rigorous science: it cannot, its circular essence prevents it. By contrast, it is necessary to invent a rigorous non-empirical science, a theory that would precede philosophy and be its science. Becoming scientific is the essential predicate and telos of philosophy, but the science in question remains a mere philosophical predicate, an indeterminate project or a Greco-unitary fantasy. *It is necessary to think science straightaway from its own phenomenal requirements and to cease moving in the aporetic circle of philosophy, to which belongs, like an unresolved dream, the obligatory goal of a scientific exit from that circle.* Such an exit renews the aporia and gives it a higher form: yet a science does not generally become rigorous except by being deprived, for reasons of positive sufficiency, of the aporetic essence constitutive of unitary philosophizing. The essence of the science of the (empirical or individu-a-l) real is its non-circularity, its non-reflexivity, its naiveté. This principle of the sciences, which we will not specifically discuss here, but which is itself based in the One, is the *Principle of Real Immanence or Identity*, a principle unknown to philosophy, but which holds for the empirical and transcendental sciences.

On this common basis, the characteristics of the science of man are obviously not at all the same as those of the empirical sciences, in which philosophy sees – perhaps wrongly, for that matter – an inferior naiveté, a powerlessness, and a defect. Concerning man, the Principle of Real Identity must receive a transcendental specification. The science of individuals therefore possesses a transcendental – and no longer empirical – naiveté, which, without being "superior" to philosophy (nothing is superior to that which is the very spirit of superiority), is not accountable to it and determines it without reciprocity: the science of individuals suppresses the circle and no longer passes through a circular process of determination. This is because the setting-outside-the-circle of science in general ensues from the real itself, which has never been circular, above all in its essence, here given by individuals. This is not a disguised philosophical operation, but the experience of the positive phenomenal content of individuals or of ordinary man – the very foundation of this science. The science of the real (the real par excellence or the human real) is a non-positional science (of) the real. It is not constitutive of its object, but merges with the immanent, non-thetic, and finite experience it has of its object. It is, of course, a transcendental science, but one in which *empirico-transcendental parallelism* is definitively broken, as are all modes of difference, particularly anthropo-logical difference.

From this comes its ante-philosophical and completely positive naiveté, which is no longer philosophical because it is not merely ante-predicative or ante-reflexive. The real is not a presupposition of thought; at most, it is a presupposition *of* and *for* philosophy. By its very nature, it is already thought, but thought that is non-thetic (of) itself, that is unreflective or individual. Therefore, we lay claim to a *transcendental naiveté*, real but precisely not philosophical, at the foundation of the absolute science of man. An absolutely naive science, devoid of constitutive philosophical operations and whose naiveté can no longer be – like those of the empirical sciences – critiqued, reflected, overcome by philosophy and its Consciousness, deferred by philosophy and its Other, etc.

(2) It does not begin with the *cogito* – which has always been preceded by idealizing philosophical operations and has never been a real beginning – but with individuals as non-positional transcendental experiences (of) themselves. This is to say that finite individu-*a*-lity is likewise not a principle, always primary according to the *ratio essendi*, the *ratio cognoscendi*, or the unity of difference of the two. These are refined forms of the circle, and not yet the finite transcendental identity that is the essence of the real and that is no longer a concentrate, a condensation of the relative-absolute, logico-transcendental, circle of philosophy (thought *and* the real, being *and* thinking as the Same, etc.). Such a radically finite transcendental identity exists: man in his non-anthropological experience. This identity is neither logico-formal, nor logico-real – it is nothing-but-real, and not at all "logical" in the sense in which logos is always a circular relation to the real.

Here again, a science of people is completely different from a philosophy. Philosophy is a science of real possibility, not a science of reality *before* the possible. It is a transcendental logic, with some variations, not a transcendental reality: for fear of transcendental realism, which is essentially an absurdity, it confuses the real with either Logos or with the Other of logos. Philosophical magic denies the authentic real in the name of a fantastic image, sometimes ideal, sometimes empirical, of the real. Philosophy is not and has never been an absolute science: it is only a relative-absolute "science" with an irreducible hypothetical moment. In his own way, Nietzsche offers the key to philosophy: the real is an interpretation, interpretation is the real or represents the real for another interpretation. This is the absolute-idealist mixture of the real hypothesis or the real interpretation that the absolute science (of) the real excludes in order to move straightaway onto this anhypothetical terrain that philosophy has always viewed as a promised land.

(3) Greco-unitary philosophy is originally and essentially practical: it is an essentially superior praxis and/or techne. For three complementary reasons too lengthy to analyze here: it is a form of knowledge that does not have absolutely given objects, only *ob-jects*, which is to say *stakes*, or that has its own circularity for its ob-ject. Next, it is a knowledge whose essence is care, concern, or interest, rather than disinterested contemplation; finally, it is a mixed, logico-real knowledge that precludes itself from knowing the real as it is or in its "real identity" because it organizes the intervention of thought into the real to make the real occur.

As such, Greco-unitary philosophy lacks a rigorous theoretical foundation. It is not that it has too much theory – it does not have enough of it. It leaves *theoria* unelucidated in its essence. Of course, philosophy has theoretical aspects, but it includes *theoria* only as a predicate for activities, values, and goals that are mere socio-political or other prejudices and are not elaborated in their real phenomenal content. This makes philosophy an opportunistic and unrigorous activity, an antimythological strategy rather than a science. Philosophy does not have to "become" fully theoretical, that is, be suppressed and realized, but it must be de-rived or, as we will say, unilateralized as a secondary activity by theory unfolded in its essence. The theoretical can cease to be merely a predicate of praxis; it is this mixture that must be broken. Even in its Greek states, which seem to give primacy to the theoretical, to "contemplation" over action, the insertion of *theoria* into a structure of mixture is enough to subvert the irreversible, real order, which runs from the theoretical to the practical.

It goes without saying that these terms can no longer retain their common and/or philosophical meaning, otherwise such an order

13

would appear paradoxical, an idealist prejudice, or even the return to a Greek prejudice, a misunderstood one at that. Philosophy, let us repeat, has up until now always been a *praxis* with theoretical aspects, and not at all the experience of the real essence of *theoria*. How, then, to conceive of the latter?

Theoria ceases to be a universal predicate as soon as it is the essence of science, though an essence that itself has never been a predicate. Theory is a radical subject, an experience (of) inherence (to) itself and essentially individual. It ceases to be an attribute and a unitary goal as soon as it identifies itself with the individual, finite, or radical immanence of the subject; as soon as "contemplation" is its own essence (to) itself; or, as soon as it is inherent (to) itself, a rigorous transcendental – that is, non-thetic and finite – lived experience, *before* contemplating the World, Object, Unity, etc. This excludes the *self*-contemplation that is proper to Unity rather than to the One such as we understand it as "individual." This specifically excludes the *cogito* or the *transcendental ego*, which are nothing but transcendent modes of self-contemplation through the mediation of the World, precisely due to all the philosophical operations, praxis, or techne of doubt, of suspension, of the return to the foundation, etc. that they still circularly presuppose.

(4) Thus returned to its essence, real theory, undetermined by philosophical operations or prejudices, is *a non-positional contemplation (of) immediate givens or (of) unreflective transcendental experiences.* These are the material of this science, which describes the content of the finite phenomenal experience of man and his relations to the grand authoritarian attributes of History, Language, Power, etc., and to their totality, which is the World, without intervening in them. The theory of man is not a theoretical practice, an intervention into an object and a transformation of that object. It is rather – we will return to this – a non-positional but also non-deforming description (of) positions (philosophical for example, unitary in general): an immediate or unreflective description (of) the phenomenal experiences that are the real content of the life of man and his relations to the World. Passive thought, but not *before* an ob-ject (where passivity is the counterpart to a production), doubtless because rigorous science (in connection with the necessary destruction of the Copernican Revolution, we will suggest) is a thought devoid of *ob-jects* (but not of "contents" or of "objects" in the broad sense), a science that has no vis-à-vis, which does not mean that, in the idealist manner, it is devoid of reality or materials: it is content to describe strictly immanent phe-

14

nomenal experiences *before* (and outside of) all unitary-philosophical prejudice. In particular, outside of any phenomenological prejudice, it emphasizes phenomena as immediate givens rather than as still-transcendent intuitions. Finite thought gives up reflection, analysis, and construction, entrusting itself to the unreflective, to phenomenality devoid of phenomenological operations. Phenomenal givens are not remainders, they are that which is straightaway real and which thus possess the power not only to possibilize, but to really ground the latent phenomenology that is the essence of unitary thought.

This is why this treatise of ordinary man is made up of *theorems* that are transcendental and not empirical. These are less "the eyes of the soul," as Spinoza said of his own theorems, than the soul describing itself in its radical individual immanence. They merely describe phenomena lived by ordinary man, phenomena that are invisible to philosophy and its phenomenology as a matter of principle.

(5) Finally, unlike the Sciences of Man, which are only anthropological and usurp the title of "human," the transcendental science of individuals is "human" because of its very scientificity. The science of people must be written the science (of) people: they are its inalienable subject without any ob-ject. The theoretical and the human have always been opposed: but far from opposing their communal essence, we merely oppose prejudices that are transcendent and devoid of phenomenal rigor. In reality, man is the only living being there is that is nothing-but-theoretical, a mystical living being: the unreflective contemplation (of) himself is his essence, though not the entirety of his relations to the World. There is no theory but human theory, not in the anthropological but in the individual sense of these words.

4. The Scientific and Positive Meaning of Transcendental Naiveté

(1) Any comparison of one science to another, particularly of a science as peculiar as a transcendental science to the empirical sciences, is dangerous and rarely transcends metaphor. Nevertheless, we have seen that the one and the other have in common a pre-philosophical naiveté and a non-reflexivity, and that this feature, *if it is positive*, is in all likelihood essential to their definition of science. The transcendental theory of individuals has a second shared characteristic, this time with a particular empirical science, which, even if it is a mere metaphor, could give philosophers a better way into this project. It is

quantum mechanics, and its foundation in objects, let us say particles, which qualitatively and by definition escape from the earlier modes of visibility and objectivation specific to classical mechanics and thermodynamics. *At least from the standpoint of habits of thought* – if not from the standpoint of the type of rigor according to which we cannot claim to compare an empirical and a transcendental science, for reasons, moreover, that are not one-sided – the introduction of the individual conception of man supposes a qualitative leap in relation to unitary presuppositions, and cannot occur within the framework of existing philosophical conceptions being merely questioned, renovated, or deconstructed. It is also different from a "revolution of thought," because, as will be suggested here and there, it is the renunciation of all "revolutionary" ways of thinking. Undoubtedly, this requires psychic efforts that are different, and perhaps more difficult, than those required by a revolution.

Indeed, it is less a matter of questioning, fracturing, or displacing objectivating or metaphysical representation, than of *resolutely thinking outside of it, without ever giving oneself ob-jects, which does not mean that this thought would be empty and without "objects" – on the contrary.* But its objects are not ob-jects, that is, realities slightly affected by transcendence: these are individuals, defined by their transcendental immanence alone and by the experiences they have in their relations with the World or Authorities, which are themselves, moreover, also not ob-jects. Unlike unitary or authoritarian thought, individual or minoritarian thought moves in the utterly positive sphere, neglected by philosophy, of a radical invisible, perhaps of an "unconscious" (but which would be purely subjective, if we can say so), of an unconscious that would be nothing but subject without in addition being transcendent or ob-jective (linguistic, biological, etc.) and constituent of the subject.

This is a different paradigm, not a supplementary variation on the unitary paradigm. What we call the minoritarian paradigm entails the abandonment of Greek ontological habits and their deconstructions. It opens a field of realities that have been absolutely hidden since the origin of philosophy, concealed for reasons even more profound than the existence of Greek forms of philosophy, even if these forms have in the West almost completely killed the vague desires to shake off the yoke of unitary hallucinations. It is not at all a transcendental field of individuals that is proposed here, like a new transcendent hinterworld[2] of philosophy, but a dispersion of purely transcendental rather than transcendent individuals, whose essence, therefore, is to no longer obey the laws of-opening-and-ofclosing, the always unitary laws of a "field," of a "body," of a "continent," of an "epoch," of an "episteme," etc. From the perspective of theoretico-psychic habits, there are as many efforts to be made to penetrate the laws of these entities that are individual or outside-the-field = outside-Being, absolutely unnoticed by ontology, as there are to penetrate the domain of "particles."

(2) To identify and determine any object whatsoever, the unitary paradigm must resort to the variable and relative combination of two philosophical parameters: immanence and transcendence. Because they are relative to one another, they are each partially indeterminate and are only determined reciprocally. The space or field is called unitary because it is made of the circularity of these two dimensions, which are together necessary to identify any entity whatsoever. Now, let us suppose that entities exist that to be fully and sufficiently, if not completely, determined require no more than one of these parameters, the first. Minoritarian or individual thought is the experience of these entities that do not fall under the scope of the unitary field and are determinable not by that relative combination, but rather by a single dimension thought independently of its unity with the second; and only after, by a combination – but not reciprocal, not relative – of the two. These entities are not determinable in a unitary manner because they are already determined through themselves, or as terms prior to any relation or reciprocity. Finite individuals are real entities before they are magically captured by the unitary field. It is a question of thinking terms first in their finite transcendental identity, prior to any relation, then of describing what follows for their eventual relations with the unitary World. The relation of the two fundamental parameters changes completely, and perhaps here the comparison with quantum reality ends: it is no longer exactly a relation, that is, a reciprocity or a reversibility, or even a relativity. First, there is a primary immanence devoid of any transcendence and, if it is correctly understood, it is sufficient to determine finite individuals and to ground a science of individual entities. The parameter of transcendence only appears with the World or unitary thought, but itself ought to be elaborated according to the first. Unitary reality, which we call effectivity, thus ought to be rethought according to the individual or minoritarian real. From the first parameter to the second, there is no longer a unitary relativity/reciprocity, but a strict asymmetry, an irreversibility or an order in sharp contrast to the more or less decentered circles to which aporetic philosophizing is accustomed. Philosophy is relativist in the bad – Greek, sophistic, and empiricist – sense of the

word, but true relativity is based in an absolute and unsurpassable (finite) experience of individuals as finite.

We will thus not confuse minorities or individuals with the micro-political, the micro-psychological, the micro-sociological, the micro-sexual, etc. The micro is always molecular, not a true particulate; it remains in continuity with the quantitative, qualitative, or intensive scale of the macro-. It is not a question of suspending (phenomeno-logically, for example) the modes of unity that would hide an invisible world, giving it over to the light of reason or the philosophical day, but rather of dealing straightaway with the real in the strict sense as philosophically uncreated or non-constituted. This is a world that is immense as well as invisible, intangible, unobjectivable, but which is perfectly thinkable once it is thought and the unitary hallucination has been dispelled.

We describe here the immediate givens of the invisible. But the invisible is what is seen in the One; it is not the Other, even an Other or an Unconscious of our World. These givens are distinct from objectivated or empirical realities, and from the philosophical pro-cesses of their objectivation. *Objectivation thus can no longer serve to experimentally verify essentially transcendental theorems whose only pertinent criterion is the unreflective immanence of the One that serves as their common thread, that is, the descriptive fidelity to the real.* It is from or through these experiences that are non-positional (of) themselves that we contemplate and describe the aporias of lan-guage and philosophy, the agitation of the World, the benevolence and the barbarism of the State.

Understood correctly, these principles will perhaps allow us to denounce the so-called legitimacy of a question someone, unable to resist objecting, will not fail to pose. In the event that someone is searching here, in a traditional manner, for a new object, a political object for example, an extraordinary issue to defend, or the possibil-ity of a politics of minorities that ultimately would rest on principles, they will inevitably ask: well then, show us your minorities, give us examples or cases, stop talking about them abstractly. Is it a matter of a new interpretation of a political and juridical status of national, linguistic, cultural, sexual minorities – or else, if not, according to what conditions does one *become* a minoritarian or a "man" of the sort you claim to describe?

These questions have become so obvious to us that the response they receive here will seem rather casual. This essay is written to show that this sort of question has no bearing on a rigorous conception of the essence of minorities or individuals, in other words, that its relevance is only polito-logical or anthropo-logical, that it has its possibility in (polito-logical, etc.) Difference, which is the matrix of Greco-occidental or unitary thought. This sort of question must now be abandoned in order to reach a problematic of minorities and a science of man that would itself be minoritarian rather than an ultimate concession of the State or of Philosophy. The minorities in question do not receive a new political and juridical determination; they are not raised to the state of a stake in a new style of revolutionary practice. However, the pre-statist determination of their essence permits a rigorous critique of the political, the statist, or the anthropological, without overwhelmingly denying their order and their existence.

From this proceeds a thought without examples but not without precedents. There are no *examples* or *cases* of minorities described in this way. They are certainly the object of an experience, but one that will be defined as strictly transcendental and no longer as *simultaneously* empirical: they are thus not givens in a universal horizon of power and governmentality, of culture, of language, of sex, etc., nor are they, in the contemporary manner, modes of that horizon. Not only do they refuse for their part to enter under categories or into types, but they are that which enables the exclusion from thought of the descriptions and arguments of examples, cases, or facts, which are always interconnected with these great universals. They are par excellence the absolutely invisible of the State, of political or philosophical practice, of language, etc.; this is what grants them their own relevance and their capacity to resist these Authorities. If they become visible on the social, historical, or linguistic surface, they will once more become more or less constrained and integrated parts or members of the State. Finite minorities are the definitively invisible essence of Authorities, though denied as such by those Authorities. Destroying this denial by respecting the absolute invisibility and inaudibility of finite individuals entails the renunciation of rational philosophical demonstrations based on the primacy of Unity, Universality, Logos, Being, the State, History, etc., and the clarification of the immediate givens of the One. Generally speaking, *there is no minority question*: real minorities are absolutely silent in History and the World. That is why, ceasing once more to be a stake, they are the object of a science. Only for the State is there a minoritarian question, only for the World a question of individuals, only for those who ask how to tolerate them, to define their difference or margin, put otherwise and always: how to integrate them? Minorities become a problem or an issue for philosophers and intellectuals-of-the-State, who claim to determine their cultural and political, linguistic and sexual, specificity. It is a task by and for the

State, which can only work out a tautological, vicious, and already compromised concept when it makes them into a question. To put it rigorously and more succinctly: it is a question of breaking (with) the empirico-transcendental – we might say, stato-minoritarian – parallelism in the thought of minority; of preventing allegedly minoritarian cases, facts, or givens from coming to be reflected in their essence, from which they draw an existence and a reality that owes nothing, for example, to the universal horizon of the State and to the rules of governmentality that organize that field. In general, individual thought gives up concrete representations, representation in all its forms. It defines the essence of individual multiplicities in such a way as to exclude any figuration whatsoever – as though passing from a macroscopic, even molecular, sphere to a particulate sphere, where laws would be entirely different from the figurative laws of the first. The One is the criterion that enables a leap from the enclosure of representation once and for all and the abandonment of the aporetic knowledge of philosophy in order to establish a necessary science of man.

We will not believe that, because of this refusal of all empirico-ideal experience, minorities are a concept without reality, the object of only nominal definitions. They are true immediate givens, real essences lived in pre-political, pre-linguistic, etc., experiences. Their necessity, *provided we stand by it*, is shown to be the necessity of an ultimate and absolute requisite for the existence of Authorities themselves, and the necessity of the effects their conception produces on the State, on polito-logical, anthropo-logical, socio-logical, etc., Difference, that is, all the ancient Greco-occidental couplings that lose their validity and are no longer thinkable circularly and viciously starting from themselves, but only starting from individu-a-lity. But although the exploration of these effects confirms the reality of finite individuals, it does not demonstrate it. This essence of minority is positive, concrete, and open to a rigorous transcendental description, which involves notions whose content and organization are articulable and definable.

(3) Clearly, the realization of a theoretical science of man entails a complete shift not of the philosophical problematic, but of the paradigm of thought in general. It entails the end of describing, in the guise of phenomenal givens of man, modes of the *Philosophical Decision*, which are always mixed and circular operations or processes, and generally vicious; and it entails that we first confide in the real in its individu-*a*-lity, which philosophy cannot claim to still determine, save through a unitary illusion whose mechanism we will analyze.

However, a resolutely naive science is intolerable for unitary philo-centrism. But, it will be said, can philosophy be made into an abstraction in this way without manifesting a highly philosophical innocence? We precisely do not make an abstraction out of philosophy, because that would still be a final philosophical operation, a hopeless attempt at an "exit." We begin with the real, which does not need philosophy and determines philosophy without reciprocity by assigning it a place whose specificity we will soon see. The science of the real, that is, of individuals in their individu-a-lity and in its immediate givens, absolutely precedes philosophy and the Sciences of Man, that is, the unitary mytho-logical sphere, with a precedence without counter-part. All of these essences (the finite multitudes, and even the Philosophical Decision) are immediate givens and presume no passage of philosophy "to" the real, as one would pass to the Other, no transcendent and universal operation going to lose itself in exteriority. The unreflective real, in its *veritas transcendentalis*, is not a potentiality-for-being, a "real possibility," but an immediate givenness even more originary than the distinction between Being and being [*de l'Être et de l'étant*], being and the Other, Being and the Other, the Same and the Other, etc. The problem of knowing whether it is possible to "leap" out of philosophy (out of its discourse, out of reason, out of its texts, etc.) into the real is obviously a false problem, a unitary problem that is only relevant inside the dominant paradigm, which asserts itself through these sorts of intimidation effects.

The problem is not of knowing *whether* there are immediate givens. Immediate givens are transcendental, immanent, and prove their relevance from themselves. In any case, it is more scientific and less vicious to admit, or settle straightaway in, this sort of immediate givens than it is to transcendently posit, in the unitary style, rational *facts*, scientific, ethical, or aesthetic facts; or else semi-empirical and semi-transcendental facticities; or even the *Other*, transcendence par excellence, the immediate givenness of transcendence or of the Infinite. In all of these cases, the real is only tolerated, filtered, mastered by its falsifying blend with a form of possibility or transcendence; in extreme cases, it is even reduced to transcendence or to the Other. As though philosophy could "leap" over its shadow, its essence as mere possible, to "pose" – only to pose . . . – reality. The "ontological proof" was nuanced, differentiated, de-rationalized, softened, etc., but it has remained the heart and breath of contemporary philosophy: passing – it passes and does nothing but "pass" – from the possible, from the Other, from transcendence, to the real or to immanence, or to the mixture of the first group and the second group. Until now, philosophy was the under-taking of the real and the possible, their non-scientific confusion, the falsification of the nevertheless absolute essence of individuals.

The real is indeterminable philosophically and determinable through itself, a priori, before any philosophical intervention. Philocentrism responds that this is impossible, that philosophy is always necessary, when this would only be because one speaks of the "real," of the "apriori," of "singularity," etc., the entire *textuality* of philosophical discourse. We will respond by and large that this objection is not pertinent, demonstrative, or scientific because it is vicious, circular, and simply reproduces the requirements and pretensions of philocentrism, which has decidedly no reason to abandon its narcissism. Philocentrism turns its fact into law, adduces its de facto existence and its brutality to block any attempt that would radically limit it. This argument returns to say that philosophy is everything, or rather that the Whole is the absolute or the real: the mytho-logy par excellence of unitary philosophy. Here as well, philocentrism manipulates an argument that is a sort of displaced, expanded, and apparently reversed "ontological proof": it always infers essence from existence; or, more precisely, *from effectivity* (the World, Society, History) *or from the mixture of the real and the possible, it infers the true real, which is also essence . . .*; from predicates, it infers a subject-without-predicates; from Authorities, it infers minorities, etc. This is the vicious argument, the paralogism at the heart of unitary thought, which the individual experience of man, scientific in its own way, must reject as a superior form of mythology.

The transcendental naiveté we invoked is an aprioristic indifference to the philosophical such as it exists; it renders all philosophies contingent. But absolute science or the real is such that indifference or non-participation in philosophy do not belong to its essence, do not define it, but ensue immediately from it. Indifference to philosophy, no doubt, but this is no longer the indifference that philosophy secretes towards itself; that of skepticism from too much dogmatism; that of the Other = real (nihilism, then counter-nihilism); that of the Other as Other-than-real (contemporary deconstructions), etc. A priori indifference, whose precedence over that which it indifferences would be absolute and without reciprocity and would finally allow the dissipation of the unitary magic that is Greek philosophy – and the Other . . .

5. Towards a Critique of (Political, etc.) Reason

(1) The scientific biography of ordinary man is the true critique of Reason, political or other (polito-logical, socio-logical, psycho-

logical, etc.) A non-circular, non-vicious critique: not an auto-critique of Reason across its diverse modalities, nor even a hetero-critique by man assumed to be the Other of Reason . . . Ordinary man is neither in Being, nor in Difference or the Same, nor in the Other: he is the essence that determines rational Authorities in the last instance, and who conducts a critique of these Authorities that is at once immanent and radically irreversible. The authoritarian essence of Reason is difference – polito-logical, socio-logical, anthropo-logical, etc. – and it must be irreversibly derived from this foundation of ordinary man, which it will have scorned and hidden under a growing heap of universal determinations.

This ordinary man exists from his finite essence alone; it is a Solitude that enjoys an absolute precedence over the authoritarian continua: ethnological, sociological, techno-political, linguistic, sexual, etc., which are constituted little by little and intersect on the unlimited surface of the World. The emergence of new social logics, new technological logics, new sexual or political logics, etc., beyond the old authoritarian stock, passes for the major event of our time: but these do not destroy the unitary essence, which remains, even if it is in the plural and according to an experimental mode, precisely that of logics. Ordinary man is not the ultimate product of these recent social or technological practices. Rather, he is the requisite, or even something other than a mere requisite: the real that they hallucinate with a view to inserting it into their unitary schemas. Individuals who are finite or without qualities, they are straightaway the actual critique of these social, psychological, or political practices of an authoritarian style that cannot but deny the individual structures specific to the human existent, and through which alone it is the object of an original science.

(2) If, taking a special case from the Sciences of Man and of Society, we attempted to give a political version – or rather, a *political simulation* – of this minoritarian program, we would say this: in the case of minorities and their relation to the State, this essay develops a thought that touches on the essence of the political (and of the State, of course) that can no longer be called a "political philosophy." This is because its point of view on the State, powers, and minorities itself ceases to be statist, as it is traditionally in this sort of philosophy, with slight variations. Instead, it becomes purely minoritarian, merging with the gaze minorities themselves can cast on the State. From this standpoint, we could pursue two goals: giving a new definition of the State according to individual structures; defining in general a minoritarian

23

line of resistance to the State that would no longer be a "struggle," a "strategy," or a "class struggle." The new paradigm is opposed to traditional conceptions of minorities and of their relation to the State, but what is the non-political concept of minority in question? Concerning the relations of minorities and the State – but they can be extended to the individual in general – the traditional paradigm of "political philosophy" and Greco-occidental metaphysics, which constitutes its necessary background, is based on the following two premises:

(a) Minorities, in the historico-political sense, are always more or less expressible in terms of fringes, margins, sub-systems, and sub-ensembles of the State, when not in terms of relics and archaisms, which modern States or Nations endeavor to contain, master, and integrate while granting them the juridical guarantees of a relative and always-specified autonomy. To think such relations, traditional philosophy – contemporary philosophy included – puts into play the two categories of *mode* and *difference*: minorities as modes of these totalities or universals that the State and the Sovereign are; or else as groups that identify their existence with the claim of their "minoritarian difference." This concept of minority as "difference" can itself be interpreted in two ways: as difference *in* or *under* the Nation or the State, a particularity within a totality that has the privilege of unity; or, in a more revolutionary manner, as a difference *identical* to the Nation or the State, a singularity or individual *as* State and no longer *under* the State. We will necessarily return to this second – contemporary – conception of minoritarian difference, which no longer subsumes minorities under the State or any other political entity. But either way, these two concepts of *mode* and *difference* will be excluded from the new paradigm.

(b) Minorities are thus definable not in themselves according to strictly transcendental or immanent criteria, but according to quantitative, and, more often, qualitative, criteria that are always drawn from the experience that is immediately – purportedly – that of *citizens*: criteria of language, culture, history, sex, law, race, etc. Variously combined among themselves and hierarchized, these predicates clearly converge with the foregoing. This is the system of politological difference, difference of the Polis *and* of the citizen, into which one intends to insert man by force.

Together, these two premises amount to giving minorities a largely political evaluation, which, accordingly, is carried out for the benefit of authoritarian universals: State, Nation, People, Sovereign, Classes, etc. To exclude them altogether, all of "political philosophy" and its metaphysics must be eliminated and replaced with a paradigm based immediately on the essence of minorities themselves, on a directly minoritarian criterion, which no longer passes through political, linguistic, sexual, etc. quantities or qualities called "minoritarian," and which would be elaborated independent of the point of view of the State and those universals that are joined with it. It is a question of reversing [*renverser*] – though this is different from an overthrow [*renversement*] or a revolution, which are always ineffective – the terms in which the problem has traditionally been posed, that is, *the statist hypothesis on minorities*. Instead of conceiving of Minorities as modes or differences of the State, let us form and develop the *minoritarian hypothesis on the State*: let us attempt to understand whether there is an essence specific to minorities that allows us to recognize in them an absolute autonomy with regard to the State or any other universal, and let us draw the conclusions or effects of this new paradigm on the essence of the State. Let us attempt to experience the State based on minorities as its essence, rather than the reverse.

Therefore, the first step is to build – under the name of "minority" or "individu-a-lity" – the new paradigm not only of political thought, but of thought in general. Before legitimating existence, within absolute limits, in the State or in Philosophy, we must work out the "primitive" and only real condition from which the State itself draws its degree and mode of reality for finite individuals. To define individuals in a non-empirical way, it is necessary to give up ordinary – political, historical, cultural, sociological – criteria, which are always indeterminate and contradictory because they only know how to arrange individuals for the State. The new minoritarian criteria are strictly "transcendental," not, to be sure, in a philosophical use, but rather in a scientific one; that is, they are real and not ideal, a "unary" use of the transcendental motif. They pertain to an experience of multiplicities: minorities only exist in the state of multiplicities, but *absolute* and not *relative* to each other. These are "parts" that exist *before* the Whole, events before their setting in history, dispersions before any continuity, singularities before their insertion into Being, Logos, the World, Reproduction ... minorities before the State, taking their existence from themselves rather than from Institutions and Classes. They are the real condition (of possibility) of the State, but are not conditioned by it in return, at least not in their essence. To avoid being empiricist, this thought of minorities does not establish a revolutionary practice, but rather a resistance to the Revolution, resistance that is essentially pre-revolutionary, pre-activist, anterior even to "struggles."

All of these notions are described on the basis of an experience that contrasts those overly famous "differences," such as *continuous relations* (political, economic, etc., relations), to *"individual" multiplicities anterior even to relations, social or not*. Such multiplicities are no longer called continuous or ontological, but "unary" or individual. No philosophy, political or not, has ever done without the concept of *Unity* in one form or another: it has always and everywhere been an operator that is even more effective since its necessity remained unnoticed in its essence. Here, it is precisely no longer Unity that is operative, but the One, which we formally distinguish from Unity, not by this or that predicate, but by a sufficiency of essence-without-predicates. A thought of the One in a finite transcendental sense is the same as a thought of multiplicities prior to any Unity, and particularly prior to the modes of Unity par excellence – the State and the other fetishes of political thought. Such as we understand it, according to principles that will be developed below, the One is that which expressly allows the elimination of any reference to Unity and the liberation of individuals – the "individual" reality of minorities – from the State. From this springs the fundamental opposition – as well as the correlation – that we draw between the "minoritarian" and the "authoritarian," these two categories that distinguish minorities and the State, respectively (also the World, Philosophy, etc.) according to relations that are all the more complex because there no longer seems to be a "face to face" so much as two terms left to their solitude, happily abandoned by all "mediation."

(3) From this comes a new experience of what should be called and denounced as *the political forgetting of the essence of the State*.

What some thinkers have said of Being can be said of the State: the essence of the State was always forgotten and unthought, in spite of or precisely because of political reflection, which did not know how to unleash its own mode of power, its essence and its truth. We ought to highlight this thesis by adding a second: the function and essence of "political philosophy" exhausts itself in the hallucinatory repression or denial of the essence of the State, whose "forgetting" is not accidental. However, the thought of minorities likely does not experience the forgetting of the One the way Heidegger thinks the forgetting of Being; nor, consequently, the withdrawal or resistance of minorities in the same way as the "withdrawal" of the essence of Being. Details on all of these points, including the distinction between several conceptions of withdrawal or forgetting, will be given when necessary. Nevertheless, to avoid a common interpretation of the thesis of the political forgetting of the essence of the State and of the political – as though we meant to proclaim a long-deferred revelation, and were satisfied with that sort of effect – and also to distinguish the minoritarian interpretation of this thesis from its Heideggerian interpretation, which is always possible, we must qualify it, and begin by bringing together two apparently contradictory propositions: a) the essence of the political, of power, and of the State, has always been thought by all philosophies, political or not; b) the essence of the political, of power, and of the State has never really been thought in its proper truth, origin, and autonomy by philosophy, political or not, whose purpose was rather to conceal them.

It is not these two propositions – hardly original in themselves – but their way of uniting in a thought that is neither dialectical nor differential, that distinguishes their minoritarian truth from both their "Heideggerian" interpretation and their prior interpretations. These two propositions come together in this: *philosophy in general, and politics in particular, use an essence of power, of the political, and of the State that is constantly indeterminate, hallucinated rather than really experienced.* Of course, we cannot know if that essence is insufficiently determined and individuated unless we measure its degree and mode of individuation according to the criterion of a radical individuation that we possess a priori in a finite transcendental experience. This criterion is the One in the transcendental, not the metaphysical or unitary, sense; it is minority or individu-a-lity that ensues from the One reduced to its essence and thus distinguished from Being. From this point of view, unitary metaphysics and its political offshoots do not pose the question of the radical individuation of the State and the Citizen, precisely because they make do with the Greek paradigm of the *difference* of the Polis *and* the Citizen. As indissoluble or indivisible as it may be, difference remains fundamentally indeterminate in its terms and their relation, even more so when it is posed in the form of the traditional thesis, also born of this Difference, of man as a "political animal." Whether explicitly political or not, philosophy has always prematurely understood essence in general, and the essence of the One or of individual multiplicities in particular; it has, for example, always reflected in itself given empirical, cultural, and historical models of the effective exercise of power. These models range from God and the Father to the Proletariat, passing through the Citizen, the Tyrant, the Law, the General Will, the Sovereign, the Owner of the Means of Production, the Signifier. Political philosophy is an imitative activity, cheaply copying the essence of power and the State from their historical forms, from their institutional instances or modalities. It is a fundamentally vicious thought, the reflection of the conditioned in its condition, and one damned to confuse an under-determination of the essence of the State – supplemented in the best of cases, those of Marx and Nietzsche, with a determination in progress, a becoming or a "revolutionary" direction of history – with a completed and sufficient determination of this essence.

However, we have not yet understood how these two propositions are identical beyond any contradiction or simply formal identity; how, that is, individual thought can dissolve this semblance of contradiction.

(Polito-logical) Difference is indeed the forgetting of the essence of the State, but forgetting in a new sense. For this essence – minority – can no longer be subject, for example, to the interminable games of veiling *and* unveiling. The fundamental thesis on the finite essence of minorities is that this essence is *in itself*, an object of an immediate givenness that precedes even the transparency of a logos (of a polito-logos), which is always the transparency of Unity rather than of the One. The individu-a-lity of minorities does not reconstruct a transcendent, ideal, and logocentric essence or completeness; it exists straightaway in the mode of an unreflective immanence. In other words, this essence, which is also the essence of the State in the last instance, is rigorously inalienable and un-forgettable, and political thought has never been able to really forget it.

How, then, to dissolve this contradiction, this strict identity of a total forgetting and an absolutely un-forgettable? The thesis of *the political forgetting of the essence of the State* is not only a minoritarian thesis; it is also itself intra-statist, a last effect or final polito-logical confession. *Only the State can believe that it has truly forgotten its essence: and this belief is the real content of that "forgetting," a hallucination.* The true forgetting and its real content is the belief or the illusion of a forgetting of the essence of the State. "Forgetting" thus changes meaning from when it was first invoked and denounced in the name of minority: it exists only to be confirmed in itself of its own belief; it becomes an event that depends only on itself, a unitary hallucination that is absolutely contingent and absurd. It is tangled up and sunk in itself, taking on a gravity, a responsibility, and an absurdity which are its only existence and which are joined to the existence of the State. It is not that it affirms, re-affirms, re-flects itself in itself, employing thereby its traditional modes of exercise, which always follow the paths of transcendence. Rather, it receives, even in the statist denial of minorities, the unreflective mode of existence that comes from the One. When the State, in its own way, becomes minoritarian, it does not stop repressing the minority, it but does so through an existence that has become immediately accountable and responsible (for) itself to the point of absurdity. We will necessarily return to all of these difficult points about the existence and the critique of the *Unitary Illusion*.

(4) Finally, to complete this sketch of a Real Critique of Reason, political or otherwise, we can juxtapose Political or Philosophical Faith with Minoritarian Knowledge. Against the always-vicious polito-logical interpretations, the minoritarian way of thinking can be summarized by this one rule: the essence of power contains, but for positive reasons, absolutely nothing-of-the-political [*rien-de-politique*]; the essence of the State contains absolutely nothing-of-the-statist; the "withdrawal" of this essence must be conceived of in an absolute way, as a strict irreversibility of the condition to the conditioned. The State has always been studied from the point of view of the State itself – we will criticize this paralogism – instead of from the point of view of its real, and not vicious or circular, conditions. How to think a "withdrawal" – this is no longer the right word – of essence that would be neither an "exclusion" nor a "difference" in relation to empirical properties and to the immediate logic of the State, that would not be a "relation" in general. What is this "*nothing* (of-the-political)" that appears to define essence? The stated rule has precisely no minoritarian meaning until the essence of minorities – which is also, but only in the last instance, that of the State – is first determined in itself and through itself, without relation to history, without reference to politics, *the "nothing" being only an effect proper to the State and the political themselves, but not at all constitutive of minority, in which it has its essence.*

Like the Sciences of Man, (political) philosophy is a mixture that identifies philosophy (the *essence* ... of power) with politics (the *power* ... of essence): it is the first obstacle to a rigorous thought of Authorities and of the State. The correlation of the philosophical *and* the political – their reciprocal determination, partial and deferred, but always reversible – is the never questioned Bible of traditional-and-contemporary reflections on the political and the statist. This vicious circle, this latent but authoritarian hermeneutism of all thought that moves in the relation (even if it is "indivisible") of polito-logical Difference, indicates that the determination of essence is in turn a power, and is thus at stake for itself, not immediately given but in becoming or in progress. Not only is power its own stake and must assert itself, manifest itself, and take hold in its parousia, but philosophy must become political or effective as a fusion of the philosophical and the political. Essence is thus never actually given except as a process. We call "faith" the relation of what is at stake to itself or its effective becoming: faith and violence co-belong to power, which has to manifest its power, while they abandon science, which has no stakes. It is a question not of a mere secularization and metaphorization of religious faith, but rather of an "essential" – if not always "rational" – "faith," which is identical to the distance the essence of power maintains from effective power and is the practical Greco-unitary essence of philosophy. For example, the Revolution as a theoretical and practical project does not rest on the *knowledge* of the essence of the State – its immediate or unreflective givenness – but on *faith*, which is objective, to be sure, and makes power into a process. Faith proper to power itself, whether political or philosophical: Revolution is not a faith *in* the becoming of power and of the State – that would be to object to it only superficially – but the becoming of power through class struggle, which is itself an objective and structural faith, that is, a completely different thing than an object of science. The faith intrinsic to the workings of power is the objective structure of class struggle and of Revolution. With the individual minority, it is a question of substituting for political and philosophical faith the actual knowledge of the essence of power insofar as it is no longer understood politically, but scientifically.

From this springs the necessity – but we will have neither the time nor the place to get so far – of substituting for the auto-interpretations of the State a new point of view ensuing from the use of the minoritarian paradigm that we call "Techno-statist." The Techno-statist is the essence of the State understood from minority; it is the fundamental concept of a minoritarian theory of the State, one that allows us to understand to what extent the State is the universal field of governmentality and its proper technologies – from the point of view of the finite individual. It is thus a matter of the State as well as of minorities: we will not ask for an example or a case of it as proof. A finite transcendental theory of the State, of History, of Revolution, is not an empirical description of facts or givens that would presuppose the universal horizon of governmentality as already known. It describes essences, but which are real because they are experienced as immediate givens, absolutely required and necessary for there to be something like "the" political, "the" historical, etc. These essences are here concrete apriorises, absolutely "universal" invariants, but which are not formal (in the sense in which formality is distinguished from empirical generality and even from its rational, scientific, and ethical contents). This accounts for the blueprint character of this essay, which elaborates the fundamental concepts of a rigorous – if not empirical, at least "scientific" – discipline of man, and, therefore, of minorities and their (non-) relation to the State.

— I —

WHO ARE MINORITIES?

6. The Two Sources of Minoritarian Thought

Theorem 1. There are two sources, two paths, of minoritarian experience and thought. Minorities as "difference," grafted on the body of the State and of Authorities in general. And minorities who are real below difference: individuals as such, or without qualities, "ordinary people," who precede the State, and whose concept is no longer difference.

Here and there, in the warp and weft of games of power, marginalized individuals or collectives obsessed by their identity claim their "difference." De facto differences (historical, cultural, political, institutional, linguistic, sexist, ageist, etc.); de jure differences (ethical and juridical); the right to difference . . . These are effective minorities, and they are found in the World, History, Language, etc. But they are not the subject of a specifically minoritarian experience and thought, which could be said to be only for and through them. This type of minorities, whatever more or less elaborated concept philosophy provides it, is well known: they are nothing but margins, gaps, lateral effects of games of power, their foam and their scraps. To think minorities as "difference" is to reduce them to their fusion with or – which is not very different – their difference from the State, conceiving of them as stato-minoritarian mixtures, as modes or projections of power relations, profits and losses of an indefatigable grind – history.

The other thought, properly minoritarian and no longer stato-minoritarian, radicalizes the conditions of the problem. It asks what would minorities be who would not form an additional universal – the intersection of the great authoritarian universals, Language, Sex, Culture, Desire, Power? Who would be par excellence real or formed of individuals as they are? It demands that we think people as nothing-but-individuals: *before* the State, Language, Text, Authorities, etc. But what is a thought that would only be by and for minorities, not too broad or too universal for individuals, and one that would ensue from them irreversibly as from the real itself?

The solution resides in a "Minority Principle," which, being itself minoritarian, is no longer exactly a "principle" – we will return to this point – and which requires that the authentic minority, that is, individuality, be laid bare and decide to think through itself.

Theorem 2. *Minorities determine Authorities in the last instance, who do not determine them in return.*

"Determination in the last instance" is a formulation whose Marxist use, completely pervaded by empiricism and materialism, could not elucidate it radically enough to dispel its mystery. It has two sides: first of all, it registers the pre-statist autonomy of minorities and the pre-authoritarian existence of individuals; then, it draws the consequences this has for their "relation" to Authorities. This order is decisive: we will not grasp the truth of this formulation until the essence of minorities is clarified; it alone will explain why they form a "last instance" in a radical sense that is no longer entirely philosophical. How can minorities distinguish themselves from the State and its sub-systems and constitute an absolute sphere of individual existence, irreducibly autonomous from all relations and games of power? This is the first question. The second: why do the various aggregates of these relations, which have the form "institution" and the form "State," enjoy only a relative autonomy, and why do they remain paradoxically dependent on "minoritarian" – which is to say simply real – individuals? "Determination in the last instance" is the key to these relations. It contains the novel meaning of a unilateral – non-reciprocal or non-reversible – determination. The stake of a thought of individuals as they are, or as minorities, is the experience of a radical irreversibility or uni-laterality in thought: how can individuals act on these universals, which seem to crush them? How can determination (and which one?) go from the individual to the State, rather than in the inverse direction?

It will take time to learn how not to inscribe minorities on the body of the State, to unlearn this immemorial philosophical gesture, and to no longer believe that we do well when we reduce them to more or

33

less marginal or partial members of the body-State, to mere modes of Sex, of Language, of Traditions, etc. Ontology and politics, which serve us as thought, have never been able to conceive of individuals as anything other than modes of the State or of the great universals. What good is the deepest thought to us? A certain unitary complex, "metaphysics-and-its-surpassing," "metaphysics-and-its-difference," "representation-and-its-difference": this unitary paradigm has never been able to conceive of multiplicities that would not be of Being or of the State, even when it claimed to "destroy" them. Even more so, onto-theo-politics, including the interrogation it carries out of its own essence, has been content to prematurely determine the essence of minorities as multiplicities-of-the-State, of-Language, of-Text, of-Desire, etc. This is what must be unlearned.

Theorem 3. *Minoritarian determination in the last instance, which is the specific causality of the finite individual on the World, History, and Authorities in general, institutes a bifocal or two-pronged thought. It distributes the matter of existence or the life of the existent in a "uni-lateral" manner.*

On the one hand, there are individuals *as they are* – we will return to this expression – who escape at least in their essence from Culture, History, and the State, and disappoint the hope Authorities have of ensuring their mastery. On the other hand, there are all of the powers of regulation, without exception, which produce or maintain a social or political body. These are overwhelmingly unitary Authorities or games of power, which are seductive but no less unitary. The "last instance" demands a strict respect for the uni-laterality of these rela-tions and, above all, of these non-relations, which metaphysics no more than Marx or Nietzsche, not to mention the cultural and his-torical sciences, knew how to tolerate. The entire power of singularity or individuality, without any synthesis, must be put to one side only, and the entire power of synthesis must be cast exclusively to the other, and this without exchange, fusion, or reversion ("dialectical" or not), even if by definition the institutional and statist forces of the production of power (juridical rules, political institutions, economic exchanges and struggles) always tend towards the encompassing of minorities.

We do not yet know how this economy is possible. The claim to elevate unilaterality to a principle, to insert a radical irreversibility into thought, to elucidate a specific causality of the singular over the universal in the ordinary – without qualities – individual, form

34

the coherent body of a nothing-but-minoritarian thought. But these claims so violently collide with common sense and Greco-unitary philosophy that they must be brought back to their sole "principle," that is, based in the "real" in the rigorous sense of this concept, in the intimacy of the most incontestable experience. How could such a split – which claims to cast de facto and de jure minorities to the side of the powers of the State and denounce them as mere margins, necessary for its functioning – be anything but abstract and fictive from the perspective of philosophy and politics, without support in cultural and historical diversities? How will it be anything but overwhelmingly "metaphysical" and "ideological"? An objection without an object. On the one hand, the essence of real minorities will no longer be defined philosophically, politically, or culturally, etc., but by a *real* essence that does not participate in these universals. On the other hand – and this is a consequence of this way of thinking – what we call unilaterality will no longer be, in a "critical" and classical manner, a line of division or demarcation, or even a synthesis, a continuity, or a continuation. There is no "line of demarcation" or even of "difference" "between" minorities and Authorities, between individuals laid bare and the powers of the World. We renounce these politico-philosophical processes, which regularly amount to making minorities into a sub-system, at best a "member" or a "difference," of these great entities – the State, Culture, Language, etc.

Theorem 4. *Nothing-but-minoritarian thought begins neither with God nor with things, neither with Being nor with the Other. Nor even with "man," insofar as he comes together with or forms a team with these unitary fetishes. It begins with the real, that is, with the One or the ordinary individual. It is the One that grounds "individuel" causality, unilateral or in the last instance determination.*

A real and scientific concept of minorities is a discriminating concept, a criterion that finally distinguishes individuals from all the subsets of Authorities or of universals. We find this concept immediately in the "One" rather than in "Being." The last presuppositions of a minoritarian thought are those of the One, and no longer those of Being (of its meaning, its truth, its place, its difference, etc.). The One is only real – this is the hypothesis that will constantly guide us – but Being is a real that is merely possible, a "possible experience." And it is in this One that the power to uni-lateralize is rooted insofar as it forms an order that commands that the rest, that is, Authorities, be thought after the One, starting from it and according to an irreversible order

35

of experiences. This division is only legitimate if it merges with the experience of the real, determined and described under conditions that are rigorous, that is, phenomenal and not – since we begin with real rather than with philosophical universals – phenomeno*logical.* This nothing-but-real on the basis of which we move and think is thus the experience (of) the One, which will also prove to be the experience of determination in the last instance. Meditating on the essence of the One, then on its consequences for the philosophical and the political – these are the first steps of a nothing-but-minoritarian thought.

Theorem 5. *The political forgetting and denial of the essence of the State originate in the forgetting and the denial of the essence of minority or the One.*

The restitution of this essence to its truth produces more than one reversal of the traditional relations of the State and minorities, of the World and individuals. Different than a new economy, an effect that is other-than-economic: the essence of minorities has no need for the essence of the State, it is the essence of the State that needs the essence of minorities; it is the State that cannot be correctly defined except from an absolute and positive essence, that of finite individuals – as is the case in general with authoritarian Universals, which are thus determined without reciprocity. If the minority principle is of interest, it is due to the rigor of its interpretation. It no longer entails "distinction" or "difference," but the independence of minorities – at least when grasped in their real concept – with regard to any power, that is, any *relation* of power. And inversely, it entails that relations, which we will call *games of power*, have no real possibility or existence except as uni-lateral in relation to these minorities, which are their determination in the last instance.

Doubtless, as soon as the minoritarian becomes "effective" and extends its essence into a political existence, as soon as it is inscribed in communal and political lines, continuities, and becomings, as soon as it acquires goals and means, it cannot avoid appealing to the State and to Authorities to carry out its work, cannot avoid mixing its responsibility with that of the State – a process through which the State has always known how to render itself indispensable. But this is the great danger proper to "effective" minorities alone, to those that enter into politics: by dint of crossing swords with the State wherever it is present, they confuse their means with those of their adversary. In one sense, it is true that these individuals know no enemy but the

State and its institutional variants, nor have they any seducer more impressive than them; and, in any case, it belongs to the essence of these minorities that are inscribed in the World and History to be vulnerable to seduction, to be able to be imitated and compromised by powers that are hardly "minoritarian," simulated by Authorities with which they form a "stato-minoritarian complex," whose tricks, illusions, and paralogisms we will continue to explore. But a theory of "real" minorities describes these minorities as by definition inalienable: the individual, real rather than effective, is not a part of the machine of the State, despite the minoritarian mimesis the State develops as its motivation and innermost goal.

It is obviously the One, insofar as its causality is that of "determination in the last instance," that carries the possibility of these relations and non-relations of unilaterality, and thus also the possibility of a description of the individual without qualities, of ordinary man as distinct from man defined by the World or by anthropo-logical difference in general.

Theorem 6. *The two experiences of minorities are not entirely foreign to each other, because Authorities (and the effective minorities who are inscribed in the sphere of Authorities) are determined in the last instance by the minorities we will call "individual" or real. We call effective minorities, those of which authorities are capable, "stato-minoritarian."*

The minoritarian individual (or the individual "as he is") is a Janus-faced being, who only communicates unilaterally or with a single side. Multiple and dispersed straightaway, he is constrained by his essence, the One and its positive in-completion, to refuse to be defined by a group, a community, a commerce of any relations whatsoever. Not only does he not fall under regularities and continuities, but he refuses even to elevate his singular case into a rule, to make a law from his singularity, to identify the latter with the former: this is the minoritarian properly speaking, the dispersive or the positive diasporic, the One rather than the Other. Then, in a seemingly contradictory manner, even though it ensues "uni-laterally" from this first definition, "the man of the most comprehensive responsibility, who has the conscience for the over-all development of man"[3] (Nietzsche): this is the stato-minoritarian, the individual who justly makes law or who merges with the State and becomes an Authority in his own way. In requiring the absolute autonomy of minorities with regards to the State, the Minority Principle demonstrates that minorities, at

37

least as they are traditionally defined as "differences," are nothing but powers of the State; and inversely, that the State's own becoming constrains it to merge with minorities to constitute a stato-minoritarian sphere. From this arises a second, onto-theo-political, definition of minorities, a second source of minoritarian thought, the one of which philosophy has been "capable."

"Double" knowledge, two apparently contradictory knowledges, both necessary, but which have different and perhaps incommensurable values. On the one hand, real minorities, who know that they are inalienable in games of power, who do not fall under these Relations that try to negotiate them even though they are the non-negotiable. And, on the other hand, effective minorities, those unitary philosophy hallucinates as being the essence of minorities. Of these two concepts, the first describes an absolute, pre-political, pre-linguistic, etc., essence of the individual and determines in the last instance the other and its political, linguistic, etc., content.

7. How to Think Individuals?

Theorem 7. Individuals are not modes of transcendence, that is, of scission, of identity, or of their combination in a higher unity or objectivity. Neither are they modes of transcendence as Other or Beyond.

The task of contemporary thinkers, the forced march of frontier intellectuals, is well known: the hunt after the "beyond." Beyond the pleasure principle, the power principle, the principle of being: everything began with "beyond essence" . . . This indestructible ideal that exhausts so many thinkers still dares to appear on the threshold of minoritarian thought: beyond the "political vision of the world," to find and determine the common people [*la plèbe*]? The last resistance? The most secret margins, . . . minorities? Still, should it not stop there, where the marchers stop, and be able to determine a radical "beyond," a diaspora that would not be the sublimated projection of the political, an ethical or juridical hinterworld, but the instance of individuality as real? How to apprehend this absolute im-potence that contains power and the State in their specific and limited order? We abandon the project of a "reconversion of politics" (Nietzsche), of a reversion of the political to its still-political *beyond*, of a *Kehre* or a return, of an ascent towards the essence of the State, of a "revolution." Individuals laid bare refuse to identify with the Statist Ideal that still fills this beyond: to think minorities, the entire thematic of transcendence, of the Other, and of the Beyond . . . must be abandoned.

This is the great danger, the temptation of all minoritarian thought: to be so dazzled by the State, so bewitched by Authorities, that we would be tempted to raise our eyes towards minorities as though help would come from that direction. There is a minoritarian ambiguity: to think with the help of "transcendence," of the beyond, of the distant; to imagine reality as deep, high, and hidden, and minorities as crushed by the base of the State. Those are unitary customs: individual as a remainder, as a game, or as an effect of a game, of several universals: the concrete as becoming-concrete and overdetermination; the singular as identical to the universal, the part as arranged according to the whole; the individual who is never the essence but always subsumed under the essence, etc. Unitary philosophy is the interminable confession of the martyrdom of the individual – a hypocritical confession – and it is not certain that we will escape this unitary police if we continue to seek the individual beyond the State . . .

"Stato-minoritarian" thought, Nietzschean and postmodern, already distinguishes factual minorities – defined by criteria of culture, language, history, sex – and minorities as *continuous multiplicities*, as reciprocal differences relative to one another, as differends that cannot be inscribed within the social fabric and on known political chessboards, but that still form exceptional and fluid regularities. From this point of view, we would call minoritarian, or, more precisely, "stato-minoritarian," "the individual who is the entire chain" (Nietzsche), the singular case that is identical – without mediation – to a regularity, or that "makes law" from its singularity as differend. This is progress from the "national" and cultural concept of minorities, which can be excluded from our research because these minorities are not a source, except an external and empirical one, for minoritarian thought. They are not experienced as continuous parts of the State or the social body, as sequences taken from the regularity of laws or as limits in the continuum of games of power; they are only organized from the outside under the generalities of the State, the Nation, Constitutions, Laws, Languages, Cultures. These are what the sociologists, historians, "regionalist" militants, each in their own way, discern starting from goals, demands, and affects that are already socially coded and hierarchized in accordance with the machine of the State. But eliminating them is useless if the Authoritarian Ideal in the form of a "beyond" of Authorities is retained. There is a minoritarian amphibology that derives from the amphibology found in dominant, Greco-unitary thought: it is condemned to remake minorities as a beyond of power, a beyond of the power principle. This is the contemporary solution whose arguments and foundations come from Freud, Nietzsche, Heidegger, the great seducers of the individual as such: the beyond of power remains in the web of power that merely has been loosened. *Beyond of* . . . a Greek and Jewish form of the question, a form of unitary compromise. The beyond is the Other, the real-as-Other, or the Unconscious of . . ., the Other is always the other of . . . the Same, the Identical, the State, the World, the Greek – without which it is nothing.

Reduced to their essence, devoid as much as they can be of their socio-political-psychological and even philosophical attributes, individuals instead form pre-statist diasporas, positive dispersions that are no longer set upon the screens of history, psychology, culture, sexuality, languages – but also not on the screens of transcendence in general. Unlike "minorities-of-the-State," they do not pass through these empirical givens or attributes in order to continuously include them in the flux of power, by way of thresholds or cuts – they do not "surpass" them: it is necessary to think otherwise.

Theorem 8. *Minorities are not the Other of History, the unconscious of the State, the repressed of Authorities, the beyond of power. It is the powers, Authorities, the State, etc., that are beyond minorities. It is not the individual who is beyond the World; it is the World that is beyond the individual.*

The minoritarian essence of individuals, or the essence that we will later call "individual" rather than individuel, of minorities, must be sought in a different way than through philosophical desire, the meta-physical, transcendence, the Other . . . Individuals do not fill the beyond of the World any more than minorities are the ungraspable cut or the indisputable malaise that renders Authorities incomplete and puts them "beside" themselves. Let us stop imagining them as remote, caught up in interminable flutters and waves of veiling and unveiling, devoted sometimes to techno-political parousia, sometimes to endless withdrawal. Minorities are invisible in the sense that invisibility is their positive essence, or in the sense that the real can be invisible (to) itself due to transparency. We obviously do not yet know why, but it is no longer necessary to imagine them as edges, margins, marginalities, archipelagos, systems of chicanes. We are minorities, they are us, they are not others. Thinking is beginning with real individuals in order to go towards the State, and it is the State, the World, History that are distant and strange. It is necessary to "invert" or rather *uni-*

40

lateralize the World and the State by changing the content of terms
– precisely of individuals – so as to never again reverse them, so that
thought finds its real basis and is no longer tempted to give itself
over to see-sawing, to the reversibility of the Cartesian diver who
so enchants contemporary thinkers and gives them the impression
that they are thinking because they are given the means to be clever.
This is the meaning of the injunction: change the paradigm. Not even
change the base or the terrain, but secure the base, which was never
abandoned except by an illusion still to be analyzed. Are individuals
the base for which the World would be the superstructure? Minorities
are not a base, nor are Authorities in general a superstructure. Two
worlds, then? Still no: a single World, that of games of power or of
Authorities. As for real individuals, they do not make up a world,
even though they also are not of this World . . .

Theorem 9. *Individuals are not "beyond," they are "before" . . . the
World or Authorities, but in an anteriority that is only ungraspable
for the latter. For in their essence they are inherent (to) themselves
and begin through themselves. Therefore, their anteriority is not the
anteriority of an Other or an Unconscious.*

The great anti-Greek and anti-postmodern rule: to no longer think
"beyond," but "before," in an absolute anteriority, indisputable for
the World as well. In an apriority that would be an *a priori defense*
rather than a defensive reaction a posteriori. Even more, it is a positive indifference to the World rather than a defense against it. But
this anteriority is not constitutive of the essence of individuals – it
only affects the State and the World, not individuals themselves who
no doubt think "before" the State, but from themselves towards the
State or the World, in an irreversible direction. Therefore, they are
not structured by a Beyond and are not desired like an Other or an
Unconscious: they are subjects or finite, which is to say, inalienable.

In its non-philosophical, or as we will say, "ordinary," essence,
thinking is an irreversible activity because it is the very experience of
irreversibility. Authoritarian thought, however, consists in guarding, in
taking care of and being concerned about, in being interested in . . . ; it
moves in a circle or slits it; it prolongs and intellectually extends what
takes shape in the World. Intellectuals trace a continuous circular line
in their heads, they only want compromise, unity-in-spite-everything as
long as it is based on difference, which is the "honor" of Intellectuals.
But ordinary man, the individual without predicates, does not feel
himself to be first and foremost of all *in-the-World*: this is the slogan

41

of intellectuals and Greco-unitary philosophers. He has no basis (the World) and is not a basis for the history of the World any more than he is a line or a game of positions to maintain or stakes to defend: he indifferently contemplates the World and the State, where nevertheless he is also found though not through his essence: this contemplation is by itself an irreversible order of experiences.

Theorem 10. *All of these characteristics have only a transcendental meaning, and certainly not a transcendent or empirical (political, cultural, historical) one. Minorities or finite individuals are not accessible to the false sciences of man: to politics and polito-logy, history, psychoanalysis, ethnology and all the "social sciences." Ordinary man resists all historical and cultural, linguistic or sexual, etc., characterization.*

All of these characteristics return to the recognition of a positive content that is irreducible to these sociological, techno-political, etc., "zeros." Minorities can be made visible and described neither by human sciences and the historical disciplines nor by techno-political description and Greco-unitary philosophy. From this perspective, we might think them little more than roughly sketched subjects, hesitant larvae between social being and non-being. Even though this reluctance towards existing is no hesitancy towards living and sensing, it is not through refusals, interruptions, and becomings, that is to say, through authoritarian processes taken from the State, that minorities appear and come to know what they are. Does their positive essence derive from their membership in a State or a sub-system of the State: nation, language, culture, region, party, social class; from their identification with its values and goals; from their subjection to its power, and from the bonus satisfaction this sacrifice gives them? They do not know the inevitability of a land, of a culture, of social relations, any more than they know the overwhelming, summary refusal of the State, the relation of exclusion or contradiction to its apparatuses, against which they would carry out a politics of theological accusation (against Marxism, against the State, against Capital, against Society, against Christianity, . . . against the Greeks): to all of this, they are instead "indifferent." An individual knows (himself) immediately and in "unreflective" manner from himself; he does not wait to become a self and reach the World to be characterized as an individual and thus as normalizable, socializable, statizable. It is he alone who "determines" his essence, or who experiences himself "in" this essence and experiences the quality of what he can do. Within himself, immanently, he draws on an im-potence and a knowledge (of) himself that we will call non-thetic. These are the positive characteristics of his essence, far below, for example, his belonging to a culture or a social group, both what he "is able" to do and the nature of his adversary, which is never just any sort or in general (Power *in general*, the Bourgeoisie *in general*, Capitalism *in general*, the State *in general* ...), but always determined and specified, even as a generality endeavoring to capture him. He does not need to seek the rules or models for his activity among gregarious instances or anonymous organizations of powers or of flux (traditions, practical lines, parties, institutions). He is an absolute empiricist who combines his existence with the internal and unreflective ordeal of that existence, and not, like the stato-minoritarian, with the invention of forms of action and resistance that are as possible as they are real. He does not need to combine his essence with his effective existence in history or culture, in the relations of power (in which he is never grasped, anyway) save to imprint them with a radical uni-laterality and an absurdity that expels them from himself forever. Fascization and Revolution are always already-there, but only for the World. As for the World, it is de-rived from the start: it is in this sense that the responsibility of the minoritarian is "anterior" with an anteriority that precedes the anteriority with which the State or Being, History, Culture, Language, etc. claim in vain to anticipate, localize, and regulate it. As for watchwords or practices, he does not need to want them, to pose them, to idealize them: his minoritarian non-acting is "efficacious" before any activism. Nor does he need to fear losing that which he enjoys – he already "lost" what was liable to be taken from him: he is devoid of it. Individuals lack nothing; they are not determined according to that which is withdrawn from them, but according to the positivity of who they are as finite, which is not exhausted in their traditions. They do not "react" directly to abuses, to exploitation, and to destitution, because they do not want to stop head on, nor interrupt-and-take-over-from a movement always aimed against them but incapable of really grasping them. Their efficacy is outside of struggle: even when they attack the State, always elsewhere, on another point, establishing a new line of resistance from one to the other, these stato-minoritarian practices find their fulcrum and their bedrock still deeper, if not more in "withdrawal": absolutely below the State. This is why they never allow the battleground, the goals of struggle, and the political quality of what is at stake to be wholly dictated to them. Of course, as stato-minoritarian, they struggle in these places, for these objectives, and for a definition of new stakes. But if they resist even minimally, it is because, according to their essence of the last instance,

43

these are discrete impulses coming from elsewhere – to tell the truth, from a non-place that determines the elsewhere of the World itself – that innervate the games and systems of the State at the same time as they disrupt them. Put simply, they refuse comparisons, they who are endlessly compared, measured, defined abstractly in exteriority by the State and its authoritarian sub-systems. They never stop being defined by an existence and an impulsonnality from before the political and the philosophical – an existence unbearable to the State.

Theorem 11. *A radical thought of individuals ceases to be merely possible and becomes real as a thought of terms, not a thought of relations. A thought of terms before all relation is a thought of the One.*

What nothing-but-philosophical, and perhaps less-than-philosophical (in the unitary sense of the word), criterion allows us to see invisible minorities, to discern them from the grain of power, where they perhaps do not have their site? Where to find the instrument to discern them, if their discernment is at the highest point a science that is itself minoritarian and not at all optical? How to define a minority or an individuality capable of liquidating all the known types of causality (material, final, efficient, and formal, but also differential and techno-political) and forming a criterion of absolute reality, each time assigning to a conjuncture – an event, a practice – its determination in the last instance?

We know the dilemma: a term *as it is*, nothing-but-term, is unthinkable, because either all thought is a putting into relation or it is a disguised return to the principle of identity A=A, which would be put in charge of reality and unduly given a real or "transcendental" function . . . This is the dilemma in which dominant and unitary thought attempts to enclose the undoubtedly paradoxical thesis of a pure experience of terms. This is how the term is regularly reduced to a mere index of alterity and exteriority at the heart of the interiority of relations – in the worst case, to an absurd and unconscious manifold, in the best case, to a function of the Other. Unitary idealism has a somewhat bad conscience regarding terms and the injustice it does them: it transforms the term into the Other, into the Unconscious, even into the Primary Process. The essence of the term – which is the One – cannot, however, be granted by Relation, and the One, as we will describe later, is not at all Unity, but an unreflective or non-thetic immanence (to) itself [*(à) soi*], which philosophy is powerless to think. The One is the immanent paradigm of the term and its specificity, irreducible to any ideality or relation. Unitary thought has always been a real logic, onto-logic, or transcendental logic, a logico-centrism that drives the term back to its periphery, interiorizing it and excluding it at the same time. There will never be a thought of individuals as such as long as the term is thought residually, as an exteriority to reduce, as a support for relation, as the index of the real. The term is not the index of the real, it is the real itself insofar as the real is absolute – that is to say, "finite" or inalienable – and insofar as it does not need relation to be an "object" of thought, that is, here, by virtue of its unreflective essence, an *immediate given*.

The conditions of a pure thought of the individual are thus precise: if the individual is first or a priori in relation to universals, if he gathers in himself the real par excellence, if he is a part before the Whole, a being before Being, an event before History, etc., this is because he neither enters into games of relation and transcendence nor results from processes of cutting and synthesis – cut, recut, and overcut – that are themselves games of power. The "part" is a priori, but a transcendental or real apriori. This is the requirement and guiding principle of a thought of the individual as immediate givenness: minorities must be "parts," not just a priori, but transcendental = real and coming before the "wholes" or the "sums" (sensible, figural, conceptual, or ideal) as well as before the ideal and formal type of apriori that Western thought normally attributes to such wholes. The conquest of a formal concept of the apriori, which Plato, Kant, and Husserl contrasted with the "generalities" of the empiricists, is completed by Nietzsche, who gives the formal to itself as sole content. He re-affirms Form and places it in "affirmation," Form and its synthetic transcending towards itself [*vers soi*], thus bringing the universal or the apriori to such a power that it can henceforth claim to contain the manifold and the differential, assuming in its own way the infinite labor and jouissance of individuation. *But the problem of an apriori proper only to the "manifold" and the "differential," of an apriori that is itself "manifold," non-universal, and non-formal, suited to multiplicities or "parts" that are real as Absolute, to individuals who precede the ideality and the relativity of wholes, has only become more important* . . . The "invention" of minorities as an apriori that is itself real corresponds to the dissolution of the illusion at the foundation of the Philosophical Empire of the World, the illusion that the individuation of people, the fusion and reciprocal determination of the State and subjects, for example, is true minoritarian individuation . . . In reality, the individual is *before* individuation, he is its true, real apriori. Individuation is an impossible task.

Theorem 12. *To think a term or an individual as it is, two determinations must be combined: a uni-laterality of the World in relation to it, or of Authorities in relation to minorities; its inalienable, immanent, or inherent (to) itself reality, under the form of the One.*

How to think the term *as it is?* Thinking the term as it is does not mean thinking it *as such,* that is, in its being or its logos and, necessarily, in its unity and its unicity by virtue of the convertibility of Being ("as such") and Unity. To parody Leibniz, that which is not truly *a* term is also not truly a *term.* But we can no longer understand this "a" [*cet "un"*] as a mode of (substantial or transcendental) Unity, which – at least from the point of view of the "unreflective" One [*l'Un*] – is no longer anything but an external criterion, a transcendent predicate that brings the term back under the law of relation. The individual does not fall under the category of "unicity," and even less so under that of "unity."

Nevertheless, we do not yet know what it means for the One to be the instance of the real, and we risk going too fast and missing the "stakes" of a pure thought of terms. To the One, it is necessary to add, as we have done, this other determination, which is not contrary to the One but rather finds in it its foundation, uni-laterality. The individual cannot be thought as unicity – that is still an imagination, a transcendent image that falsifies the experience of the individual – but rather as a finite One capable of uni-lateralizing the World.

How to actually experience uni-laterality without making it into the kind of abstraction denounced by philosophy? Is it not a form of the Other? But the individual is not first of all located beside . . ., on the margins of . . ., withdrawn in relation to. . . . That would be to confuse it with a mode of the Other or of the Unconscious, an ancient confusion we have just denounced. Uni-laterality can be saved from its "fall" into the Unconscious only by the One, which gives it its reality and inverts its meaning. Indeed, the One is so immanent to itself that it needs no withdrawal to retreat into itself and that *it does not need to disengage from relation or render itself uni-lateral. But this is why it makes all things unilateral.* On this basis, uni-laterality becomes a real "principle" or receives an absolute truth and consistency. But then it also, as we well know, entails a quasi-reversal: *the individual is not uni-lateral in relation to a Totality, as an Unconscious or an Other would be, but the individual unilateralizes the World and produces a "beside" him that is relative to him.*

To reach the essence of the individual, we will also proceed in two stages. First, we will clarify the refusal of the individual to fall into relation, that is, in reality his power to uni-lateralize the World and Authorities, which is the content of the real experience of his causality, completely different from a "withdrawal." To do this, we will use a certain "principle of difference" known to philosophy, which we will alter in order to give it a "real" meaning, withdrawing its logical character and inverting its meaning or its effect. Then we will suggest that uni-laterality is real and ceases to be a relation, that it is a term or the specific effect of the term, and no longer a relation, under precise transcendental conditions or conditions of experience. These conditions are those of the One, that is, of a structure that is rigorously *unreflective* or *non-positional (of) itself*. Uni-laterality is thus no longer a logical principle, and even less a pre-philosophical abstraction; it is an immediate given identical to the individual, which, from the individual, affects the World and the great authoritarian universals.

These are the two determinations described in the following paragraphs in order to explain the real phenomenal content of the individual and his "minority," his radical or intrinsic finitude.

8. Theory of Uni-laterality

Theorem 13. *Uni-laterality, which real individuals impose on the World, is not an ("asymmetrical") relation, but a priori precedes any possible relation, without this precedence thereby being a relation.*

The philosophical tradition is familiar with a certain "principle of difference" or of "determinability." It lays out what it thinks is an asymmetrical, non reciprocal relation between two terms. Logic is also familiar with such asymmetrical relations ("son of" . . .). But asymmetry or uni-laterality simultaneously gains an autonomous reality and a transcendental value, that is, one that is constituent of experience, under certain conditions of interpretation which render it absolute and free it from the very "difference" that always contains a factor of reversibility.

Distinguishing uni-laterality from any possible relation, asymmetrical or not, is obviously a difficult task. It is not enough to desire asymmetry only to make a logical or relative use of it; nor is it enough to make uni-laterality a syn-tax and irreversibility a new unilateral synthesis, to say, for example: *minorities distinguish themselves from Authorities, who do not distinguish themselves from minorities.* This statement is a first step towards the rigorous conception of the individual. But it still makes logical, relative, and negative use of uni-laterality, such that uni-laterality needs a certain residual bilaterality as a complement, and irreversibility becomes the complement of a peripheral reversibility.

On the other hand, if irreversibility must no longer be inserted *in* a relation, it must also no longer be posed *in relation to a relation*, which it would reject only on one side in order to place itself on the other. This essay has proceeded a bit like that in its initial descriptions. But the most insidious error would consist in re-introducing reciprocity by putting the relative or the relational *on one side*, and the unilateral or the absolute *on the other*. This would plunge the whole thing back into a relation of higher power – that of the existence of two sides in general. On the contrary, "uni-lateral" means that there will be *one single side* that will take root in an instance, which will in no way itself be a higher or more powerful side producing a synthesis of the two. If it becomes real, as an unreflective experience must be, uni-laterality excludes all relation, which is always reciprocal in spite of everything. It excludes, for example, asymmetrical obvious statements such as "son of . . .", which are complemented by "father of . . .", and which still presume a reciprocal, encompassing, and higher relation, that of "the same family."

Two cases can be examined:

1. Real uni-laterality must be liberated from the form of predication that is both substantialist and logical. It is a matter of giving asymmetry or irreversibility a meaning independent of the game of general predicates, of recognizing in it a direct effect of the most individuated subject, a consequence of its finitude. Minorities are not empirical individuals herded under general codes: cultural, historical, regionalist, biological (age, sex), or capitalist; they are distinguished from what sub-systems of the State designate as "minorities." We can hardly even say that they are always on one side, never determined by the other side, that of the State. For that remains an ambiguous formula: they are not on any side – we have just spoken out against this illusion – it is the State that is by their side, or, more precisely, that forms their possible surface or their exteriority. Whatever the predicates attributed to them, individuals are irreducible solitudes: they are not determined by those predicates; the solitude of the subject does not even stand "facing" the attribute; it does not tolerate an attribution, which its essence excludes or to which it is indifferent. The radical thought of the individual entails the exclusion of the logico-real model of predication, which remains a transcendent model.

2. Real uni-laterality falls outside the logic of relations in general, not just that of predication, because more generally it liberates itself from the complementarity of "terms" and "relations," from this game that wants relations to be sometimes "external" and assuming points or terms in themselves (Russell), sometimes "internal" and interiorizing terms to their advantage (Leibniz, Hegel), sometimes mixed or simultaneous with terms (Nietzsche) as is the case in games of power. Uni-laterality does not become transcendental or real before being a mere apriori, that is, still a universal, unless it ceases to be a relation, to belong to a genre of relation, and unless it ensues from the unreflective essence of the term itself. Instead, it is relation understood globally that enters as a "term" into a uni-laterality to which it is subordinated and which subordinates it to the One. It is still necessary to find the instance capable of grounding and determining uni-laterality as real. Only the One will guarantee that the individual will no longer be a term merely opposed to a relation or supporting it. It will not be satisfied with deferring [*différer*] logico-centrism, the traditional couple of the relation and the term. It will eliminate the holistic conception of terms along with the logical conception of relations: their idealist conception as the interiorization of terms into the relation, as the absolution of the relation and its primacy over the terms (Hegel); or even the becoming-terms of relations (Nietzsche). It will render not only the ideal conception, but also the idealist use in general, of "relations" (and, thus, of "Relations of Power") useless for defining the essence of individuals. But it will only eliminate idealism from the theory and politics of minorities because it will take relations in general for a non-determinant and non-essential moment of their reality.

This has obvious consequences that concern the political even though they themselves are not political. Absolutely "before" relations (Marxist Relations of Production or Nietzschean Relations of Power), the essence of minorities or of individual multiplicities determines around itself an absolutely originary asymmetry rather than continuities, relativities, and differences. For example, a minoritarian practice is autonomous even before being distinguished in a more or less clear-cut way from social relations. It appears already before the suspension, which it actually induces, of the relations of causality and motivation. Ideally and ontologically indeterminate, minorities are not too distant, too high, too remote. They are too much "in themselves" to still be determined according to modes of generic social representation (bourgeois), specific social representation (Marxist), differential social representation (Nietzschean). A constant thesis of this essay is non-Nietzschean and non-structural, and not only non-unitary: the minoritarian perspective, unlike the stato-minoritarian perspective and the perspective of games of power, rejects posing the problem of the individual not only in general terms of "relations," but also in terms of "difference" or "differend," that is, of fluid relation or becoming. In his essence, an individual is first of all an im-potence, a non-acting in itself that is experienced positively, more than a resistance, an indifference to coded social practice, more than a way out of Relations of Power: the individual never entered into games of power. This is why he can uni-lateralize them.

Theorem 14. *The One is not uni-lateral in itself or in its essence, but only it can induce around itself a real uni-laterality, an original and primitive dimension of laterality that affects any given relation or transcendent causality.*

Uni-laterality only becomes real and ceases to be merely logico-real if it simultaneously ceases to define the very essence of individuals in order to become a consequence of that essence, belonging to it virtually as its principal effect. The insertion of uni-laterality into a non-unitary thought of the One definitively transforms its concept and experience.

The paradox of a positive – that is, real – conception of unilaterality is that unilaterality itself changes sides, so to speak. More precisely, it "inverts" the only side in question in relation to the terms of the One and the World. To explain it in a very external way: the more we try to radicalize the unilaterality of a term, its characteristic of always being to the side, ill-placed, dehiscent, etc., the more it becomes necessary to leap: to attribute to this term a consistency that it draws absolutely in itself and that it experiences from itself, and thus to reject any other term *beside it* and as *its* side, even though it (if we can put it this way) remains at the center (of) itself – an unreflective or *non-thetic center* (of) itself. Unilateralizing a term renders it absolute; but as soon as it is really absolute, it is relations that are cast to its side, down-graded, completely dis-placed or de-rived. It is they that en-sue irreversibly from the term. First understood as essence of the term as it is, unilaterality ends up constituting an original and primitive dimension (of) "side," a veritable intention (of) laterality, in which this term as One does not fall, but into which it makes all the rest fall. This dimension – which is not in turn "beside" the One or the individual, but rather is its originary dimension of "side" or "laterality" – is directly or immediately rooted in the One.

The Absolute certainly "has" a side, or rather it determines a side, a primitive ir-reversibility, a unique and absolute direction that it itself is not, but which is the element in which the World, Authorities, the State, Universals, etc. will take hold.

This is how one avoids a conception of unilaterality that is still unitary, as absolute by itself, and thus relative-absolute: the Other or the Unconscious. No a priori primitive uni-*laterality* that would not be a real *uni*-laterality: uni-laterality determined by the One, which is its essence though itself no longer uni-lateral or beyond, a below of the World, a withdrawal, an Other, etc. Now is the moment to recall that this necessity for the World to en-sue from the One, and after it, is what we call *Determination in the Last Instance* – we will return to this point. It is also the moment to recall a thesis that is now more understandable: it is not minorities who are beyond Authorities, or the One beyond Being, but Being that is the beyond of the One and that is taken up in this primitive laterality (to) the One. It is the Whole that is uni-lateral . . .

Theorem 15. *The uni-lateral is the specific form of order of the real, which is not rational or rationalizable, not "logical" in any sense of the word. It is as distinct from the "relational," as from the "trans-versal," the "logo-centric," etc.*

All philosophical thought seeks a "form of order" – dialectics, syllo-gistics, the order of reasons, analytics, structure, being-in-the-world, difference, différance and supplementarity, etc. – which is for it the ultimate rationality of the real, one that it in part helps to determine. Insofar as it no longer falls under philosophy and rationality, the form of the order of the real is uni-laterality as irreversibility, induced by the One inherent non-thetically (to) itself. That is the "form" of order specific to terms as they are, when they are experienced as immediate givens, no longer falling into a relation and under a logic. The indi-vidual is not that which is beside . . ., on the margins of . . ., on the edges of . . ., beyond . . . it is instead that which induces around itself a side, a margin, an edge, a beyond.

Uni-lateral: a single side, a single edge. After the One, the origi-nary structure of our experience is not a bilateral relation, but uni-laterality. There is no bi-laterality, inter-subjectivity, relation, unless it is interior to the World . . . However they are specified, the *relational* or the *inter-subjective* is the point of view of the philosopher, who surveys the situation, denying its radical individual finitude, its proper essence, to better ensure his mastery over others, whom he plunges

51

back into the neutral and partially indifferent element of the relational, of the differentiel, of the differential. Unitary philosophy only scorns universals because it arises as an over-universal, an encompassing element that allows it to judge from on high the stubbornness of the individual, to incriminate his refusal to identify his reality with rationality. Unitary philosophy is the delirious form of the rationalization of the real, directed, among other things, by the sciences. But surrounding ordinary man, everything – the Whole, philosophy itself – becomes uni-lateral: *the Whole is a margin and the only margin that the real induces.* The One "in itself" suffices for a primitive – in the sense of irreversible – dimension, a *rection* that is not a di-rection, to take shape.

We will not mistake this laterality for a transversality. It is more originary than a transversality, which runs from point to point, each time forking at the crossroads, its impossible yet obligatory waypoints. Transversality is one of the final surges of unitary thought, the point where irreversibility still touches reversion – the "ideology" of the margin, the beyond, the deviation or the drift, the infinite course of difference, the continuation of the differend. In contrast, *uni-laterality is em-placement without dis-placement and without return, being derived without derivation or drift*, to which the One that is inherent (to) itself in a non-positional way constrains all that it is not, Being in particular.

As for the thesis of the "logocentrism" of metaphysics, it seems that neither it nor even perhaps its deconstructors have rigorously thought the centrality of the center and of logocentrism. When they speak of the need for a fixed point and for a center of metaphysics, they precisely still do so as philosophers, with a split double gaze, one eye on the center, one eye on the periphery, traversing the relations of hierarchy between the center and the periphery. But if the split squint is *the* unitary, that is, philosophical, method par excellence, the experience of the center as it is, of nothing-but-center, compels us to abandon the constraint of circularity and place ourselves *really* in the "center," that is, in the One itself as non-thetic (of) itself. Thus everything changes: for *if* something appears, either in the horizon, or more originarily as horizon, it will give itself in that which is not a horizon that is already there, but in that which inscribes every possible horizon, in a certain irreducible laterality. This more profound than the horizon is defined in relation to the One and thus is not circular. This is an originary dimension of down-grading, of being-derived, of en-suing, or of ir-reversibility. It is buried and lost in the metaphysical survey of the center. It thus seems that philosophers of the center or of "metaphysics" have never examined closely what a center is. If, like the metaphysicians themselves, they are content to survey the center from the periphery in a unitary round trip that is the utmost adventure allowed by philosophy, this is because they took logocentrism at face value and considered it logocentrically, leaving the essence of the center unclarified or indeterminate. This fault is the essence of philosophy, and extends far beyond "logocentrism," because it still reigns in its deconstructions. *All of philosophy is at once released from its pretensions when the center is really experienced in its non-thetic inherence (to) itself, before being experienced in its possible relation to a supposedly given periphery whose genesis moreover cannot be produced and whose essence cannot be elucidated.* The essence of logocentrism is not at all the need or desire for the center, it is purely and simply the lack of a center and of its real experience. It is vicious circularity and, for this reason, the mere "need" – but how "peripheral" – of a center. This need is, more deeply, a "forgetting" of what is, in its unary essence, the center as it is.

Theorem 16. *Real or absolute, and no longer relative, uni-laterality is what we call "Determination in the Last Instance." This is the specific causality of the individual or of ordinary man – a "minoritarian" causality.*

Uni-laterality is the non-philosophical but real or transcendental form of causality. When thought abandons the system of four causes and seeks the specific causality of the real or of the individuel (later we will say "individual"), it finds uni-laterality, the rigorous concept of determination in the last instance, which is the form of causality based on irreversibility alone, devoid of any "relation." It puts an end to the constitutive use of the category, philosophical by definition, of "reciprocal determination." Only the real, the individual as absolute, can without reciprocity (even deferred or delayed reciprocity) determine in the last instance that which it is not – the World, History, etc.

We miss the truth of the last instance when we think it as "in the last place," according to derived and conditioned instances; or as "in the first place," in the sense of a principle or a Unity. The "last instance" begins from itself, but not in a philosophical gesture of auto-position or of a principle; nor even in a leap more originary than the principle (the *Satz* in the *Grundsatz*. . .): it is a non-thetic beginning (of) itself, and the "last instance" finds its truth in a thought of the One rather than in a philosophy of Unity. Understood correctly, as an unreflective transcendental experience, the "last instance" eliminates the aporias and false problems born of its metaphysical and unitary interpretation.

Generally speaking, uni-laterality is no longer a mode of scission and transcendence, a separation or a secession – an abstraction. Instead, it is uni-laterality that forms the only content of real = unreflective phenomenal experience in transcendence. The State is beyond minorities, and its own transcendence falls within this beyond, which no longer has the form of transcendence, but the form of that which de-rives or en-sues irreversibly as de-distanced or dis-engaged. "Determination in the last instance" is par excellence the possibility of dualism and whatever of causality it still tolerates. It is pointless to mention how its mechanistic interpretations, but also their dialectical and structural correctives in various Marxisms, have distorted its meaning, lost its truth, rendered its thought impossible. It was an attempt, each time, perhaps even in Marx, to normalize it, to re-inscribe it in the more or less open circular schemas of the dialectic; to hide the radical dis-placement of "ideology" and politics in relation to the real, to subordinate it to visions that were sometimes materialist, sometimes mechanistic, sometimes dialectical, which, themselves, finally seemed "thinkable," whereas they were, as mere projections of unitary prejudice, great absences of thought and coarse tautologies.

Thus, the "last instance" is not a distant instance or a hinterworld, present in flesh and blood in spite of everything, or else present through its absence as "absent cause," as certain Marxists say, continuing Marx's error with regards to his own concept. As inherent (to) itself in an unreflective or non-thetic way, it induces an asymmetry from itself to the World that is no longer vulnerable to a corrective, a reversibility or recurrence of the World on it. Individuals dis-place the State, and minorities dis-place Authorities with a distancing [*d'un écart*] without relation, without possibility of the recurrent objectivation, thematization, and alienation of individuals. This dis-placement is first *with* the One, before any philosophical and political operation; it will not have been preceded by a reversal, an inversion, nor will it be followed by a reversion, a return to the "identical" state of things or the "same." With determination in the last instance restored to its transcendental essence, thought is able to limit the influence "topology" (of the logos of place inserted in the place of logos) exerts over it in the work of contemporary thinkers. The endless games of the relational, of chiasmus, of difference, by which unitary philosophers attempt to seduce, capture, and violate the real, are finally derived from the One from which they irreversibly en-sue by the force of the One itself.

It is now a question of grounding this solitude of the individual, solitude of beginning, solitude of reality, in its reality as an immediate given, as absolute experience "before" any principle. It is not enough to subtract uni-laterality from its logical, relative, or negative use: it is still necessary to ground the new use in a real, that is, transcendental, essence.

9. The Essence of the One or of the Finite Subject

Theorem 17. *The forgetting of the essence of the One grounds the forgetting of the essence of individuals and of their capacity to "uni-lateralize" the World, the State, Authorities.*

Thinking individuals from their power to unilateralize means risking another sacrifice to relation, at worst to "representation," at best to "difference." It is still necessary to root this power in an absolute and indisputable experience. The fundamental characteristic of minorities is the absolute refusal, even the before-refusal, to enter under totalities or to themselves form regularities and lines of becoming. However, this power must be recognized in its positivity, that is, as an effect of the One, of an essence ("unary," and not, we will repeat, "unitary"), which alone can give them a reality or immanence to which the Idea and Being, Institutions and the State, cannot lay claim.

We have suggested that there is an absolute, non-thetic givenness (of) itself, of irreversibility, an experience of the last instance of asymmetry, starting from which we can know, for example, what an asymmetrical relation in the World is. It is time to elaborate this factor = x for itself, because it is the foundation of everything. It is not added to uni-laterality as a complement or a supplement, but as its immediate reality, its actual experience, and thus as the individual's experience of individuality. As we have said, this factor is the One, and thus is more than a factor. Unitary metaphysics will have recognized the One only as a mere Unity, transcendental, to be sure, but in the mixed, logico-real, manner of a unity that *is added* to the empirical or ideal manifold, just like a supplementary factor. But the One is something else entirely.

The difficulty in understanding that uni-laterality can cease to be a relation to ..., or relative to ..., that it can become an *in itself*, as irreversibility no longer coupled with a reversibility and finally forming an autonomous instance, comes from whatever of the essence of the One has been forgotten and denied for the benefit of that

Unity with which the One has always been confused. Uni-laterality or ir-reversibility is by itself nothing other than that One: not insofar as it would always already have refused, as absolute, to enter into a relation – that refusal does not constitute its essence – but because its essence is autonomous from the beginning in such a way that it determines or induces an effect of ir-reversiblity around itself.

Must we bemoan the forgetting of the One the way some philosophers complain endlessly about the forgetting of Being? In one sense, this forgetting of the One is much deeper, more extensive, more ineradicable. The forgetting of Being could never have become the guiding principle of a thought save on the insistent and much more decisive ground of the forgetting of the One: attention to the forgetting of Being finds its condition of possibility in inattention to the One. But according to another turn of thought, the One does not have the same essence as Being; its forgetting is not the forgetting of Being, and perhaps we should even inquire into knowing whether the essence of the One is such that the One can be forgotten or be made itself forgotten? From Being to the One, forgetting and anamnesis will probably change mechanisms, because the One, upon whose essence we propose to meditate, refuses its convertibility with Being. Uni-laterality will be based in the One but only if the One "unilateralizes" Being itself, and does not enter, has never entered – the way Unity in reality does – into relations of intrication, blending, or conversion with Being. *The One is absolutely distinct – without itself being unilateral – from Being, which is only relatively distinct from the One, thus according to a mode of unilaterality. The One does not need Being, while Being needs the One.*

However, it is not yet time to describe the forgetting and remembering of the One. That time will come when we describe the resistance of the World, History, the State, and Universals in general to the One, their repression of the immediate givens of the individual or the minority (Chapter III). We will merely point out the absence of any meditation on *the specific essence* of the One within the core of Greco-occidental philosophy, that is, within the unitary paradigm. Indeed, we will not confuse ontologico-philosophical aporias and projections onto the One with a meditation on its specific essence. Against this paradigm, but particularly against Hegel, Marx, or Nietzsche, against their idealist or materialist uses of it (both of which remain empiricist), we must redefine what henceforth we will mean by the One, the individual, or the real. Their definition quite obviously assumes a problematic, techniques as well as criteria of thought that are quite different from those of Marx, Nietzsche, Heidegger, etc.

We will analyze the concept of minority in terms that challenge the Greco-occidental style and its ontology, its politics, its political ontology, and first of all its use of the One, which confuses the One with Unity and Totality. A radical thought of individuals as absolute of reality preceding Being and the State is impossible, and indeed useless, if we do not begin by awakening – against almost the entire tradition of "metaphysics" and its "surpassing," its "overcoming," its "différance," etc. – the specific requirement of the *veritas transcendentalis*, and if we are not capable of thinking it as an experience prior to all philosophical operations.

Theorem 18. *The experience (of) the One as without-division is thoroughly positive, and precedes the experience of division, of nothingness, of the Other, etc. No philosophical Evil Genius can deprive us of that experience that we "do not have," but that we are.*

To phenomenally describe the essence of the One, it is necessary to think two things together.

The first is that the invariant kernel of the One, once relieved of its fantastic and religious attributes, is the "exclusion" of all division: the without-division, the indivision. This insufficient definition lets us think that indivision is negative, a result of removing division. Indivision is thus a mere predicate, the highest no doubt, but still transcendent, just like any other predicate. This transcendent indivision is, at most, the indivision of what philosophers have called Unity, or sometimes the One. Such a Unity already had a transcendental meaning, but this term, "transcendental," designated for unitary philosophers only a logico-real or mixed point of view, or in any case a representational and transcendent point of view, not a fully – that is, "only" – immanent or real point of view. Unity is the unity of immanence and transcendence, whereas the One is the experience (of) immanence alone.

The semblance of a relative and negative indivision, devoid of specific and essential reality, suspended in the exteriority of the predicate, must thus be removed. It is removed when we turn precisely to that other essential characteristic – non-positional immanence. We in fact have an "idea," or rather a wholly positive experience, of the One in itself, because the One is, among other things, necessarily the essence of any experience and that we have it – *we are it* – before having the experience of division, of nothingness, of the Other, etc. I must not imagine that I only experience the One or immanence alone, without division or transcendence, through the negation of that which is multiple and divided rather than through a real experience. Not only would this confuse the One with what the philosophers commonly call "transcendental" Unity, and the experience of the real in its essence with an inferior experience – not a real experience but an "effective" experience or an experience of the World. This would reduce the One to the experience in particular of the unity-of-division [*de l'unité-de-partage*] of two contraries: Day and Night, Being and Nothingness, etc. Greco-unitary philosophy held onto this peri-worldly experience in order to avoid going any further, taking Unity, that is, thwarted Unity, as the prototype of all experience and bequeathing this prototype to Western philosophy. This is what contemporary thinkers still endlessly vary and extend under the name of Difference, Différance, Differend, etc. But, above all, this would be to sink into the nothingness and irreality of transcendence. I have the experience of indivision in its solitude anterior to any experience of division, or else I would have no experience in general, not even of myself. Only a super-Evil Genius could want to deprive me of this experience (of) experience. Furthermore, he could deprive me of this experience of the One only by recognizing in spite of himself that I am this One. The hypothesis of a will capable of depriving me of this real essence, which in truth I do not "have," but which I am, is fatuous and heralds the immediate suicide of this all-too-evil genius. All the more reason why these unitary philosophers, from Heraclitus to Heidegger and beyond, these semi-evil geniuses who are ultimately so ineffectually cunning, had to recognize the existence of the One, assume it as the keystone of Being or final requisite, and make all of philosophy rest in indivision as such. But they are satisfied to merely requisition indivision, to use it functionally as a mere limit on division; to give it a manifold of Being and Nothingness, of Same and Other, to conceive of the One not as the intimate experience of the finite Absolute that we are, but as a super-genus, an ultimate category, the highest of the transcendentals. In truth, it is philosophy that experiences the One through privation of division and of heterogeneity, which thus reduces the One to mere Unity. Furthermore, all philosophy can do is eternally reproach the One for its alleged relativity to division, to nothingness, to transcendence, and eventually to Being, and return to the games around the convertibility of the One and Being, to the entertainment of the "highest" tautologies of Same and Other, of Difference, etc. The foundation of the philosophical West is not the confusion of Being and being, but the confusion of the One and Being, of the One and Unity.

Theorem 19. *If indivision is an experience that precedes the experience of division, this is because it is given to itself according to the specific mode of indivision. The One is an unreflective or non-thetic (to) itself immanence, devoid of transcendence, nothingness, alienation, etc. This is the "veritas transcendentalis" in the rigorous sense or the "mystical" kernel of all thought.*

How do we "pass" from indivision that is still relative, in danger of drifting off into transcendence, to indivision as essential reality, "passing" from a relation to an absolute, from a negation or privation to an affirmation? Certainly, the One is not such a passage, an exit, or yet another transcendence in relation to the transcendence of Being. It includes in itself no philosophical operation or decision. That would only introduce into the One a relativity in relation to division, to nothingness, to transcendence – to Being. Indivision is not experienced or won against division, nor is it merely identified with division without mediation – as in Difference – or through mediation – as in the Dialectical Contradiction. *It absolutely a priori precedes division because it is given (to) itself and as itself.* It is immediately real from itself, without the mediation of transcendence in general. It draws its reality from its identity (to) itself. But its identity is not logical, that is to say, analytic; nor is it real in the sense of synthetic; nor is it the difference between these two modes. This identity is indivision itself, which remains immanent (to) itself and does not exit itself – it is irreducibly "finite," or condemned (to) itself. This is how indivision "becomes" real through and through: it experiences itself, gives itself (to) itself, but in a mode of givenness specific to it or a mode of which it is capable: precisely that of indivision or non-distance, non-objectivation, non-difference, non-alienation. Even though these terms are unsatisfying, the reality of the One is to be *only* "interior" or "inherent" (to) itself without needing to pose itself. Absolute interiority, and thus without manifestation in the World, without a common surface with History, without a border with Being and Games of Power. We will call this kernel of immanent experience without exteriority, this immediate givenness of the One-without-transcendence, "the mystical." *The mystical* is pre-philosophical, or, as we will say, "ordinary."

Theorem 20. *The One and the experience of the One are identical: this is its transcendental truth.*

The One is not given before its experience, before experience *in general* [l'expérience]. The essence of the One is its "reality" in the sense of its purely transcendental experience, insofar as the essence of the One – and in spite of the so-called "transcendental" tradition, although for the same reasons – is the essence of the *veritas transcendentalis* that was lost as soon as the autonomous or unitary philosophical decision came into being. The transcendentals themselves, in particular *ens*, presuppose a specific truth that only the One, and not Being, possesses: transcendental truth, truth that is autonomous in relation to all the transcendent forms of truth, not only scientific or religious forms, but ontological and logico-real forms as well. Unitary philosophy is identical with its bad conscience with regards to truth. We will not believe that philosophy clung dogmatically to "truth": at most, philosophy was subjected to its inferior and transcendent forms to the point of becoming that nihilistic hatred of truth that constitutes the essence of contemporary philosophical activity. The essence of truth is not of this world, of this history, of this philosophy, none of which know it at all. The *veritas transcendentalis* is unreflective immanence, without alienation or nothingness, and thus without a self-position: non-thetic or non-positional (of) itself. Without position and thus without topology: *there is no topology of the One*. The "transcendental" instance par excellence is not Being but absolute immanence, indivision insofar as it is its own "object" in a strictly immanent or "unreflective" (rather than "internal") experience. Prior to any other definition, "transcendental" means a radical immanence, devoid of distance to itself or of nothingness. This is the very definition of that which is only absolute, the absoluteness or the finitude of the absolute. The One is given *in itself* or in its own way: there is in it an identity of its "content," indivision, and of the mode of givenness (to) itself of that content. This *real identity* is the mystical; it is the foundation or the essence of the individual existent. Ordinary man is a "mystical" living being.

Transcendental thus signifies – more than ever – real *or* immanent: reality as immanent, immanence as real. This rules out the mere *condition of real possibility*, which is the unitary form of the transcendental. In fact, it is posed as still relative to a transcendent experience (perceptual, natural-philosophical, moral, linguistic, aesthetic, etc.), as unitary philosophers usually do. It thus includes in itself some transcendence, some separation, some negation – all ideal and relative to the empirical given. Unitary philosophy includes some of the transcendent in transcendental immanence; to transcendental immanence it gives an empirico-ideal *support*; to the One it gives the support of Being. Once again it is incapable of thinking the One in the rigor of its essence, which it cuts in two; it detaches indivision from itself or from its reality, functionally requisitioning indivision to place it in the service of transcendence, thereby confusing the essential: Unity with the One, transcendence with transcendental immanence.

A rule of anti-unitary thought arises from this: if a transcendental condition (of possibility) is to determine the conditioned, it must be indeterminable from the perspective of the conditioned and be determined first of all by itself. Too often – always . . . – unitary philosophers lazily rely on the conditioned to help them think the condition, on the transcendent to help them determine the transcendental: there is the infinite, the interminable, time, and history, etc., for this. The rigor of thought stems rather from its irreversibility, requiring that the One be completely and actually determined by itself before determining any other type of experience. The only rigorous thought is the *descending* "dialectic," one that starts from the One. Any dialectic that starts by ascending is circular, vicious, and ignores the unreflective essence of the *veritas transcendentalis*. This is why the essence of individuals (minorities as they are, irreducible to all the universals or to all the totalities) must be inscribed not in the interval or gap between the empirical (culture, history, languages, customs, etc.) *and* the transcendental, but in the essence alone of the transcendental itself. The One is that which breaks the empirico-transcendental parallelism.

Theorem 21. *The unary and the unitary are really distinguished according to whether indivision is immediately and non-thetically given (to) itself or given to itself by and with division (scission, nothingness, transcendence, etc.)*

We differentiate between the *unary* and the *unitary*, unreflective immanence and reflexive-reflective immanence constituting itself through the mediation of a scission. Here, "unreflective" does not quite have its Sartrean meaning. It denotes the non-positional or non-thetic (of) itself immanence that is no longer the immanence of a synthetic substance but rather that of a pre-ontological or pre-substantial individual. The real immanence of the One as non-unifying principle, neither synthetic nor analytic and repulsive, does not know the "self-presence" ["*présence à soi*"] of consciousness. It forms a light, if you will, but an absolutely coherent light that does not proceed by reflection and is not itself open to being reflected, divided, and captured. The absolute "autonomy" of the One means, among other things, that it is in-alienable or finite, that it cannot even be grasped by the mirror of representation, be reflected as self-*same* and by means of a division *of* itself.

61

The essence of the One is indivision, but this is not the function of indivision as Unity associated with a Form, an Idea, or a Difference. Unity is in fact given by and with something else: a division or a transcendence. On the contrary, indivision is here given in itself, in its own immanence, in a strictly unreflective way – this is what constitutes its absolute reality – instead of being given, as is that of Unity, with and through its contrary: scission, nothingness, and finally the universal and mediation. Thus deprived of transcendence, it is devoid of ideality or formality. It no longer bathes in the neutral or indifferent element of universality. The Idea or the Relation is also indivisible or "undecidable," but it is a totally relative indivisible, one that still tolerates specific division, which it overcomes. For example, when Marxists say that the "One divides," they are thinking not of the One but of something else, of Unity, of the *relation* of the scission of contraries, of Scission-as-Unity, that is, of the Idea (in which, moreover, they still reflect inferior forms of unity: these are empirical idealists who have not yet attained the Heraclitean or Nietzschean state of the purification of the relation of contraries, their pure coincidence, that is, absolute idealism . . .). If the One, on the other hand, does not tolerate division, if the cuts are not reflected in it, this is because the One is not Unity, the transcendent Unity of the mathematico-moral Idea, or the immanent Unity of the Relation of Power. Unity is nothing more than the reflection of the minoritarian One in and as transcendence, a self-synthesis that is split and reflected for itself. The attribution of the One to minorities will surprise only the philosophers, who confuse the One with Unity and with a relation of contraries, and who give – this is a contemporary example – a techno-political interpretation of the condition that ought instead make individuals independent of the World or the State.

Thus the One is not unifying, and even less unified, even for itself. Nor does it divide itself, and for the same reason: the One is not synthetic outside itself or in itself. Its mode of efficacy, lateralizing rather than unifying or positional, knows no operation of synthesis on an exterior and received manifold, nor on a manifold with which it would be joined ("continuous multiplicities"). Knowing no form of synthesis or unity, no form of division or reflection, the One is independent of all forms of relation, be they "logical" (mathematical relations) or "real" and synthetic (self-consciousness). We will not confuse the One with the reflexive syntax of "self-consciousness," nor with that radicalized and becoming form of the Unity-of-Contraries, the thwarted unity of the Same that is "Difference" or the "Differend." It is experienced in an immanence that is heterogeneous to any *interiority* (psychological, logico-ideal and formal, phenomenological) because it excludes the scission that defines either the self-consciousness that projects itself as horizon (Hegel, Husserl), or Being that projects itself as relation-(of)-relation (Heidegger), or Difference that projects itself as techno-politics (Nietzsche). Instead, the One should be experienced as positive indivision, as lived and received non-distance, living coherence or inherence (to) itself. This indivision is not the result of a re-unification, and it is not an effect or a product of synthesis. It is the real immanence of the One that allows us to avoid transcendental realism, that is, the projection of an empirico-ideal immanence of a given object, of a unity-of-thing or of *res*, in Essence. Essence is devoid of all ideal interiority because it is devoid of Unity. We will thus distinguish between undivided immanence or immanent indivision *lived* in a non-positional way, proper to the dispersions of finite individuals, and the ontological, onto-theo-political, techno-political interiority of a synthesis or of a relation, of a presence *to* itself [à *soi*] or a being *in* [*être* à] . . . (being *in* the world, *in* history, *in* itself [à *soi*]), which, thus separated or detached, becomes incomplete or abstract. Immanence that is complete, or rather finite or without remainder, is not the immanence of a unity that would receive itself.

Nothing-but-subject devoid of attributes, the One ceases to be a logical or ontological entity. It is a real and living "principle," a lived essence, an "internal," or, more precisely, unreflective experience (it is the unreflective that constitutes the internal, not the inverse) that is below logico-ideal essences as well as logico-real essences (relations or games of power, for example). Furthermore, individuals are not the objects of a production that presupposes a reproduction. Any philosophy of the Idea or of the Relation, even when it assigns to the Relation the Idea itself as content, reduces production to reproduction (the West has never been able to make production anything other than a reproduction) and makes re-affirmation penetrate into the heart of affirmation. The unary and non-synthetic conception of the real ought to free us from the dilemma in which philosophy has been trapped, of essence as logical or as real = productive or synthetic and thus reproductive.

Theorem 22. *Individuals are immediate givens prior to all unitary, that is, dialectical, scission. The dialectic assumes the real, which determines it, like everything else, in the last instance.*

Individuals of the last instance begin through themselves, that is, through an im-mediate multiplicity that is not a withdrawal or a scission. This multiplicity is experienced in itself and is not divided, but receives itself or possesses itself immediately such it is according to its specific mode. Individuals are filled up (with) themselves, without division and thus without Unity, synthesis, or self-presence. Finding themselves and experiencing themselves as multiple straightaway, they have nothing to decide, too passive to be taken up in a becoming or inserted into a process, to accept the humiliating terms of "difference" or "contradiction."

If minorities combine their being with the unreflective, they do not know division "in two": "One divides in two," one side of contradiction is divided in turn, division reflects itself on each side, etc. The unreflective does away with such games. There is never one minoritarian, then two born of that one through cut and addition, scissiparity, supplementarity, or even rhizomaticity. The One-without-scission, unilaterality without division, is "first," anterior to the relative unity of the One-that-divides. It is thus straightaway multiple and excessive, always in excess over the 2 and not only over the 1. The minoritarian subject only exists as dispersive, not as several and repeated. There is never any preliminary or latent unity (or scission, as the one is inseparable from the other) as in the dialectic, but a uni (-laterality) without-unity-and-without-scission, but not without immanence. Unity-as-scission is that which alienates itself and returns – this is the State or the World – as the *antecedens* of a horizon of universal power, as an objective techno-political appearance, a preliminary or presupposed authoritarian condition that constitutes a symptom to which philosophers of "Relations" (of production, of power) and of "Difference" confine themselves. That which is divided, that which divides-itself is already in itself division; that which cuts-itself is already in itself cutting: Unity. But the One and its own multiplicities do not recut or overcut themselves. Furthermore, this is not the primacy of Unity over contraries, over their scission, or vice versa, which remains the last criteria of this essential dialectic, which is coextensive with the unitary paradigm, but rather the primacy of the Unity-Scission over the One, of the unitary duel over the unreflective: the denial of the real, the Greco-occidental confusion or paralogism of Unity with the One, of the Polis with minorities, the stato-minoritarian paralogism such as Nietzsche, for example, carried out. This primacy of Unity-Scission, of Unitary Scission, of Difference, is an appearance (Whole = Absolute), and it is that of the State and its form. The Statist Ideal, or the Unitary Illusion, is a "symptom" that is consubstantial with the Western dialectic, be it negative (Hegel) or positive (Nietzsche), but this affinity is only visible from a totally different point of view and certainly not "from within" Marxism and Nietzscheanism.

In fact, the dialectic functions not only transcendently, but also, in spite of itself, as a transcendental principle. It exists like a decision that decides in advance that reality is subjected to the jurisdiction of the decision of contraries, of their scission, and of their unity. The dialectic decides that the One is undecidable or has the form of a contradiction, or else of a difference, the form of Unity-Scission or else of Difference, which is Form par excellence. It hardly leaves itself open to error: having given itself the One as a presupposition, it is silent about its essence so as to insist only on the final One of the identity of contraries, thereby avoiding the appearance of a vicious circle. The dialectic begins neither with God, nor with people, nor with things, but with Authorities, with the State. With Unity, even when it begins with Scission: above all with scission. From this arises its completely unitary hatred of individuals and the activism it sets in opposition to the "passivity" of minorities. The dialectic, in all its forms, is one process of power among others, and among these others it confesses its affinity for the Statist or Authoritarian Ideal. It is in this way that the dialectic becomes no longer a political problem – it is one by its mere existence – but a minoritarian problem through its claim to count for the real and the way it proceeds with the primacy of scission, that is, – must we repeat it? – with the primacy of Unity, ideality, and synthesis. No surprise here if, with such a claim, the dialectic and philosophy in general were always conceived of as laws of history, of society, and of nature. The law is always simultaneously above the law; a law only rules when it is relatively absent from itself and the world, in the manner of Authorities and the State, which simultaneously fall and do not fall under their own legislation. This is the authoritarian truth of the dialectic, the point by which, appearing as the universal that holds for all of the real, it poses itself as an absolute fact, reflects itself into itself, and claims to legitimate itself in an absolute autonomy. The unitary dialectic that we use as thought is the Statist Ideal in theory and practice.

10. Minorities and Authorities

Theorem 23. *Minority is an unreflective transcendental experience, which, like the real itself, determines Authorities in the last instance.*

As unreflective transcendental experience, the One is that which "grounds" uni-laterality and ir-reversibility, that which removes from them their relative character and gives them their reality. Experienced this way, this One is the essence of the individual. We call this essence "unary."

"Unary" does not mean uni-city. Uni-city refers on the one hand to Unity, from which it is inseparable, and on the other hand to real or finite individuality, not individuel but, as we will now say, "individual," which is the token of radical singularity. The One is so in itself that it refuses to enter into an empirical or ideal Whole (perceived object, duplicating optical image, logical signification, conceptual generality, ideal relation or function). The finite individual retains its absolute autonomy without needing to receive a complement or to serve as a complement for another so as to form together some sort of totality. Minorities are neither identifiable under a universal nor as a universal, a horizon of light, an ecstatic transcendence or a project, a rule for the organization of powers or for the governmentality of multiplicities, all of which would act as a "complement" to their "unilateral" character regarded as an insufficiency. It would only be insufficient if they were modes of division and if they needed the aid of Unity. Minorities are instead this absolute solitude of "being"-without-World, without-Being, without-History, without-Program, without-Project. They do not allow themselves to be divided like institutional continua or relations. These are the Techno-political Universals that claim to complete them, to fill their "lack" according to their own organization, either inserting them into their horizon and sub-suming them under their rules, or joining so tightly with them that they give the illusion of having captured them in their rules, their becomings, political lineages, or paths, of marrying them without their consent and then refusing to divorce them, having in any case no existence, no breath, and no life, save from these dispersive "objects."

Defined in this way, as real rather than philosophical or political, minority is an unreflective transcendental experience or an experience completely devoid of transcendence. Minorities are the only immediate givens in historical and cultural experience. Immediate, because they expel the mediation of a relational horizon (which is always, sooner or later, technopolitical objectivity) as alienating, useless, and uncertain for their reality. They are real straightaway through and for themselves, in the form of a lived *in itself*. From this springs the "inversion" that is essential for thinking the individual: they are no longer beyond the Universal or the Idea, as in Platonism, which makes of the One the Idea of Unity. They are in themselves [*en soi*], and any "beyond," that is, any transcendence, is deduced from this in itself [*en soi*]. This is not a more or less refined supplementary mode of transcendence. It is rather the State that is "beyond" (but in a new sense of this word) minorities and transcendent to individuals.

They thus form the in-audible background noise of culture and history, a noise completely in the background, uncreated and thus inextinguishable, even though games of power try to imitate them, to pro-ject them as the relative-absolute limit of history. They form the real non-objectivable phenomenal content of techno-political strategies in general; they join with the test of power reduced to its essence. It is obvious that techno-political experiences, always mediated in spite of everything by the machine of the State, are possible, and that there is a pure historical experience of the universal techno-political field. But these tests of Authoritarian Institutions and of States are always linked at least peripherally, with the universal element of power. Techno-political experience (the institutionality of institutions, the statism of states, the State-form, the State-type, the Statist Ideal) is simultaneously self-mediated and transcendent, and not only transcendental and subjective. The experience (of) themselves of minorities is the only experience that is simply transcendental, the only experience that does not fall into techno-political universals. It is almost inevitable that this im-mediacy of subjects (to) themselves and (to) their culture, their past, their world, their gods, their earth, is confused with a self-presence [*une présence à soi*], a self-consciousness [*une conscience de soi*], a self-will [*une volonté de soi*]; with a stubbornness, a natural particularity, or with the substantiality of a subject inscribed in these universals; but this is the illusion of those who make "mediation" their trade: politicians, functionaries, revolutionaries, philosophers . . .

Theorem 24. *The individual and the relational are distinguished from one another as the unary and the unitary.*

The essence of the individual in its transcendental truth is thus not unitary, but "unary." To distinguish this essence and its rigorous phenomenal description from their unitary conceptions that re-inscribe them in the game of relations, we create the adjective "individual."[4] It designates the finite transcendental essence of the individual and thus contrasts with the individuel, which is always relational. We speak of individual structures of the subject, of the individual essence of ordinary man. "Individual" refers to a rigorous description (from the triple and unique transcendental, phenomenal, and real point of view) of man as such [*comme tel*], or rather *as he is* [tel quel], and is opposed to every relational, that is Greco-unitary, conception of subjectivity and man. The *relational* is as broad as the unitary paradigm itself, above all when it becomes the higher mixture of Idea and matter, this hylé of the Relation of Power in which the Idea is raised to the power of Good or of the Idea-of-the-Idea. True minorities must not surpass it, below or beyond, but rather determine it as uni-lateral. This is real determination, which no longer proceeds in an ideal manner or through a "withdrawal" – still a distant mode of the transcendence of the Idea in relation to the empirical or in relation to itself. We "posit" – in reality this is the a priori experience of minorities – that they form a true absolute, an autonomy that is no longer gained through relativity, an instance so real it cannot be deduced from a multiplication, an intensification, or a re-affirmation of ideality as such of Relations. The phenomenal real contained in the Idea or the Form is not – as almost all contemporary thinkers, for unitary reasons, believe – exhausted in the destruction of the inferior forms (perceptive or conceptual) of the blending of the sensible and the intelligible, or of the gregarious forms of their community. This is merely what is established by, for example, unlimited becoming-revolutionary à la Nietzsche. Its effect is rather – and even this effect does not exhaust it – the "destruction" of the Idea or the Relation itself as a "higher form" of any pure thing or mixture. Apparently the Idea is "surpassed" in a non-ideal way "towards" the real, the way the fulfilled Polis is surpassed non-politically towards the beyond of the State – though in reality it is the Idea and the Polis that "surpass" or "transcend" the real. Minorities are most certainly not like *Dasein*, which Heidegger, in a very "Western" way, still says transcends towards the Good, that is to say, towards the Polis. On the contrary, these are all forms of the Polis, even the completed fusion of the State and minorities organized by *Technopolis* as *Infinite Revolutionary Empire*, which leave outside of them even more irreducible dispersions and an invisibility without withdrawal that no longer has the form or figure of transcendence. It is no longer beyond the limits of that Empire, which during the unlimited Revolution invented the supreme means for subjugating individuals, that we must seek a pre-statist and pre-technopolitical apriori. In truth, it always already preceded them in a non-ontological and non-ideal way. Minorities are no longer understood as a process of transcendence or surpassing, but as the in itself of a radical immanence that repels them "beyond." The ordinary individual is not, therefore, a new supplement to the Overman; it is the Overman who, at precisely the moment that he thinks he "overcomes" man as this "all-too-human" with which he is interconnected, is constrained by ordinary man to a form of transcendence he did not will, and which contains no promise of returning to or having an effect on man. Because man is unsurpassable, because he is finite, the philosopher, who always claims to surpass man, is condemned to a transcendence stronger than the one he has mastered – to a unilaterality that, without alienating him, loses him for man.

Theorem 25. *There is no minoritarian difference. Minority is an immanent and unreflective multiplicity prior to any difference, differend, or différance. The equation minoritarian = relative or different (from) is the thought of the State and the State's final ruse.*

We must abandon the stato-minoritarian point of view: not politically, but in the experience of the essence of ordinary man. Minoritarian does not mean "relative." That mixes up the multiple with the relative and does what the West, its philosophers, and its politicians have always done: identify minority with a "difference," that is, with the indivisible or undecidable kernel of a Relation. Minority is the power to uni-lateralize or, if we can put it this way, to "irreverse," but experiencing itself in itself, starting from its own essence, in an unreflective way, and, from this, truly determining Authorities as uni-lateral. Through its positive sufficiency, minority is "deprived" of all relation. Only the State and Authorities conceive of minorities as "differences" or fluid relations of power that they seek "beyond" reified political relations that are stripped of dialectical movement or flux. Moreover, it is impossible to continually, through successive distortions, bring the traditional concept of "minoritarian difference" to the state of an "individual" concept; impossible to pass via transitions from the "relative" to the "finite." To destroy the equation minoritarian = relative = different(ial), it is necessary to cease saying and thinking that the minoritarian "differs" from others and from itself, and to stop believing that we are right in doing so. The minoritarian is absolutely different because it rightly foregoes being "beyond" institutions and the State, foregoes "differing," forgoes "making a difference," and because it experiences its existence in an immediate and unreflective way, without any distance to itself. This finitude, which was never a relativity but instead contrasts with all relativity, is able to downgrade or de-rive the State, which thus irreversibly follows individuals in the order of immediate givens.

Theorem 26. *Minorities in the rigorous sense of the word are singulars, individuals, multiples; not singularities, individualities,*

69

multiplicities. Unlike the latter, they are radically invisible in the horizon of universals of power, sex, language. They are pre-political, pre-sexual, pre-linguistic, etc., secrets.

The individual or diasporic-finite real is inseparable from an unreflective transcendental experience of the One that is immediately a "multiple" without the universal of multiplicity or of individuality, a dispersion of individuals that does not reconstitute a Body, a Continent, a Substance, a State, even if they were specific to that dispersion. The minoritarian "gnosis" does not proceed by projecting an ideal horizon of intelligibility taken from the World (Logos, Intelligence, Analytical or Dialectical Reason, Self-consciousness, Class Struggle, etc.); it is the knowledge that precedes the light of the Idea and that turns thought into the immanent contemplation of unilaterality that the One "decides." The theory of minorities is nothing other than the immediate given of the One – of the One that nevertheless "multiples" are when they are no longer continuities, unities, or regularities – relations.

Because minorities are radically invisible politically, invisible in any possible unitary mode, there are no known examples of individuals. When minorities meet historical, cultural, and political criteria, they are thereby responsible and disputable groups, countable and speakable in institutional spaces and according to supposedly given codes – groups that are more or less identifiable and that agree, whether they like it or not, to enter into the authoritarian parousia of the World. This is not the case with finite individuals: they are not a secret only *for* History – they themselves are such secrets, or have the secret for their essence.

Theorem 27. *Real individuals are uncountable, unspeakable, indisputable.*

When, as in the contemporary thought of "Difference," individuals are raised to the state of continuous multiplicities, of completely relative minorities equipped with a techno-political concept, they no doubt cease to be empirically speakable and countable through reference to units of measurement or historical, cultural, natural, political, sexist, etc., codes. But the pure possibility of counting them, their ideal enumeration and qualification thus become their essence and replace their statistical definitions. Indeed, in the technopolitical sense, "minorities" are what we call collections of those special unities, differences, that are relative and objects of repetition: the

matrix of these stato-minoritarian minorities is and . . . and . . . and
. . . etc. The essence of these collections is their ideal enumeration or
their quantitability. On the other hand, the real or individual concept
of minorities rules out the possibility of producing them through
repetition of those unities (even partial ones) that relative cuts are.
For the power of uni-laterality through which we now define them
is absolutely a subject non-thetic (of) itself and can no longer be
subjected to a repetition. Abandoned to the solitude without return
of their finitude, they are definitively "deprived" of this characteristic
of collection or open whole, of this side that is synthetic or unifying
in spite of everything, of this unity of "same," repetition or reproduction, that makes every multiplicity also *a* multiplicity or a "body."

Neither the dispersive nor the individual is a fantastical redoubling
of continuous minorities into even "higher" and rarer minorities that
nevertheless would remain the same type and grounded in the same
syntax. Individual dispersions form the multiple par excellence, but
because the multiple is finite it does not retain the form of a quantifi-
able and enumerable object, either empirically or ideally. Thought
finally emerges from the pure image, from the representation of the
multiple – "multiplicity" – as from a collection or a "several" liable to
be counted according to an ideal world. Because of their finite immanence, minorities are the "multiples" that are inalienable within a
unity. These are the continuous multiplicities of games of power, produced through the repetition of cuts or differential relations, which
are reducible, fugitive, effaced by the very operation that repeats or
affirms them, reduced to a play of disjunctions and collective traces.
When thought finally dispenses with this final representation of the
multiple, when it suspends not only the enumerations and the pre-
conceived quantities, but also some of their transcendent(al) forms –
which are only ideal and relative, rather than simply real – it discovers
the remainder, the resistance of dispersions without countable unities.
Dispersives are absolutely *un-countable* minorities, whose positivity
entails the immediate absence, without negation, of ontological and
onto-theo-political power, that is, of the allegedly essential power of
self-counting and being counted.

It is representation, or what is left of it in the technopolitical
perspective of contemporary thinkers, that intentionally mistakes
minorities (we should say: *minors*) for pluralities, thus risking confusing them with social, cultural, and historical formations that are
presumed to exist in themselves. The concepts of the unreflective and
the finite ought to free us from this doublet of de facto – historical and
cultural – minorities within continuous minorities. It is not, therefore,

a supplement of ideality, of universality, of pure relativity – a supplementary repetition – that can absolutely "surpass" or "reverse" these ideal collections of cuts or of differences. The One is the supracountable, or rather, of the last instance, dispersive factor that keeps differences alive while nevertheless refusing to yield to repetition and to enter, in its turn, into the flowing form of difference. However, as soon as the One is assumed to be "invested" in the technopolitical or institutional continua of which it is the determination, it forms multiplicities with them that are always unary in the last instance, and that are as liable, through their continuous side, to give way to empirical or pure enumerations as they are to qualifications and specifications. By themselves, uni-lateralizing dispersions are neither dispersing nor dispersed, nor both at once. They are no longer images traced from a known type of multiplicity, as in the monstrous union of the Multiple and Unity that representation has always opposed and reunited.

Theorem 28. *Individuals refuse to be compatibilized in a universal calculation, a calculation for the end, the gathering, or the limit of history – for the Revolution or some other fetish.*

Any notion of minorities that is at all transcendent, exterior, or objective must be "renounced." Any notion that would make minorities the result of a process of idealization and reproduction, a system of synthetic cuts deployed as a new universal, a minoritarian continuum in the World or on the edges of the World, which would be the relative-absolute limit of history, and which, because it would be ideal and continuous, would be not only transcendental or immanent, but also transcendent – a new Authority. Individual minorities do not redouble, divide into two, purify, or "pro-ject" factual minorities and those constructed by contemporary techno-philosophy; they do not form a hinterworld of resistance to the natural abuses of history; they are not traced from a historical or imaginary model of minorities. Instead, they amount to the sole impenetrable real, uncreated and identical to immanent experience, the only thing capable of keeping "differences" open, non-idealizable and non-negotiable; of setting an absolute "end" to the process of universal auto-consummation not of history, but of the real by history.

We need to stop imagining individuals and searching for them in the cracks of power, like searching for a speck even subtler than the micro-political games that occupy Intellectuals. Neither "disciplines" nor any other historical-political formation can generate individuals.

72

The actuality of the radically finite subject, that which permits it to say "I," has no historical dimension: only political and philosophical Authorities interpret through extension and intensity, through activity and power, the impenetrable secret that is not of this World. A historical figure of man fades away in the same movement in which it is born, but man, the actual subject, is without figure. Were it not for philosophical and historical smugness, there would be no figure of man, and no part of him, at least of his essence, would be destined to fade like a ripple, die like a wave, pass like a river. History is an undertaking of auto-liquidation that sings the glory and the toughness of man.

Theorem 29. *Minorities are immediate givens that precede power games, language games, philosophical games: they are thus the real critique of Authorities.*

We seek the condition of the sphere of stato-minoritarian Authorities in the minoritarian sphere properly speaking; the condition of continuous or ideal multiplicities, of power games, in unary or real multiples. This second type of "multiplicities" does not cancel out the first, but subordinates it by imprinting an insurmountable uni-laterality upon it. The *real* – non philosophical – *critique* of onto-theo-politics (that of Nietzsche, for example, but first of all that of Plato and philosophy as a whole) looks nothing like "reversing" and "displacing" them. All of these gestures are both philosophical and onto-theo-political: minorities are no more an operation, an activity in History, the World, etc., than they are an object or a concept. They do not belong to this gesturalism, to this activism, to this philosophico-political practice. They are the immediate givens of the transcendental or unreflective experience of the One. They are the Peoples (-of-) the One as experience of indivision in itself, of uni-laterality experienced positively from itself, turned around into a uni-laterality affecting the State.

When they maintain their existence within the limits of their real essence, individuals perform the real critique of the State. By their essence as individual existent, devoid of the universality of existence, they are the actual critique of the State and of Authorities. They do not have to inscribe that critique, this *Krisis of Authorities*, in the World or in History because they themselves are already this *Krisis of the World-in-totality, of history-in-totality*, etc. (these points are developed in Chapters III and IV).

— II —

WHO ARE AUTHORITIES?

11. Individuals and the World

Theorem 30. *The real critique of the Copernican Revolution demanded by a rigorous science of man presumes that the finite subject is located at the center (of) itself, and no longer of the World, and that the World ceases to revolve around the subject so that it can be determined in the last instance by it.*

Up to this point, we have only recognized the essence of ordinary man. We know that he *really* exists and that he is *really* distinct from the World, from Language, from Philosophy. This is the first moment of his biography: the description of the fact that he is, in his essence, uncreated, and the recognition that this is the condition from which we will achieve a rigorous science of him.

In our Western thought, man has always been a great, unstable figure, a moving idea, a historico-philosophical event with traceable origins and a predictable end. A river with a source near Greece, which ends several thousand kilometers downstream after a meteoric course, in the eddies of a brief history. This was man as support and periphery of logos; as foam, ripple, or fluctuation of history; as play at the intersection of the great authoritarian universals: Sex, Language, Power, Will, Meaning, etc.; man whom philosophy only agreed to recognize as a desiring being, a speaking being, a capable being, a signifying being, etc. As a subject, certainly, but not yet as the subject of a specific science. Merely the subject of the anthropological myth, always finding himself, in the obsessive presence of these universals, facing if not objects, then at least objectivity, and being himself only on the condition of *reaching* himself, of being alienated in these universals and *returning* to himself, reconquering his essence. It was man who lost his finitude because of philosophy, an infinite as much as a finite being, as heterogeneous, overdetermined, and ephemeral as History: the man of anthropo-*logy*, or else (and not all that different) of the death of anthropology. The one we were told was dead, without quite realizing that the "death of man" was itself a thesis corrupted by history and reliant on the same fundamental prejudice – the unitary prejudice – as "anthropology" and "humanism," which were promised Gehenna, but deserved something else entirely: indifference. The rigorous science of man begins with the rejection of these unitary myths and the affirmation of the radical autonomy of the subject, of its finitude "below" universal predicates. The final yield of Greco-unitary thought is the confusion of the exhaustion of anthropology with a death of man.

We do not know, perhaps we will never now, if this epoch of thought is over, if thought that still thinks according to epoch and in bondage to history is destined for complete domination. Is the goal still to "complete" the "Copernican Revolution," or rather to suppress it by liberating the subject of all "revolution," by placing it at what undoubtedly is still the "center," but the non-positional center (of) itself, not at the more or less decentered center of Being, of World, of Language, of Sexuality, of Science, etc. At the non-thetic center (of) itself, the subject ceases to be weighed down by these predicates or these vis-à-vis that offer themselves to it and solicit it, with which it seems to conclude a philosophical pact, no doubt determining these universal spaces, but only provided that it is determined by them in return, and in an increasingly prevailing way. What must be eliminated is the subject that believes it is only itself when the army of these stars turns *around it*, and which seduced by the World, agrees to negotiate the non-negotiable, that is, its finitude, its real separation from the World and Being, in the name of so many possible "alliances" that only express philosophical narcissism and authoritarian tricks.

We have placed him at the beginning, this subject-without-Object, without-World, this man-without-Being, who, because of his extreme finitude, has no vis-à-vis. Without once more inverting the Copernican Revolution, we change the hypothesis, abandoning the almost immemorial philosophical gesture of seeking man sometimes at the center, sometimes on the periphery, in a game of coming-and-going that makes up the entirety of dominant philosophy and the only reality of the subject philosophy experiences. We start with originary or ordinary man, as from this center that is finite or non-positional (of) itself, that is, from the absolute (non-relative) center, devoid of periphery, of locality, and of all universal space in general. This, as we have said, is only the first moment of his biography. Is it a question of solipsism, of a solitude artificially deprived of World, of Language, of Authorities? Not only is this solitude positive and, as individual rather than individuel, adapted to the multiplicity of individuals, but the subject, which is without-World or without-Language, etc. in the sense that it is not co-constituted or co-operated by them, encounters the World or Language in a way that is no longer reciprocally determined by them: it encounters them unilaterally and no longer as an ob-ject. The destruction of the unitary conception of the subject, which is still that of the "Copernican Revolution," does not redouble the individual or essential solitude of man with an existentiell or intra-worldly solitude: as we will soon see, the individual implies a duality with the World, and his solitude is completely positive and ensues from a sufficiency rather than from a privation. *The individual is radically finite, though also affected by the infinite. Instead of man being an infinite subject affected by finitude, he is a finite subject also affected by infinitude.* Instead of man being surrounded by a World, he is a subject-without-World, who, for this reason, encounters a World across the absolute emplacement he imposes on it.

We will now describe this second experience of the life of ordinary man.

Theorem 31. *The ordinary individual experiences his reality and thinks from himself, in the radical finitude of his essence as inherence (to) himself: he is for himself an immediate given. But he also produces a second type of experience, that of universals: the World, History, Sexuality, Language, Power, Philosophy, etc.*

It so happens, without us being able to "give" any reason for it derived from the World itself, that the individuals that we are, despite being radically finite or inherent (to) themselves as the One, and being identical to a non-thetic (of) itself experience, *also* lead to experiences of a completely different sort: experiences of universals, of continua, of unities, of totalities, of Authorities in general. It hardly matters whether we know why: the order of experiences is such that, as finite individuals, we now encounter an aggressivity, a frenzy, an interminable grinding through which what we call History, the World, etc., are made. These are entities which, *without being objectivated*, are globally unilateralized: what should be called "Theworld," "Thehistory," "Thestate," etc., a likely unlimited series of activities, each unlimited for itself. It is characteristic of unitary philosophy to explore these attributes, to experience them sometimes as rather infinite, interminable, sometimes as rather finite, but in any case to take them as an object, to use them as a vehicle, to cling to this agitation and to draw movement, being, and thought from it. Thus, in the World and on its edges, finite individuals also find Philosophy, an entity that also ought to be called "Thephilosophy," and they find it intertwined with History, Authorities, etc. We do not yet know what they will do with all of these great authoritarian universals. But if the order of immediate givens here offers a new test for thought, it is important to pause at this encounter itself.

Theorem 32. *Even though any possible experience of ordinary man is carried out from the immanence of his lived experiences or from his finitude, nothing in his finitude or his essence prevents him from also producing another experience, but already unilaterally.*

Finite individuals are not a beyond of the World, and minorities are not the unconscious of Authorities. They exist straightaway from themselves, and are not acquired through an operation of reduction or suspension. Furthermore, they neither negate the World or the State nor destroy them. Nor do they nihiliate them. Phenomenological "bracketing" was already a softening of destruction, and even of doubt: it left the World there while depriving it of its natural authority. But individuals have as their essence the One, which is more positive, more contemplative than the "Transcendental Ego." The One retains and protects the World more positively: it uni-lateralizes it – this is its operation of suspension. Individual or ordinary experience is able to bring the World to phenomenality less reluctantly than phenomenology, which was too eager to negate it *logically* after having reduced it to an unavowable empiricity. If the World is not necessary for the test of the essence of the One, if it is contingent and indifferent to it, then correlatively the One neither repulses nor negates the World: finite subjects phenomenalize the World radically or unilateralize it *if* it appears and only if it appears. Now, we have admitted that it appeared, that something like the World appeared from itself, without us, as finite individuals, knowing why. In this way we have conformed to its claims, and nothing from the essence of minorities – if we are faithful to its positive indifference to Authorities, to its unilateralization of them – bars us from it or constrains us to negate or nihilate them in their existence "in themselves." The State is not essential to minorities – even if it appears as necessary, this is the

Unitary Illusion – but nothing in minorities prevents the State (or Authorities) from manifesting itself as either necessary or unnecessary. The fecundity of ordinary man takes different paths than the operations of negation, alteration, and nihilation, which philosophy elaborates and, in its unitary self-resentment, needs. These are the paths of determination in the last instance of the World, its immediate, insurmountable uni-laterality: the most positive "reduction" it can possibly undergo without being negated.

Theorem 33. *The "effective" denial of the One, the resistance to the real, is no obstacle for the One or for anything that follows the order of immediate givens. Rather, it is the rock or the support that allows individuals to suspend, according to the "mystical" mode of unilaterality, the World, the State, Authorities, etc. (Chapter III), and then to undertake their own resistance to this denial, to ground an activity or a specifically minoritarian pragmatics (Chapter IV) affecting the World.*

The individual is no more responsible for the eruption of the World or of History – of effectivity – than he is for negating it. These manifest themselves from themselves and first of all – following the order of thoughts – through their resistance to finite individuals, through their inevitable denial of the One and the real.

Minorities do not negate Authorities, but Authorities negate minorities. It is enough, as the order of experiences dictates, for Authorities to appear *after* minorities for them to make their existence a universal protest against the One and to situate themselves as a philosophical and political defense. This resistance is so violent that it goes without saying (and is not even formulated most of the time) but bursts out against the One as soon as its essence is restored to it as unreflective. That the One be devoid of transcendence; that the World, on the other hand, be transcendent, "unilateral" to the One rather than the inverse (Platonism and Neo-Platonism, etc.); that individuals precede the World, History, Language, Authorities in general; that parts be independent of Wholes; that being radically precedes Being and imprints it with an unmasterable irreversibility, etc. – these theses are received as impossible paradoxes that defy reason and the reasons of philosophy no less than those of politics.

This unitary resistance to the One is a phenomenon as necessary or as unnecessary as the very existence of Unity and the World, depending on whether one evaluates that resistance viciously according to them, or rigorously according to the One. In any case, the order of thoughts finds this resistance and, far from resenting it as an obstacle or an impossibility of going further – this is precisely what Authorities count on from their resistance – the finite subject uses it first of all as a phenomenon to "analyze" to the advantage of the One (even though that resistance no longer resembles a symptom), as a philosophical, political, etc. defense mechanism against the finitude of the real. Ordinary man denounces resistance, suspending its impact and effects simultaneously, imprinting an ungraspable contingency onto the World, a definitive lag behind the One: its uni-laterality, its determination in the last instance, inscribed directly upon the real (Chapter III). But this denial is even more "useful" for individuals when they, at the very center of this suspension with which they have always-already affected the World, attempt to carry out a practical, or, as we will say, *pragmatic*, "analysis" of this resistance. They certainly do not treat resistance as a symptom – because the One, the real, is not an unconscious – but rather as an illusion that can be uni-lateralized a second time according to the new mode of activity, this time with the finite subject conflating its being and its acting "on" the World in totality. After the contemplative or quasi-mystical suspension that is the individual causality of the last instance, there will be a practical relation to the World, the pragmatics of ordinary man facing Authorities (Chapter IV): these are the two great experiences that the subject has of the World and that a transcendental science of man must describe as a matter of priority.

Theorem 34. *In his second experience of himself, man is not only thrown-into-the-world, which is the specific causality of the World on itself and on man, but is more profoundly remote-in-the-World, unilateralized with it.*

Individuals are thus not only absolute lived experiences in their individual finitude; they also have something to do with the World. From this latter point of view, they are not first of all and essentially *thrown-into-the-world*, into-Being, into-the-State, into-Authorities, or into any other universal.[5] "Into-the-World" expresses an indivisible relation or a relation of difference between man *and* the World, a relation of neighborhood or proximity: this is the World itself, thought unitarily as transcendence or throwing-into-the-world. Insofar as they are finite, however, individuals can no more be affected in their essence and determined by this relation than this essence can prescribe – or prohibit – this affection. Therefore, if they and the World are in fact affected and determined (even if this is an illusion forced upon them by the World and Authorities, it is perhaps not only, or from every point of view, an illusion), they do not know why they are this way: the way man as finite in spite of everything belongs to the World and to Reason is not rationally explicable. It does not have reasons drawn from the World, because the World is, in any case, already uni-lateralized by the finite subject and thus without effect on it. This radical contingency that is joined to the World will be one of the conditions for the creation of an absolute science of the World and of man-in-the-World. But if this affection is contingent on their underlying finitude, individuals know this contingency itself insofar as it has its cause in the One. They are undoubtedly affected the same way the World auto-affects itself, but this affection, which makes them a mode of the World, is for them in the One without reason and is put-in-place in the irreversible space of uni-laterality or determination in the last instance. This auto/hetero-affection of the World, which *is* the World, which *is* History, which *is* Philosophy, etc., is already globally suspended by their essence and their life as "individual" existents, and this situation is known to them immediately.

This yields an absolute, irreversible contingency prior to any decision – philosophical or otherwise – that affects the insertion of minorities into Authorities, of individuals into the World. We will therefore call being-remote-*in*-the-World not at all the presence of man in-the-World, seen and regulated by the World, but the fact that this relation of man in-the-World is already uni-lateralized and suspended in a finite em-placement. Being-remote-*in*-the-World does not indicate an inherence or a belonging of man to the World under the law of which he "would fall" or towards which he would once more be "thrown," but must first be understood transcendentally as the unilaterality that straightaway affects "Theworld," and man as well insofar as he is found there. *Because the World is uni-lateralized, marginalized with no possible recourse, our experience of being-in-the-world, in-desire, in-power, in-text, etc.* (which contemporary unitary philosophers have described) *is lived as being-remote or "in Theworld."* This is the core of the real phenomenal experience foreseen, but falsified in a mystico-religious way, by the heresies, dualisms, and gnoses at the beginning of the Christian era, which coarsely and mythologically interpreted that experience as a quasi-spatial insertion into the World and as a topography (which nevertheless anticipated the topics of ordinary man), which the "topology" of contemporary thinkers could never entirely overcome because it extended what remained of the unitary in these dualisms. Real, immanent, or indubitable experience is in fact this: the World, with man in it, is straightaway downgraded, de-rived by "individual" finitude; when it appears, it does so as em-placed and without recurrence, in a state of irreversible dereliction.

This *in* must be understood rigorously and transcendentally, and not empirically, from finite man and not from the World or the human moment enclosed in the World. It is not the World that decides that we are remote-in-Theworld, because the World is also remote-in-Theworld. Therefore, the finite individual does not know why he is also being-in-the-world and a mode of the World, but he knows why he is ignorant – his essence is this why – why he is *in* Theworld, why Authorities are so radically contingent.

Theorem 35. *The duality of Authorities and minorities is only meaningful and necessary for Authorities, precisely because they deny it or only recognize it through the denial of minorities. It has no meaning and necessity for minorities, for whom it is contingent, and who are not constituted in their essence by it.*

Duality is not inscribed in the One, and Authorities are not the becoming-universal of minorities, but minorities also do not prohibit authoritarian experience from "happening." Duality, and the dualism of thought that ensues, does not come directly from the One and is not the philosophy of minorities, who, either way, do not need philosophy, but can determine one in their wake. Dualism is the thought of Authorities: it has a proximate authoritarian cause. More precisely: Authorities are both constrained to dualism by the One, because the One is henceforth the guiding thread of thought, and can only deny dualism by denying the One. This contradiction will be resolved by contemplation and above all by practice understood in its individual essence. It follows that duality and, above all, dualism are a globally contingent experience and philosophy, without direct genetic necessity in the essence of ordinary man, and which are only necessary for "Theworld" or Authorities. Dualism is the philosophy of the "second principle." There is no *philosophical* dualism prior to immediate givens that poses them: philosophy is finitely localized and em-placed in-Theworld and as it.

12. The Absolute Science of the World and of Authorities

Theorem 36. *The mystical precedes existence. The World, and the individual insofar as he belongs to it, do not appear in a position, a*

81

being, an existence – but in a primitive uni-laterality or in the form of As It Is [Tel quel].

The mystical is not the *that which* shown by language, nor the *that* language sometimes shows as its Beyond, identical to its limit. It shows itself non-thetically (from) itself, before language shows it inside or else outside of itself. The mystical is the real: it is thus "below" the ideal or "eidetic" essence, but also below existence, beyond the *that*, the *there is*. Finite pre-linguistic phenomenality, which does nothing but show itself without saying itself, is not brute existence below or beyond essence; it is that which determines in the last instance both ideal essence and existence. *The real precedes existence*; this is sufficient to distinguish a thought of individual finitude from all those existentiell or existential efforts that remain unitary. Against categorial (ontological) and existential ways of thinking, we offer an "individual" style based on the precedence without recurrence of the individual and its mystical kernel over Being, ways of being, and modes of existence.

If the mystical precedes existence, existence does not return as such, unchanged or merely deferred [*différée*], from the "other" side, the side of the World. Because *Theworld* is the only possible side of a uni-facial reality, the only face the One tolerates, "existence" as much as "essence" and "Being" are uni-lateralized and enter into the general form of the *As It Is*.

Thus, the As It Is is not, strictly speaking, existence, that is to say, that which shows itself in a *position*, but rather that which shows itself in or as a *laterality*. The As It Is is a form of the showable [*du montrable*], but one that en-sues as uni-lateral from the showable quality of the mystical [*du montrable du mystique*]. It is not a limitation, like the opening of an open, and the World is not limited, without thereby reforming a unity with individuals. Therefore, this de-rived showable is not a *that* or a *that which*, any more than the first was. The World is presented in an irremediable exteriority, which penetrates or pierces the horizon of existence, and which is capable of radically or finitely inscribing it. Although completely different from the essence of individuals, the essence of the World is likewise not a mode of that which metaphysics calls existence or Being, in the primacy of which it seeks in vain to think them. For the finite subject, nothing shows itself starting from a limit and as a unifying (first relative, then absolute) transcendence: these are two complementary models of existence – the factual and the ontological – that are invalidated by the uni-lateral As It Is. This is no longer a pointing out, an indication of existence, a sign towards an unthinkable alterity, a pure remainder beyond a limit enclosing an interiority. All the metaphysical games of the *that which* and the *that* (*dass, quomodo, die Weise*), of ontological *as such*, and those still metaphysical games of the *beyond-closure*, of the *Other*, of *Différance* or of the *Differend*, which do not fall into interiority, etc., are eliminated as well by the As It Is, or limited to the World [*au Monde*]. (All these points will be developed in Chapter III, which contains the positive description of the As It Is or uni-laterality).

Theorem 37. *Finite individuals, ordinary man rather than the philosopher, possess the only "absolute science," which philosophy seeks in vain. Furthermore, this transcendental science is the only science that has as its "object" the World as it is rather than a sector or a mode of this World. Correspondingly: minorities possess the absolute science of Authorities.*

This situation, that of Determination in the Last Instance, makes possible a phenomenal description of Authorities and, in general, of effectivity, that is to say, of the sphere of Mixtures, Unities, or Totalities. Rigorous description is first of all merely *possible*: the essence of the One is such that the individual who em-places the World in a finite optic can contemplate it without transforming it, by suspending its validity without negating it or nihilating [*néantiser*] it. Individuals neutralise [*neutralisent*], or rather, they "nihil-utralise" [*"né-untralisent"*], if we can so put it, the World, which they grasp along with its Mixtures and its Totalities in a unique or finite experience, that is, an experience without remainder or recurrence, as "Theworld."[6] Whereas empirical science unfolds – perhaps ... – inside of the World presumed to be given as a horizon or totality, as the sufficient principle under which empirical science develops; whereas unitary philosophy reaches the World from the inside *and* the outside; and whereas these two forms of knowledge are doomed to becoming and illimitation; only ordinary individuals possess the absolute science of the World or of Totality *as they are*. This science is absolute because the essence of the individual is outside of the World, and because it is the individual who determines the World as it is. If philosophy is only the science of the World when it is simultaneously included in and deducted from the World, then it is not the absolute science of the World, contrary to its pretensions (it confuses the absolute or the finite with the Infinite – this is its amphibology). Ordinary man, himself, *is* this science of Universals and Totalities. Through his finite topics and then his pragmatics, he imposes a new type of objectivity on them and renders them rigorously describable. Minorities are the concrete experience of Authorities and the absolute science of the State because the State ceases for them to be an *ob-ject*, and becomes a given subjected to a uni-lateralizing topics and pragmatics rather than merely objectivating ones. Of course, this rigorous science is no more a politics than it is a philosophy, because politics must also be included in and deducted from its ob-ject, and thus has only a relative knowledge of the State (all of these points will be developed in Chapter III, Section V).

Theorem 38. *The science of Wholes or of Mixtures in general, whose principle lies in the One or ordinary man, develops in several specific times: two positive moments, and two critical moments.*

1. A mystical-ordinary acting, determination in the last instance, that indifferences the World, making it contingent or unilateral without negating or objectivating it. It has a first effect: allowing for the description of the World in its remoteness and its strangeness, of its heterogeneity – the heterogeneity of philosophical logics – as fundamentally undecidable (Chapter III).

2. A pragmatic-ordinary acting, always unary in essence, developing inside of the first while adding a supplementary determination. It allows for the description of a pragmatics proper to finite or ordinary man, and its correlate: an essence of the World that would be its meaning or *its apriori*, that is, the *Transcendental Apriori of the World as it is*, something like *the genetic code of the World, and of man as he is affected by it* (Chapter IV).

3. The first acting – in a mystical mode – has a second effect: denouncing the illusion and resistance of the World as regards the One or the Real. This is the first moment of real critique (Chapter III).

4. The second acting – in a practical mode – has a second effect: to continue to denounce, but also to legitimate, according to dimensions to be elucidated, the authoritarian/unitary illusion of the World when it denies not only the One, but also its Transcendental Apriori. This is the second moment of real critique (Chapter IV).

There is a minoritarian or real critique of Authorities. It is located in the simultaneously contemplative and practical, mystical and pragmatic, acting of which ordinary man, not philosophizing man, is capable with regard to the natural and inevitable claim of Authorities to count for human reality, of the State to exhaust the real. The existence of Authorities, the practice of the State, the interminable process of History, etc., all these things are part of an illusion about what man is, part of the pretention to make of man a *homo ex machina (publica)*. We can describe this illusion as polito-logical or onto-theo-political, if we are determined to narrow it in this way and to emphasize its political effects, but its scope is completely different since it is that which animates, beyond politics, philosophy in its enterprise to subvert man, and the World in the enterprise of his capture.

Chapter III develops the mystical moment of this science of the World as it is and its suspensive effect (and theorizes its concept in the final section) and Chapter IV develops the practical relation to the World or to Authorities.

Theorem 39. *The first moment of the rigorous science of the World and of Authorities can – though this is not absolutely necessary – be preceded by a description of the principal forms of Authorities or of the most general structures of the World insofar as it appears from itself and if the point of view of the World on itself is taken as the guiding thread of this description.*

We should now describe the most general structures of Authorities, or more precisely, Authorities as the a priori structures of the World, of unitary thought, of games of power, etc. But these descriptions are long – unlimited by definition – and *necessarily unoriginal because we can take unitary philosophies to be these very descriptions, at least in their essential aspects.* We thus will not describe – for lack of space – these principal authoritarian or unitary structures, which are the aprioris that hold for any experience (*but only insofar as it remains in the World*: experience that is political, statist, sociological, technological, philosophical, etc.). We will limit ourselves in general to defining the concept of Authorities and authority according to the definition of minorities. This definition will suffice to presume, and no more, individuals affected in the mode of being-in-the-world, and to locate this affection in the irreversible order of their most immediate experiences; then to describe the authoritarian illusion, the worldly denial of the One, in a phenomenally rigorous way, from the immanence of mystical acting, which unilateralizes them; and to demonstrate the illusory character of this resistance to the real, etc.

What is the status of these descriptions of Authorities – those that we will sketch out and those that we will assume in various places – and from what point of view are they made or ought they be made? Doubtless, they are made from the inside of that uni-lateralizing suspension of the World and of Authorities. But they can use philosophy and, in any case, they describe what are for the most part philosophical logics.

This paradox must be clarified. On the one hand, such descriptions are constructed from a non-philosophical experience: we see all things in the One, particularly philosophies; these descriptions are thus inscribed partially in the World, but totally in "Theworld" such as we experience it from the One; they are semi-contingent and semi-necessary for he who, like the philosophers, thinks the World from itself; they are absolutely contingent for individuals. But on the other hand, for the moment, the point of view of the One and of its specific suspension (uni-lateralization) does not yet have to be actualized, and its consequences for the World do not yet have to be drawn. And above all, we know that the World and all that is found in it is not, in any case, negated or nihilated by the One, but only determined in a finite way by it, and conserved in its "in itself." For this last reason, we can still use philosophy (ontology and political philosophy, on the one hand, and their deconstructions, on the other) to help us in these descriptions or to suggest what these descriptions ought to be. As this does not contradict the efficacy of the One, which still allows us to make use of the World and Philosophy, we can take advantage of this generosity, more phenomenal than phenomeno-logical, and describe in an authoritarian or philosophical mode the essential parts of these structures of the World. Finally, the description of the aprioris of Authorities, of Authorities as an apriori, is still, in its content and its form, a philosophers' science. Nevertheless, we will suggest that, even with these reservations, we can already preemptively interpret Authorities from the perspective of minorities or individuals.

Other nuances are even more important: we will carefully distinguish between these descriptions, which are apriori only inside the World, the State, Authorities, etc., and their transcendental or real apriori, which are the object of the science of the World as it is (in its second, pragmatic, moment). We will distinguish just as carefully between the forms of heterogeneity and undecidability tolerated by the World and programmed by particular philosophies – particularly such a philosophical logic – and those the One assigns to the World and to philosophies *as they are*. Even in the first case, these are heterogeneous experiences of Authority (as the presumed essence of the individual), and it is not a question of blending them, especially if one takes their point of view, which they share without knowing it, the point of view of Philosophy, of the World, etc., which wants them to unleash a war without mercy. But we cannot linger with the World for too long: even perceiving this war, this impossibility, in principle, of choosing in the struggle of multiple logics and Authorities, requires another point of view, the only one that can be called real: the One.

13. On Authority as Individuel Causality

Theorem 40. *Because minority is the inalienable essence of man as ordinary individual, authority and Authorities remain an interpretation of that essence, a conception of man and of the individual: authority is not an ethico-political concept. It is a logico-real concept. But it assumes a point of view on that essence that is different from the essence itself: it is indeed a real or transcendental concept, but one that remains logical, philosophical, worldly.*

Authority and Authorities must be understood in a broad and essential way. Rather than their political, ethical, and juridical concept, here, as we have said, it is a structure, an essence, an apriori that is valid for all particular phenomena that take place in the World (for example, if not for science, at least for its philosophical and political interpretation). Compared to the aprioris of political, economic, ethical, etc. regions, this is an apriori of a higher degree that applies to them all. This point must be explained.

Authority and Authorities are traditional concepts of political science and of classical conceptions of power. But, just as the essence or the immanent phenomenal givens of the State have been forgotten by political philosophy, which itself *is* this forgetting, their specific essence has remained as such indeterminate under the mass of all sorts of determinations with which that essence was confused. In the political domain, where these concepts have remained wrongly confined, their forgetting has not been lifted - to the contrary - with the contemporary techno-political philosophy of power, with Nietzsche-inspired micro-political descriptions. The latter, under the pretext of multiplicities and games of power, lost the "individualist" meaning of Authority, its meaning of individuel causality, to which we must return in order to finally retrieve its truth, though likely not in a classical way.

The truth of the concept of authority thus requires the elucidation of its content of real or phenomenal experience, which must be our guiding thread if we hope to avoid wandering in political indeterminations. *Authority must be treated not as an ethico-political concept, but as a logico-real concept.* First of all, as having a real ambition or claim to legislate experience, to constitute it, then, as an apriori. Then, and more radically, as itself being real in a non-empirical sense of the term (political, administrative, etc.), thus as a *transcendental* apriori. This content of phenomenal or real experience, although still described logically or philosophically, that is, unitarily, can now be explored under these two conditions. First, Authorities are not particularly political and administrative; they are the aprioristic structures of all experience in the World, History, the State, etc., the most general forms of power, and, for example, of games of power, which are only one of its modes; they are thus real essences and have an onto-(logical) content. Second, they are only semi-real, being moreover mixtures of reality and logicity, which is what makes them Authorities. For example, these are the most universal structures of polito-logical and socio-logical difference: if we interpret the polis and its content of real or immediate individual experience in polito-*logical* terms, or the socius in socio-*logical* terms, we free the universal type of aprioris that are Authorities. But they themselves are a priori authoritarian, since they are thought circularly: from the World as an apriori of the World; from the polito-logical as an apriori of the polito-logical, etc.

Theorem 41. *Authority must be understood according to minority or according to the specific causality of the real individual, though this is a transcendent interpretation of this causality. The author is the actor, the agent, or the actant, but he and his causality are here given "unitarily" or "effectively." Authority is a "worldly" and "philosophical" conception of finite human causality.*

We have described the individual essence of ordinary man (first chapter), and that which, in it, makes him really distinct from the World. But this essence is transcendental: even if it is not alienated in the World, it necessarily emerges in it, but not for reasons that would be proper to it. It does not emerge to be what it is: it is what it is without having to emerge in the World and in the mode proper to it. But it is the World that, itself, in its uni-latrality and its finitely determined being, is constrained to manifest that essence in a transformed form. Individual causality, which is *before* the World, shows itself, disfigured, in the figure of the World, and this is authority. This explains why classical thinkers, among them the thinkers of political individualism, were able to enfranchise this concept. By its real phenomenal content, authority is nothing other than the causality of the agent, of the actor, of the actant, but individuel and no longer individual, the transcendent form of finite human causality. Authorities are the a priori forms of individuel causality, that is, of the causality that obeys the World. The individuel and the World – the universal then the Whole – are in fact the same thing, are obviously the World itself. Individuel causality and universal causality must be identified because the individual in the World is always a mode of a universal or an intersection of universals, and because it "lost" its individual essence. Individuel causality (authority) and individual causality (minority) are distinguished in the following way: the first is in the World and in History, or more rigorously, at once *in* and *on* the World, etc.; the second is finite, distinct from the World, but efficacious *on* the World-in-totality or finitely em-placed, on *Theworld* or the World *as it is*, etc. and this is (first mystical, then pragmatic) determination in the last instance. Causality on the universal cannot, in its turn, take a universal form or be mediated by it. It radically changes in nature to be the causality of ordinary man, distinct from the World, on the World.

Theorem 42. *The description of Authorities, however authoritarian and circular it may be, must bring to light their content of real human experience, of anthropic causality, though – it is true – in a transcendent and worldly way.*

In the exposition of the concept of Authorities, and before examining the possibilities of minoritarian resistance, we must first assert, against unitary violence and the totalitarian spirit of philosophies, the degree of humanity and the real individual content of Authorities. It is in the very posing of the problem of the State that it is necessary to cease being political or polito-logical, to cease proceeding circularly by way of abstract universals: *who* is the State and *who* are Authorities when we examine their essence from a finite real experience, from the radical human essence that is located in the One. From this point of view, it is clear that Authorities do not express radical human essence. Furthermore, even the most barbarous State must be granted a certain humanity, a certain individuality, at least in the last instance. Authorities appear as the excellent and superior form of humanity, but they miss or deny in this way the *anthropic* – rather than the anthropo-logical – essence only because they are still determined by it in the last instance.

The problem of the State as a problem of Authorities is not a political problem. There is a certain barbarism in addressing a political problem politically, a philosophical problem philosophically, etc. The problem of the State is a problem of transcendental anthropo(-logy): first, more philosophical than political, or as much the one as the other, if we put ourselves in the State to deal with the State; then, real rather than philosophical and political, if we put ourselves back in the place of ordinary man and his absolute experience. At stake is ordinary man in the State and Philosophy – in Authorities. No one can say that here we are contrasting an angelic anthropology with a political vision of the world: we contrast man as definitive and true absolute, devoid of logos, with the World itself.

Theorem 43. *There is not only a radical anthropic content in the last instance in all authority, but there is, first of all and more obviously, an authoritarian definition of the essence of man, which rigorous science must eliminate.*

Anthropology is always the authoritarian thought of man; it is proper to philosophy and the empirical sciences of man. It states that man has as his essence, being, or form a double transcendent causality, that of the universal and that of unity. Authority is always made up of these two complementary parts, necessary to define man philosophically = unitarily. Man is not for authority, and whatever his philosophical interpretation, this individual takes his essence from himself in a radical finitude that prohibits him from leaving his singularity. He is straightaway alienated by the World, History, Language, etc., by Philosophy, and blended with the authoritarian essence. Authority is therefore a causality that goes through two distinct levels and has a single-and-divided form: a universal aspect, through which man is supposed to act on the (mode of) the World, of History, of Science, of Technology, etc.; and a unifying aspect through which he is supposed to totalize and unify phenomena. These two parts of any authority are irreducible and complementary; they belong to each other in an interlacing or a difference that tears the individual from the simplicity of his essence.

This is still the classical form of Authority. This broad invariant receives historical variations, the most remarkable of which is that of authority as semi-universal/unifying and semi-real, or real-as-Other. Individuel causality rests then upon a radical Other with which it identifies. To a certain extent, it de-universalizes and de-unifies authority, but only partially, while remaining unitary at its core. This relation (to) the Other is the passage from the classical authoritarian style to the semi-authoritarian style of contemporary thinkers. It is a half measure (Nietzsche and Heidegger) that fails to shatter the anthropo*logical* myth, that is, the authoritarian experience of man. We will not examine – due to a lack of space – these two great authoritarian conceptions of man. But we can easily imagine or describe them: they both result from a blend (which is not a unitary alienation; the blend assumes a duality and is itself a sort of "second principle" . . .) of the finite individual essence of man with an abstract universal essence; more deeply, from the blend of man with the World. Anthropology is the subversion of the real distinction of man and the World preserved by minoritarian thought as a rigorous science of the subject.

Theorem 44. *Authority is a mode of the general structure of the mixture that is the content and form of what we understand by effectivity and distinguish from the real. The effective essence of Authorities is the uncreated blend, always already presupposed, of the immanence of the One and the transcendence of the Other.*

We were able to pretend that authority was a fallen and falsified mode of minority, but this was a delusion. Determination in the last instance – this is its originality – is dualist and breaks all continuity (of emanation, procession, process, genesis, etc.) between the One and the World. In reality, authority has an irreducible and specific essence: that of the "World." But here the World is not a particular totality, but rather that which has the power of totality. It is rather a law, a rule, a principle for a particular sphere of experience: precisely the one that is liable to obey a rule, a principle. But first of all, this is what we call effectivity, which must be understood as a blended structure of the One and the Other. In the sense, however, that the mixture is not created by the post-factum synthesis of the One and the Other, but rather precedes these terms, or at least precedes the Other and accompanies the One, which can take it into account as a specific domain of reality, one it cannot in any way "destroy" and re-create, but "can" only "uni-lateralize" or determine in the last instance. The World is already-World, the mixture is already-Mixed and does not allow itself be deduced from anything. The individual finds the World and is affected by it: the only thing that matters phenomenally, that is, scientifically, is what the individual can make of this affection and what he has already made of it in the very moment of this affection.

We thus distinguish between: 1. The proper essence of Authorities, that is, the mixture or effectivity that is a domain of specific experience distinct from and uncreatable by the individual real: the always-already-mixed-mixture; 2. The transcendental or real essence of Authorities, which is this immediate individual experience and which is not specific to Authorities or to the World, but is rather their determination in the last instance. Because there is an ambiguity in the word "essence" as soon as it is a question of the essence of the World or of Authorities, we distinguish their specific essence, effectivity or the already-mixed, which is always defined relative to these two in a circular manner; and their essence = "last instance," which determines them absolutely and lets it be said: minorities determine Authorities uni-laterally or in the last instance.

It remains the case that authority is not a deficient or falsified mode of minority: this would be to return to unitary thought. It is not, then, a question of anarchically refusing Authorities and the State. Instead, we can, in the World itself, dissolve them in the aleatory games of power and speculate on their decline. But this is nothing other than their stato-minoritarian fusion, the secret Statist Ideal of all unitary philosophy, still an authoritarian "politics." Chapters III and IV will examine the specifically minoritarian mode of action on Authorities, the State, the World, etc.

— III —

ORDINARY MYSTICISM

SECTION I: *The Unitary Illusion*

14. The Possibility of a Unitary Illusion

Theorem 45. *The place of the Unitary Illusion and its critique is the "dual," that is, the order of successive givenness of the One and the World.*

Insofar as man is also in the World, by a necessity that he cannot explain to himself as a finite or "separated" being, thought settles for registering this event after the One, with which thought merges. The affection of Man by the World is an absolute given in its own way, an inevitable constraint, but one that remains contingent for the One or for the individual essence of man. For his part, man affects it with a contingency or a uni-laterality that we will also call the *(non-)One.*

The current situation is as follows: just as the One does not prohibit the World or any sort of mixture from announcing itself or affecting man, this affection does not suppress the experience (of) the One, at least for minoritarian thought, which "begins" with it and takes it as its guiding thread, a criteria of rigorous immanence for all other experience. Henceforth we will no longer leave the One – it cannot be left, cannot be alienated – even when we think the World according to its own requirements, nor minorities, even when we acknowledge authoritarian demands. Moreover, it is not just unitary defense mechanisms – we will examine those shortly – that presume the actuality of the One. The argument that we will use here and there against all forms of Unity, even the highest ones, which would presume the One as the ultimate requisite even as they simultaneously deny it, remains exoteric, strategic, and exclusively anti-unitary if it is not re-inserted into the real order of experiences. We can only know that Unity is based on a presumed-One if an experience, by right prior to Unity, assures us of the existence of the One. The quasi-philosophical argument of the One as ultimate requisite and the unitary denial of the One equally presume the actual experience of the One.

These two facts, each immediate in their own way, must be kept in order, without claiming to reduce the one in favor of the other and reconstituting a unitary system. A thought open to specifically unary phenomenality can only register, after the One, the being-*in*-the-world of man, or the way he is affected by the World, and then the (non-)One with which he in turn affects this being-*in*-the-world. This order, however, is not a unitary reduction or synthesis of these two phenomena in the name, for example, of a unity of the last instance of man. Such a unity of the World and the One is precisely what we will designate as the Unitary Illusion, the hallucinated illusion that must be described and then "critiqued."

Provided they are taken in the order in which they really appear as immediate givens, and not as concepts, the One and the World, minorities and Authorities, do not form a coupling or a higher unity; in fact, they form what we will call a *dual* rather than a duality. The dual is this order of presentation of immediate givens that does not reconstitute a closed whole or a totality, but in which the World is given after the One without affecting or determining the One in return. This is the state of experience in which immediate givens announce themselves according to an irreversible order. It is not what unitary thought or even we ourselves will later call a "duality," then a dualism, which are notions that are more external, if not transcendent, to phenomenal givens. The dual precedes duality and, even more so, dualism, which is the philosophy that ensues from the existence of the dual, then from that of duality. We will inevitably return to the complex signification of the dual.

Theorem 46. *There is a unitary illusion, a resistance to the One or a non(-One) that is specific to the World, Philosophy, and Authorities, and through which they deny the existence of the One, of individuals, or of ordinary man, that is, of the "individual" or absolute sphere of existence.*

The dual does not remain inert, but is animated straightaway. Coming after the One in the order of immediate experiences, the World finds itself confronted with the One; Authorities are doomed to register the existence of minorities, whether they like it or not. But the Unity that animates them is always specular or speculative: it cannot receive as they are the immediate givens of individuals. Not only do the unitary forms of thought expressly falsify the experience of such a One-without-Unity devoid of all positionality and transcendence. They conceal its existence, reducing it to a mere higher form, an even more transcendent form, if that is possible, of "Transcendental Unity." They miss the essence of the One, the nothing-but-real form of its immanence, as soon as they settle for requisitioning the One, giving it a functional meaning, and making it useful for the subaltern tasks of philosophy. The World thus offers a *representation*, always unitary, of the One, an authoritarian or individuel image of individuals, and philosophy tries to draw minorities into a transcendent project that is too broad for them.

Why can Authorities do no more than repress the real this way? Negate at the very least the falsifying image they straightaway make of the real, which is perhaps an inevitable misunderstanding linked to the dual? The real is not accessible to any transformative activity whatsoever; it is passivity through and through and it is rigorously individual, not insertable into chains of phenomena, and not subsumable under universals: how would authorities, who belong to another principle (the mixture), not negate the existence of the real? They can imagine nothing of the sort, but, using the same words – and perhaps precisely because they take words, philosophy's words or other words, to be real, taking them rather than phenomenal experiences seriously – they merely project a representation of the real that conforms to themselves but falls beside or outside the real.

There is therefore a unitary illusion, and since it bears directly upon the real, negated or denied by the World and Authorities, it is a "transcendental" illusion, at least through its object, if not through its mechanism, which is worldly (semi-transcendent, semi-transcendental).

The Unitary Illusion has two complementary aspects. One principal aspect: it confuses the Whole with the Absolute, Unity with the One. It thus denies the One and individuals when they are presented to it in their essence. A secondary aspect: it believes that individuals can truly be, in their essence, repressed. First a belief: the belief of the World that it is all of reality, the belief of Authorities that they exhaust the truth of individuals, the belief of Unity that it covers the One without remainder. Then, a consequence that follows from the principal belief and expresses it: the belief that an alienation belongs to the essence of the real, that the real must become what it is, that individuals can be repressed, be *really* forgotten by Authorities, and that they are thus constituted, in the manner of the Unconscious, through a mechanism of "originary repression." The first form of resistance is that of classical philosophy, the second that of contemporary deconstructions of metaphysics.

15. The Transcendental Nature of the Unitary Illusion

Theorem 47. *The Unitary Illusion is neither psychological nor merely philosophical, even if it affects philosophy. It is a transcendental illusion: it is motivated by the real or its manifestation in the dual, and it concerns the real, of which it is the denial or the "forgetting."*

An illusion affecting Philosophy and the World globally cannot be psychological, social, scientific, etc., nor even "ideological," even though the elucidation of its essence is the means of giving a phenomenal content that is finally real to the concept of "ideology." We have acquired the experience of this illusion and the resistances that accompany it on the basis of the dual and its order, through an exclusively transcendental experience. Confronted with the One, the World can only presume and deny it. The One or the real is at once the "cause" and the object of the illusion, even though the mechanism of this illusion is elsewhere: in the unitary amphibology of logos and the real.

If it is indeed joined with the unitary mechanism or the World themselves, this is because it is *at least* "logico-transcendental" and stems from the mixed nature of the essence of the World or of Unity, simultaneously logos (representation or transcendence in general) and real. In this manner, it already puts the real into play, but in a way that misses its essence, because the illusion aims to exhaust it and to determine it by means of transcendence or logos, through the addition of supplementary determinations that are unlimited in number. The individual, the real of the last instance, is represented in this way and falls under a form of transcendence in general: this precipitates a unitary fury to multiply the individual, to totalize him, to surpass him, to exceed him, to deconstruct him, to make him suffer all the abuses presupposed by Unity. This indicates that ordinary man, that is, the real, is what is at stake in the conflict that opposes the World to the One, and thus also in the resistance that the One will, in

96

its turn, "oppose" to the World (the "real critique" of the Unitary Illusion).

To maintain the dual as the condition of all minoritarian thought, it is necessary to clarify that the true amphibology being denounced is not really the amphibology of the real and logos – this is the mixture of Unity or of the World, an indestructible mixture whose dissolution no critique can enact – *but that of the real and of the logico-real mixture.* The unitary defense mechanism is the confusion of the real with the indestructible mixture of the World, which is more powerful than its terms and precisely prevents them from being thought as terms. Greco-unitary philosophy is this mixture of "transcendental logic" or of the logico-real, and it is this mixture that immediately denies the real in its true essence. The problem of knowing whether this mixture is already, in itself and according to its constitution, a denial of the real and of the One is not posed: that would suppose that the mixture is creatable and destructible. The dual order excludes this supposition, implying instead that the denial of the One by the World as such is registered in its time and place.

Theorem 48. *The mixture of the World (of Unity, of Authorities, etc.) is positive in its own way, indestructible and uncreatable. Nevertheless, this is not a supplement to the real, capable of enriching it. It is already a lesser-real, even though it is not an alienation of the real, a fall or a decline of the One.*

We understand the logos we have been discussing in a broad sense, in opposition to unreflective immanence. It is a question of all forms of transcendence, of jection in general (with its principle modes: ob-jectivation and sur-jectivation). It is an expanded concept of "representation" that contemporary thinkers, generally its "deconstructors," have understood in far too simple and restricted a sense. The problem is as follows: this logos, which in the unitary amphibology "is added" to the real in the form of the mixture of the World, could make us believe that it is a supplement that does not disfigure the real, but rather enriches it.

But the mixture itself does not gain by the combination – by the addition of the One and logos – of unreflective immanence and transcendence. Not only do we not yet know what such a pure "transcendence" would be, but what is immediately given to us *after* the One is possibly *before* an experience of transcendence, and this is the mixture, the already-mixed, the World that affects individuals. The dual is composed of the One and the World, of the One and the mixture, and not of the One, or of Immanence, and Transcendence – this will come later in the order of experiences. This is the meaning of the dual and its type of distinction.

Therefore, the mixture is not generated starting from these terms or starting from the One. The One does not continue in it, as would be the case if logos were added to the One. Nothing is added to it: it does not extend into the result of an addition or into "effectivity." It is not alienated in the mixture. *The One is not alienated and, nevertheless, there is another "principle" beside it.*

The real in itself does not "really" fall under the mixture: there is no alienation, fall, or procession of the One. For its part, the mixture is a positive experience that is not reached through a decline of the real. The meaning of phenomenality, of the positivity of immediate givens, demands that the mixture not be a lesser-One expelled by the One, but that it can appear in its specificity and as an absolute experience of effectivity. The domains of reality are specific essences without reciprocal community, not neighboring domains. The law of the real is not alienation, nor even topology, the last avatar of procession; it is determination in the last instance. The meaning of determination in the last instance: the One is certainly the essence of the World, but an essence that is not alienated in that of which it is the essence, an essence that is not constituted in return by the World or by its determination of the World. Determination in the last instance is the key to a transcendentally and rigorously grounded dualism.

The mixture of the World is thus indestructible and positive in its own way. We will not, however, conclude from this that it is only the unitary representation it gives of the One or of individuals that is a devalorization of the real. It is an essence more powerful than its terms: it creates them without really being created from them. Compared to the One, however, the structure of the mixture is already a representation of the real; that is, because the real or the One does not allow itself to be represented, the mixture is something completely different from the real. That which ensures its positivity also separates it from the One, holds it remote from the real in its essence, and dedicates it to the definitive misrecognition of that essence. There is no continuity of the One to the World: this produces the autonomy of the World as a "second" principle, but also makes the World definitively lose the real, in which it never participated save insofar as it will be determined by the real "in the last instance." Furthermore, the fact that it is uncreatable and always-already given does not contradict (far from it) the radical falsification that occurs within it of the real, which it forces – even if it means losing the real definitively, because nothing can be imposed on the real that would alienate it – to blend with transcendence, to receive in itself the form of transcendence, and even more deeply, the very constraint to blend with another "principle," the higher law of the mixture. In its essence, the One excludes not only transcendence, but also that essence that is different from transcendence, more powerful than it, but less powerful than the One: the mixture. The mixture is not more than the real: its "enrichment." Rather, it is *less*: a subtraction, even if that subtraction is not an alienation but a being-determined in the last instance. It is a specific but derived and secondary reality.

Once the mixture of effectivity is given, its two components can be unitarily taken from it. But they will always be affected by the worldly conditions of their existence: not so much by the other term as by their necessary unity with the other. It is a question of unity-as-transcendence (the "real" taken from the already-mixed) and of transcendence-as-unitary or positional (logos taken from the already-mixed). These are the two minimal dimensions, or the alphabet, of any unitary system. The mixture is not produced by the post-factum synthesis of these terms, which are in fact abstracted from it. Only the already-mixed can philosophize or exceed itself (all of contemporary philosophy) by transforming itself, but without destroying itself. It cannot be exceeded, neither from the side of its pre-constrained components, nor, moreover, from the side of the One: the real does not exceed the World, it precedes it absolutely.

Nevertheless, the true situation should not be misrecognized: the mixture is an already-mixed, it exists, in a sense, prior to its terms at least insofar as they can be merely re-moved from it. This is why it subjects them to its law, which is their mutual disfiguration. More powerful than they, it causes them to betray one another by bringing them together. In it, they lose their very essence, the unreflective. It does not make them indivisible or inseparable without disrupting their relation, which is determination in the last instance, without doing violence to their essence. The law of the mixture is, for the terms, the loss of their non-positional essence and their forced insertion into a system of positional transcendence, the loss precisely of "uni-laterality" or of being determined in the last instance.

16. On the Illusion as Hallucination

Theorem 49. *The mixture of the World is not an illusion. But there is an illusion, an inevitable illusion, of which the mixture is the seat and the root. Critique is concerned only with this illusion and, in it, only with the purported unity of World and One.*

There is no illusion *of* the World, because the World is not illusory or deceptive; it is not a phantom, a cloud, a veil that would hide reality from us. The World as well as Authorities are positive if not necessary realities, or at least inexplicable and uncreatable starting from anything else.

But the World does indeed produce an illusion about the real, an illusion that is linked with Authorities. Therefore, we are not critiquing the World, but rather the hallucinated representation it produces of individuals; we are not destroying Authorities, we are "dis-placing" the magical representation they produce of minorities. Later, the World and Authorities will even find themselves delegated a certain function in the pragmatic critique of the illusion.

The critical project must be nuanced in a second way. The root or the seat of the unitary illusion is given with the matrix of the already-mixed. Because of its effective cause, which is indestructible, the illusion itself is indestructible, as positive as the instance in which it is rooted. Because of this, we do not critique the effective existence of the illusion or its mechanism, but rather its claim that this authoritarian mechanism can be the real, count for the real, that it has any relation at all to finite people, that it is something other than a hallucination of the One, than a magical animation of individuals.

Its effects can be limited by making it undergo what the World undergoes, which will be examined later: a finite em-placement, a uni-lateralization in the last instance. But even after the One is "withdrawn," as unforgettable, from its purported forgetting, and has been recognized yet again as not affected by the illusion, the illusion subsists in its proximate cause, the mixture itself, but by following it in its finite em-placement.

The root or the seat of the illusion, on the one hand, must be distinguished from its motif or object, on the other. This distinction helps to resolve the following problem: what is resistance if truth consists in saying that there is no resistance, or that resistance has no real object? Though this is not exactly what is said: resistance is certainly "real," but in the broad sense, for which the World is real in the mode of effectivity rather than in that of the real itself, effectivity that minoritarian thought registers and takes into account. And in a narrower sense, in which pragmatics will recognize in it a certain constitutive reality in relation to the "Other" or to transcendence (of a non-thetic sort).

Theorem 50. *There is no forgetting of the One the way there is a forgetting of Being. The true illusion is believing – a belief ineradicable from the World – that the illusion is real or something like a repression originarily constitutive of the reality of individuals. In truth, resistance or the non(-One) is nothing like a symptom, but rather like a hallucination.*

The denial of the One by the non(-One), if it were a *real* denial, would presume the One to be merely Unity, to be representable, an object of demonstration and argumentation, rather than that immediate given to whose essence finitude is essential. Unity believes that the One is one of its modes: it thus negates the pretentions of the One, which seem to it scandalous, or, not so differently, it admits at most that the repression, the forgetting, of the One forms part of the essence of the One: *Unity only tolerates the One as susceptible to forgetting or repression.*

This belief is particular to contemporary thinkers, and is worth analyzing on its own merits: it is not certain that the One is susceptible to "forgetting."

The dual presumes the contingent fact of the resistance of the non(-One); the presence of this fact is its condition of existence. The thinking that follows is thus suspended in this non(-One), without which it has no reason to "exit" the One and to begin to "philosophize" in a minoritarian mode. But the dual combines the contingency of authoritarian resistance with the experience of the essence of the One, which grounds the immanence of all minoritarian experience. However, this essence means the One can never be forgotten: the unreflective has none of the characteristics of transcendence. The non(-One) is certainly the forgetting of the One by the World; it is real in the sense of "effective," as real as much as its root, the World, can be. *But it is not real in the rigorous sense in which it would affect the One in its essence and be a constitutive forgetting of the One the way there is a constitutive forgetting of Being.* From this point of view, it is an absolute hallucination, which will soon be analyzed in detail and denounced as such by the unilateralization the One forces the World to undergo.

This post-metaphysical belief in a real illusion, in a symptomatic structure of the relation of the World to the One, is the height of the illusion proper to Unity. The forgetting of the One as *real* forgetting is not itself real, and this belief in the reality of its forgetting is the subtlest form of the illusion. The forgetting of essence, if it means that the World *is* identical to this forgetting, does not imply that the forgetting is essential, constitutes a symptom, or belongs to the essence of the One, which would be forgotten in this way. This forgetting only interests us here as a specific belief of the World, and this belief is perhaps the only true forgetting of the One. The true repression, which real critique will have to destroy instead of the mixture itself, and which it will have to destroy *for* the World, in the very spirit of the World or Authorities insofar as they are henceforth, for minoritarian thought, experiences of the dual, the true repression is this belief in the symptomatic reality of repression, the falsification of the unreflective essence of the individual in the form of an unconscious. Authoritarian resistance feeds on this belief that it is "possible," that the One is accessible or concealable, revealed and veiled as a mode of Unity or of Being can be.

Theorem 51. *Because the unitary illusion has no "reality" with respect to the object it concerns (the One), it is only an "effective" hallucination. It belongs only to the subjectivity of the World.*

The only reality of resistance or of the non(-One) is for the World itself. Because it does not really encounter the One, it is without object: it is a hallucination based solely on an image, a unitary projection of the One, which straightaway falls outside of the One, like the World itself. The World resists only a hallucination it forms itself, but this repression remains in itself and does not form a symptom because it is not constitutive of the One or of a relation to the One. The dual precludes the symptomatic interpretation of this resistance: the "symptom" – measured according to the One – is actually the very illusion of Unity; Unity is its ultimate presupposition. The One, falsified by Unity in the dual, is necessary for triggering the unitary defense mechanism, but it is not really affected by this fight against a phantasm.

Authorities are possessed by a quasi-magical belief, a faith, a certainty in their power to reach and determine individuals. Authority is the World's way of possessively haunting the One, the State's way of attempting to seduce ordinary man with the twists and turns of unitary thought, an entire philosophical sorcery that the World and the State deploy in front of individuals. They believe that they are doing something other than haunting them, than gliding over them like light above the night. They believe that they are mastering them, and sometimes – though this is not much different, as it is the same presupposition – freeing themselves from them. Mastery and freedom: the same illusion around which unitary thinkers revolve and which does not reside in the *real* authoritarian mastery of individuals but rather in the completely magical and spellbound belief – the ultimate form of the most "wounded" narcissism – in the reality of this mastery.

Real critique thus no longer consists of delimiting Unity from itself as well as from an Other or an exteriority, of thus surreptitiously recognizing in it an absolute reality. Rather, when and only when it is a question of the One, real critique consists of not recognizing reality (only an effectivity) in Unity, of considering it to be fiction, magic, *transcendental hallucination*, simulation of reality. Unitary philosophy is perhaps nothing more than the specific mythology of the World as such, the mythology the World produces insofar as it is capable of spirit and produces that philosophy for all spirit.

Three nuances can finally be brought to bear on the theory of this hallucination. First, as we have just seen, this magic is intertwined with effectivity and thus is only a hallucination from the point of view of the One or of ordinary man. Second, this illusion is not a mere cloud floating above experience, bound to evaporate with the sun of reason: it is a rational belief and the very fact that ought to be passed on to the riddle of critique. Finally, it is necessary to wait for another instance that is not given with the dual, *Non-thetic Transcendence or the Non-thetic Other*, to ascribe a certain relevance to these defense mechanisms spontaneously mounted by Authorities. The "symptomatic" structure will take on a supplementary *appearance* of reality when it will no longer be a question simply of the essence of the individual, but of its acting or its practice.

Theorem 52. *The dual puts into play the non(-One), the unitary defense against the One, as well as the (non-)One, the real critique of this resistance by the One and the specific "resistance" of ordinary man. This real critique takes two forms: mystical and pragmatic.*

At the foundation of the illusion and the discourses of denial that accompany it, there is an inevitable falsification of the One by its unitary representation. This necessary mechanism of the illusion means that its critique will be quite limited, that it will never be its destruction; but also that the minoritarian thinker has nothing to fear from these immediate objections, based relatively in unitary representation, that are made to him without delay against the One in which he is established once and for all. These worldly resistances, philosophical for example, to the experience of the real-as-One, far from being an obstacle to the march of thought, are instead more like a springboard or an Archimedean point for converting the thought of the One into a *real critique* of the Unitary Illusion.

We call this denial of the One the *non(-One)*. We distinguish the *non(-One)* from the *(non-)One*. The non(-One) is the hallucinatory negation or denial of the One by the World, Unity, Philosophy, etc. But the (non-)One is the efficacy of the One on the non(-One), its resistance to the unitary denial of which it is the object.

This (non-)One, the critique called "real," will have two forms. Both are modes of the uni-lateralizing or in the last instance determination, which in its finite subjective foundation was in question in the first chapter. In what follows, we will contrast its first form, which could be called "mystical," to the Unitary Illusion or to the *non (-One)*, before contrasting it in the final chapter to its second form, which is "pragmatic" and no longer "mystical." Just as there are, as in a story, at least two forms of the repression of the real or of the illusion, there will be two stages in its critique.

The first form of this real critique is distinct from what has already been done, which showed that the One is not, in its essence, representable, that is, unitarily representable, that it also is not something like the unconscious of the World, liable to be really constituted by its forgetting or its originary repression. This is the whole thematic of the so-called "forgetting of the One," which, examined, showed that resistance to the One, if it is possible from the side of the World, is not real or constitutive for the One; and that true resistance resides only in the unitary belief in the reality of resistance: in a transcendental hallucination. This critique of the illusion is like the other side or the effect of the specific acting of the One whose first – mystical – form we now must examine under the title of "finite topics."

Finally, concerning the second form of real critique, we must clarify once again that the non(-One) will recover a certain reality, which will not be that of an originary repression constitutive of an unconscious, when individual pragmatics (final chapter) will put it into relation with the element of *Non-thetic Transcendence* or *Non-positional Other*, which practice will have extracted from the mixture of the World. This is how a kernel of reality, its only reality, will be extracted from the Unitary Illusion according to the Other to which a certain repression does in fact belong, but not according to the One for which it is a radical illusion. The One is not repressed, the Other is: it is only in this sense – hardly psychoanalytic, because it does not confuse the real with the Other – that the unitary defense reactions (to the One) and the authoritarian resistances (to minorities) will be legitimated.

But first, they will have to undergo a primary analysis – a dualysis, rather, a dualyzing critique – which will consist of contrasting them with the dual type, and no longer the unitary type, of the "cut" or of the "critical" distinction: determination in the last instance as finite topics.

SECTION II: *Finite Topics*

17. The Finite Subject and the Critique of the Copernican Revolution

Theorem 53. *By his most immediate existence, ordinary man or the finite subject is the real critique of the Unitary Illusion. In general, ordinary man has no vis-à-vis; in particular, the World is not his correlate, his object, or his place. As finite subject, he enjoys an absolute precedence over the World.*

The only response to the authoritarian defense against the real, to the denial of individuals, is the real itself. But the real of before-response, thought of before-revolution, resistance of before-defense. Not a deferred reaction, an a posteriori acting that would do no more than *displace, suspend, analyze* yet again these defense mechanisms. The only response is to no longer respond, to no longer upend hierarchies, to no longer invert order, to no longer return to order by means of "Difference," or to Unity by means of "exit-towards-the-Other" [*"sortie-à-l'Autre"*]. It is enough to assert the real order of immediate givens within the dual, such that the dual no longer enters into whatever circularity may exist. The precedence enjoyed by the subject as finite in relation to the World is the best possible suspension of any unity or reciprocity. It roots itself directly in the essence of the real and no longer pertains to a philosophical operation connected to the real. It determines the unilaterality of the World; it is its real critique.

Has it been asked how the World phenomenally appears for the individual, how the individual apprehends it from the ground of his insurmountable solitude, and whether this finitude of the subject does not extend so far as to rule out the World being *for* the subject, in the unitary sense in which the subject would for example be identified with the World, lost in the World, alienated in the infinite to return to itself, to be *for* itself? Do Authorities, which stir up their processes of physical and symbolic power before the blind eyes of ordinary man, realize that ordinary man, in some sense, does not see them? Is philosophy capable of thinking man starting from himself, of doing justice to that which man knows spontaneously, of knowing that in his essence man is blind, deaf, and mute, and that everything that is given in his senses and his understanding comes first of all from the most interior part of himself? Finite man has no vis-à-vis, and yet his solitude is not a solipsism. It is more than a de-tachment *starting from* the World and *in* the World. It is more precisely a de-tachment of the World itself, which the subject forces to let go by its mere finitude. The World, History, the State "disengage" or "unclasp" from the subject, but the subject does not separate itself from them: otherwise, the subject would be separating, once more, from itself.

Theorem 54. *Finite individuals are solitudes who reject the World; its experience does not belong to their essence. Radical finitude is a "dualization" of the relation between man and the World.*

Generally, man is not defined, especially as subject, without a vis-à-vis, an object, a world, whose necessary presence indicates that it is also constitutive and that the subject partially co-belongs to it, that the subject maintains to this referent a relation essential to its own definition. When this is not the perceived object, it is the known object and science; when it is no longer science, as with contemporary thinkers, it is language, or else the Other in general; and finally, what is understood to be placed across from man is his "Humanity" – a universal that distills all the others. These games, these belongings, circles, and couplings are the element of unitary thought.

The question is now completely different. The subject exists without an ob-ject. The subject is not, has never been, will never be a subjective and higher mode of the ob-ject. Man exists without humanity; he is not the mere support of the predicate "humanity." He exists without language, which does not mean – quite to the contrary – that he cannot speak. It is not certain that the subject is good, changing nothing or because he is its condition. Nor is it certain that he is man because he maintains the gap between Animality and Humanity and is the subject of Reason: man is man *before* Humanity, ordinary man is an irreversible precedence over Humanity, the individual is not coupled with Totality, the Horizon, the World. This is not an anarchizing abstraction: the foundation of the dual, of dualization, unlike an abstract separation or an analysis of condition/conditioned, is the most positive finitude, the power of the subject to be itself without needing to be alienated or to enter into speculative and representative games, which are the tricks and seductions deployed by Authorities.

Dualization is rigorously theoretical and scientific, and consists solely in recognizing what the real is without practically intervening in it, without penetrating (*eindringen*) into it in order to grasp it (*vernehmen, begreifen*) and make it become what it is. Precisely because he is "ordinary," man does not fall under the determinations of knowledge, does not need to be alienated and to become what he is. He recognizes the real, that is, its inalienable precedence over the World, without it being a question of those "narcissisms" or "logocentrisms" that are only unitary fantasies and auto-projections.

The finitude of the non-Copernican subject implies that its essence – without being a knowledge in the form of transcendence or an objectivation, because it is the essence of the real itself – can be called a knowledge (of) itself, the non-thetic form (of) knowledge, or, more rigorously, of experience. As knowledge, it is as finite as the subject itself; the subject (of) knowledge is no longer this infinite, unlimited subject that includes objective-scientific knowledge as one of its modes, that borders and extends beyond that knowledge. The subject is impenetrable and constituted once and for all, which is to say, unconstituted.

Because it is finite, the subject is never also an ob-ject: of a constitution, of a production, of a subjection. The subject is not a fragment of the World or of Authorities, and ordinary man has nothing at all to do with this *homo ex machina*, to which contemporary thought descended from Nietzsche has clung. No process of power – political, pedagogical, statist, linguistic, etc. – reaches *the subject who has over it an absolute "advance," an irreversible precedence.* Its finitude prevents the subject from being a mode, a figure, a deformable piece of a deep or even a superficial mechanism of power, a supple and untearable topological position, in relation to others. Unitary thought always maintains two complementary theses: the real is the object of constitution or production, and the subject or man is a mode of Being, that is, precisely of a universal (and) or singular production. Both of these theses are ruled out by individual finitude, which rejects all production into another sphere, into the World, but above all into the place it offers to this World.

The real weight of solitude is not the absence of the Other, or even the presence of the absent-Other, but the impotence in which ordinary man finds himself, an impotence to free himself from himself and to alienate himself.. An intimate solitude, too inherent (in) the subject to be pro-jected, limited, surrounded, compensated by the World, or to form an economy of exchange or else of debt with an Other who

107

would be at once interior and exterior to him. But this solitude does not remain without effects . . .

Theorem 55. *Finite individuals are neither at the center of the World nor on its margins. Minoritarian experience neither continues the Copernican Revolution nor reverses it. The subject is at the non-thetic center (of) itself and because of this, its finitude, the subject does not make anything orbit around itself.*

The hypothesis, or rather the experience, that grounds a minoritarian thought is that individuals should no longer be sought on the margins and peripheries of universals, or even at their intersection, that is, as their "difference," but rather should be placed "at the center." This word "center," however, is open to many interpretations. The most common makes it the reversal of the preceding position. The subject is placed at the center *of* the World, of History, of the Sciences – this is the "Copernican Revolution" – and, *as a result, at the center of itself.* The subject only reaches itself through a secondary, but nevertheless real, mediation of the periphery. This is not the minoritarian experience of the "center." *We will say that the subject, or ordinary man, is placed at the center (of) itself, the non-thetic center (of) itself, and that therefore the subject is not placed at the center of the World, of History, of the Sciences, etc.* This is the destruction of the Copernican Revolution by the subject itself, which is too inherent (in) itself to have anything else orbit in its neighborhood: itself and the World. The radical or finite subject does not make anything orbit, it is no longer at the *center of* . . ., it is a center devoid of intentionality and relation. It cannot be said that this center, which is perhaps "everywhere," has an "infinite" and "nowhere" periphery. A "finite" center, finitude as center, can no longer be correlated with a periphery that they would place and that would re-place them: a worldly or temporal horizon, a historical dimension of project, etc. This finite subject is devoid of ecstasy and, as a result, of a universal horizon, periphery and neighborhood, world and proximity. In itself, the finite subject has no "unity": that is, it is always the periphery or margin that, in reality, brings or claims to bring unity and identity in the subject. The logocentric explanation of metaphysics is itself a unitary thesis.

As finite, through his essence at least, man remains at the non-positional center (of) himself and is not thrown into the vast World. The most positive solitude does not presume vastitude. Man is condemned to such a finitude that he cannot even glimpse the infinite on the margins of "his" world, at the periphery of "his" history.

108

Infinity, totality, illimitation: he is not, even partially, inserted into them or manipulated by them, he only sees them from the greatest distance, the distance of a finite em-placement or topics that he does not have to imprint by force in the World, but that are instead the "closest" experience of the real. This is because, even devoid of vis-à-vis, without an Other in general, finitude induces "around" itself a human vastitude in which the World *alone* takes place. Philosophy has never been able to do justice to the solitude of ordinary man, has never been able to recognize individuals as solitudes . . .

Once the Copernican Revolution is eliminated, the question accompanying the finite essence of ordinary man, of subject-man, is this: what becomes of the World, the State, Authorities in general, when the finite subject ceases to animate them and make them orbit in a circle of a higher identity, a circle of the Same? What does the substitution of the absolute, irreversible order of determination in the last instance for Copernican circularity concretely mean for Universals and Totalities? The authentic order of experience is irreversible, going from the subject to the World, without that return to the subject that would allow the World and the subject to circle each other, one with the other, one in the other. The acting of the subject is a before-reversal, a before-revolution, a subjectivity that no longer animates anything around it, but which determines in a way that excludes circularity or reciprocity. The category of "reciprocal determination" is the pivot of unitary thought, but it is the greatest threat for the finitude of the subject. The philosopher thinks circularly, but ordinary man thinks irreversibly.

18. The "Chora" in the Transcendental Sense

Theorem 56. *There is no neighborhood around the finite individual. The World has no proximity to ordinary man, and Authorities have no proximity to minorities. But there is a site, an absolute exteriority "off the coast" of man, an "open sea" rather than a "neighborhood," a remoteness or a distant without proximity.*

The subject is not the object of genesis or explanation: it is an immediate given and the "prototype" of any finite experience. But *after* the subject comes another experience that we have acquired through the contingent affection of the World, though not reducible to it. This is the experience of a transcendental structure rooted in the finite essence of the real (without conditioning it in turn).

What is this second experience that is announced *with* the World?

If the subject, as "ordinary," has no vis-à-vis, correlate, ob-ject or objectivity, thing or horizon of presence, its solitude is nevertheless accompanied by a space, a place or an exteriority that is not necessary to its own essence, but which this essence induces beyond any "vicinity." If a World is that which reigns "around" a god, what reigns "off the coast" of finite man is a site, an emplacement, an exteriority that ceases to encircle him and make him a neighborhood. Thought finds nothing in the neighborhood of ordinary man: individual solitudes have no proximity. However, because of the finitude or inherence (to) itself of the subject, *there is* a place – a unique, absolute, and primitive place, the only possible place, which is no longer taken from a continuum of positions or a topology. There is nothing in the neighborhood of the subject, the subject does not establish a topology; but there is a unique topics through which the World itself must pass if it wants to be able to be given to man in a non-objective, non-worldly way, and if it wants to affect him. This *finite topics* is necessary to explain the dis-engagment of the World, of the State, of Authorities – their "distant" essence, lived as such by the finite subject.

The first transcendental experience possible after that of the finite subject is, thus, that of this site. The subject itself is not a site, but determines one in the form of a "distant" without return or proximity. Determining the first site *before* the World itself (*before* by its essence, its real condition of possibility) is the first effect of the specific acting of the One. What must be "explained," or at least registered in its phenomenality, is this setting-into-site [*mise-en-site*], this originary emplacement for the World, which thus floats, detached, in the indifference of the One to its existence. This is, actually, the primitive and indisputable phenomenal content of what we call uni-lateralizing or in the last instance determination, which will soon be clarified while carefully respecting this absolute precedence of suspension over any suspending [*du suspens sur toute suspension*], this real and no longer operative essence of the uni-laterality of the World. It is an event of before-reduction (before-reversal, before-revolution, before-reversion, before-turning). Determination in the last instance, the uni-lateralization of the World, and its absolute em-placement as "lateral" are all one and the same thing.

Theorem 57. *This exteriority is the "chora" in its transcendental truth and phenomenal experience, below the limit or the becoming with which unitary Greek thoughts have confused it. The chora is the "correlate" of the One or of the finite subject, and, in this capacity, it excludes the Copernican Revolution.*

Devoid of horizon, finite em-placement is the positive structure, the primitive phenomenal content, of determination in the last instance or of the acting of the One as (non-)One. The emergence of the (non-)One in the form of this exteriority is finite or non-thetic. How could primitive exteriority be born of anything but the One, be relative to another exteriority? Individuals determine spaces that are not indefinitely born of other spaces, that are not even *around* subjects, but that instead symbolize infinite remoteness through their primitive quality as unique space. The *ex-* of exteriority, of ex-istence, or of ec-stasy [*l'ex-stase*] is the object only of a static genesis. It cannot itself be assumed in order to be re-born starting from itself, because it assumes only the One. Being unreflective, the *non* of the (non-) One has no time to sketch a distance, to trace a jection. Exteriority is not a trajectory, a transversal jection, an opening recapitulating itself once again in the open. Far from arising at the end of an indivisible distance that brings it into the neighborhood of the One, and far from still being that towards which the subject is thrown, this *non* is only barely what the subject, remaining in itself, throws far away (from) itself by the force of its passivity: it dis-engages absolutely, it is *the* disengagement, it is not distance or interval, that is, a relation. The *chora* is the primitive non-positional place that does not continue any other space. Before the "receivable," the "clearing," the game of opening and the open, there is this absolute site that is the site *for* Kosmos and Polis, but that does not allow itself to be defined by that which fills it. In the transcendental sense, the *chora* is the *there is* or its indisputable phenomenal content that is no longer the ontological horizon of objectivity, the objective copula that would yet again hold the World together. This is the effect of depth, of "distance" without return, the *exteriority borne* of the One and its sufficiency. The One is the sufficient "reason" of the (non-)One in which the still-unlimited World and its infinite attributes are em-placed.

Understood in its transcendental truth, the *chora* clarifies that the World and the State are deprived of action in return, of re-action against the finite subject. This is a completely positive impossibility; the World is numb, de-distanced forever from the One, or set aside. It floats far from man in an indifference that is for it a definitive site it will never leave. It cannot be said that this site is itself far from man – that would be a vicious redoubling – but only that it is the site of de-distancing, of distance without return, the site where everything that

111

finds itself loses its footing, loosens its grip, and glides into the depths of its solitude. Finitude unchains the topos from the bonds of logos, but chains logos to this absolute, which is to say finite, place. This experience is more primitive than that of the Copernican Revolution, which is nothing more than a worldification, a cosmic and cosmological fabrication of the subject.

19. Critique of Topology (Logic of Places and Logic of Forces)

Theorem 58. *Unitary thought, in particular in its higher forms such as the Dialectic or Topology, is based on the "forgetting" of the originary site. It has always given itself the primitive place, presuming it in its reality while leaving indeterminate its real phenomenal essence.*

The unitary paradigm has "forgotten" to think the originary site, the primitive emergence of place. It has left its essence indeterminate, only determining it later according to worldly or historical – empirical – contents. All the work it did on that presumed place – which was split, dis-placed, continued, dialectically and topologically interpreted – will have been no more than a camouflage for a deeper lack, of a unitary forgetting of the absolute and finite truth of place. The correlative topics of the finite subject is even more originary than topology and the dialectic, and thus originary in a non-topological and non-dialectical way. The *chora* or em-placement is the immediate "correlate" of the transcendental finitude of man, not the result of a mere privation of topological continuity or an extraction of the finite place from the continuum of positions: it is not a neighborhood deprived of its reversibility or its recurrence. The transcendental place is positive and completed; as finite, it is unique and inescapable. The *chora* is not subject to sublation, to dialectical and unitary interiorization; it only refers back to the One, and probably – we will return to this – no longer has the structure of a *position*. A place that was never taken from the World and that, because of this, can be a place *for* the World.

It is thus a place that is not acquired through the continuation of a scission or a cut. Psychoanalytic and Marxist structuralism rediscovered the virtues of that operation (combined with those of overdetermination): this was still ordering place according to displacement. *Determination in the last instance, that is, through finitude alone, cannot be an action, an operation through which the One would leave itself.* Purely passive, static genesis of place that precedes displacement and any topological operation. In truth, that is, for man, it is em-placed originarily in the distance rather than re-placing man within the World.

The dialectic in particular – it is true that it has always been that hidden magical essence of unitary thought thanks to the miracle of a production of reality called Unity divided by contraries, which is nothing other than the most constant and fundamental unitary mechanism – always gives itself the thing *and* its place, as ontology or metaphysics gave themselves being *and* its being-position, assuming them to be acquired without asking what are the originary phenomenal experiences in which they are given, being satisfied with confusing these primitive givennesses with the *and* of synthesis, or at best with the *difference* of contraries.

There is, nevertheless, an even more primitive experience than that of the *and* (relation, correlation, difference, split unity of contraries), which is the foundation of minoritarian thought against the authoritarian dialectic. *This is the experience of terms themselves as terms outside-relation, immediate givens of the sides of contradiction, of place (and) of being.* It is also – we will test this later – that of the *duality* (no longer the dual, but duality) of terms, sides of contradiction or of difference. At the risk of being a miracle or a spontaneous generation of the real, these "isolated" sides and their duality (accepted without hesitation by Greek thought) must be experienced before their contradiction, which is a secondary and superficial phenomenon. Only "dialectical" smugness could accuse metaphysics of being a thought of things and not of movement. Metaphysics and dialectics are driven by the same principle, the same amphibology: Unity as the scission of contraries. Clearly this scission is more or less hidden by the reflection of Unity in it. But, precisely on this point, what reigns in an authoritarian fashion throughout is the same superficial principle of Unity (of contraries), of their unifying scission, of their Difference: not the (not-) One or the chora, and even less the One . . .

Theorem 59. *Unitary philosophical topology only recognizes place as a positional continuum, as positions that are merely relative to one another. It confuses place and logos (a topo-logical amphibology).*

It is the essence of unitary philosophies to culminate among contemporary thinkers in a "topological" thought: structural topology of places [*places*], topology of Being, philosophical theory of place [*lieu*], etc. An additional variant is the dialectic of places, contradiction as contradiction of positions, topology as unity, divided in two,

113

of the thing and its place. Unitary philosophy knows place only within relations of structural difference or else of dialectical contradiction, and eventually in topological relations. The most complete product of the encounter of the onto-logical or metaphysical *position* and the topological *position* is place understood as a continuum of places [*de places*], the law of continuity that wishes that between any two spaces [*lieux*] whatsoever it were always possible to determine another one. The *nec plus ultra* of contemporary thought is the neighborhood, the relation of proximity or friendship, care and concern as concern for being *good neighbors to things*. Contemporary thought believed it had found the remedy for the excessively rigid aporias of ground and foundation, etc., and the means for awakening the ancient aporetic and agonistic spirit of the origins of philosophy in the higher or philosophical topology, in the thought that de-mathematizes topology and raises it to logico-real or transcendental functions of an attribute. The highest form of order for unitary thought is thus the continuous passage into (transcendental) continuity, the reversion of common, gregarious, or statistical experience into relations of neighborliness. From the fixed and transcendent places of structuralism, in which subjects were permutated, to the purely relative neighborhoods of functional places being transformed along with their own subjects, contemporary thought fulfills the topological or relational possibility that was latent in the Greek West.

This higher topology is a derived and secondary use of the phenomenality of place. It is a thought of the presumed-place: it presumes that the experience of place is given without recovering the conditions of truth of that experience. It does not undertake any radical genesis of the primitive or transcendental place, which it confuses with semi-empirical, semi-transcendental places. This confusion of the thing with logos, with the underlying unitary gathering, the amphibology of topics and logos, the philosophico-unitary myth of the "topology of thought" or of "Being," of "desiring machines," themselves also "topological" – this is the core of contemporary thought. And this is what has definitely kept it from understanding what Marx, in an empiricist and materialist way, which was only the unitary caricature of the unreflective, struggled to make understood with his distinction, which itself obscured its dual meaning, between infrastructure and superstructure . . .

Theorem 60. *The logic of places requires a complementary logic of forces, a new amphibology which is that of place and force. The opposition between a thought of place and a thought of force is the opposition between a finite or minoritarian thought and an infinite or authoritarian thought.*

Generally speaking, the unitary topics of places needs a complement to suppress its fixity, its lack of historical movement. Force, the logic of forces, is what guarantees the topological passage from one place to another and, in the worst of cases, the transgression of place.

Force is an ancient physico-philosophical concept that found a new function among contemporary thinkers: simultaneously a Greek memory and topological help. Force is required as identical to the Unity of Contraries, to the *passage* from one contrary to another, its essence is scission-as-indivision. Reduced to its real phenomenal content, force is this tension of the differend, undecidable in one way or another. It has become the basic material for theories of the text, of power, of desire, material complementary to the dialectics of place.

We understand that the topology of the positional continuum, which already crowns ontology, culminates in a thought of force, of struggle, of revolution. This is because place was at first understood as force, and force as topics: the differend of place *and* force is what makes the unitary paradigm turn. But, on the one hand, we know that place as continuation or force is the transcendent place, the place that has lost its finite essence and consequently claims, being universal, to once again grasp the subject, to localize or situate subjectivity. On the other hand, if force is required, in contrast to a reified topics, as the concrete or the real of movement (becoming, history), it is clearly, as the Unity-of-Scission, a false concreteness, a solely unitary real. Force is the truncated – representative or mixed – experience of the One. Through force, it is the unitary spirit of domination, hierarchy, and violence that usurps the real and assert its abstraction. Violence and abstraction are the same thing. The real does not know violence; only the Greeks confused *agon* with the real. Force thus does not repress the real; it immediately *is* this repression. Force is woven from fantasies of the Unitary Illusion and violence is, in the same way, the lack of the real. It is unthought in its essence: force is even the refusal to think the essence as such.

In reality, place is immediately determined in the last instance. It is the content of this determination and is no longer placed at the center of the process; it is not itself a subject. Related to a static genesis, place refers back to the finitude of a subject that does not alienate itself, a subject that does not need to withdraw towards itself or into itself: no more than it needed to go out of itself. Neither place nor the subject are forces, nor are they operations, nor are they power, a

115

desire-for-power, or a performativity. We will stop dialectically presenting place then force: not only is this actually presenting the unity of the difference between the two, *topo-potential difference*, but it also denies the real, which is the requisite of the One *in* Unity. The unitary amphibology of place and force is itself absolutely em-placed, uni-lateralized by the finite subject. The finite subject is the real that does not know what philosophy knows: Unity, scission, synthesis, difference, the relational . . .

Finally, if force, as a Unity-of-Contraries that is always deeper than place in the unitary regime, represents the logical or infinite side of representation, place as finite no longer pertains to such a logic. Logic or dialectic of places is already infinite force, illimitation that only continues in order to make a circle with itself – an infinite circle. We must choose between a topical or finite thought and a logical, topological, infinite, and potentializing thought; between the finite-topic and the relational or infinite-topic that always culminates in force and the equation force = real, power = real.

Theorem 61. *The finitude of the subject prevents the primitive chora from still being a distance of the topological type, an indivisible distance that is the final retrenchment of the relational conception of thought and of man. The World is not the great Neighbor of man.*

Topological or indivisible distance, whose two ends meet forehead to forehead, the World and man for example, is already in a sense an inalienable distance. But it is no more than relatively inalienable in its terms and their properties. An incommensurable distance to the World and to man, but all the better to couple them. Finitude excludes even this final relational essence, this transcendental *distance*, this unity-of-difference. The finite em-place is not at all a distance, an idealized higher space in a purely temporal topology; it is an irreversible order that removes the World from the subject without there once more being between them a purified distance or a relation, a neighborhood, a final possible community.

The entire philosophical practice of the *limit* is in question. Exteriority determined by the One can no longer be a finite-infinite, delimited as infinite, exteriority of a horizon of Being, or even of a totality. Neither below nor beyond a limit: we must learn to dissociate the experience of exteriority from the metaphysics of the limit. There is no dis-placement of a limit, but rather an exteriority constituted immediately, inalienable and finite in its turn, and that does not take the form of a process. It is neither the Other as internal *and* external

116

limit, nor the Other as radically exterior, in reality full of the signifying presence of the Other person [*l'Autrui*]. The *chora* is determined by the finitude of the One and merges with the indifference of the One towards . . ., towards the World, etc. It is the site as void, the void as em-placement, the void that is positive only by remaining immobile close to itself and excluding all movement.

The World henceforth is more-than-limited, absolutely em-placed and numb, incapable of exiting this place to return to the subject. The World was never the great Neighbor of man, and man never maintained – except in unitary fantasies – relations of friendship with the World. Man never really had any identity, exchange, or even reversibility with the World . . . There has never been a common border between the World and man. And if man is thrown *into-the-World* in spite of everything, he is not thrown unitarily: he is *also* grasped in this finite em-place in which the World affects him starting from its reduction to the state of "Theworld," an affection that otherwise remains globally contingent for the finite subject.

We would need a long time – is it even a question of time? – to learn that the World, Language, History, Power, etc., are not located in this proximity, this neighborhood, where philosophy, center of the World, still reassured itself. Where philosophy entrusts to the topology of thought the last bonds it maintains with things. Topology was the last form of the Copernican Revolution, in which unitary philosophy forced a whole army of its objects to orbit around itself – in, to be sure, a more and more decentered circle, but whose radius and movement philosophy still firmly grasped. Each time philosophy had to give them some leash, some distance, it was for philosophy a test overcome, further proof of its force of thought. But now this bond, held, stretched, this relation-without-relation, this distant proximity, has given way and the World withdraws from man unequivocally. There is no more Copernican Revolution. Determination in the last instance is its real or scientific critique, not its culmination or "end," its "closure," etc.

20. The Phenomenal Content of Uni-laterality

Theorem 62. *Minoritarian thought thinks in terms of side and not in terms of position (of deposition, of overposition, etc.). It thinks a single side each time, for each finite subject. Single or absolute side, uni-lateral rather than bi-lateral thought.*

117

The first place [*lieu*] is not a *position*. While Being is higher position, determining local positions, the non-thetic One is lateralizing rather than positional. Ordinary man thinks in terms of laterality and not of positionality. Ontology is the high art of positions and theses, the thetic and thematic game, the positioning order and its extension, the modern "positioning." But the One does not pose anything, not even a universal position, where it would necessarily be alienated. The One induces a primitive laterality that it does not pose and that does not pose anything, and that is thus not a ground or a foundation. Minoritarian thought experiences the pure dimension of laterality. It has already finished – it has never started – with auto-position (metaphysics), de-position (Heidegger), over-position (Nietzsche), with all the contemporary ways of thinking "around" position and partially undoing it. Just as the One is not ecstatically split in a horizontal open, it does not broach, seek, or crack this position. In the same way, laterality is not like a margin, a periphery, a limit, one of those indeterminate phenomena or, more precisely, those phenomena of indeterminacy that traverse the horizon of Being or of the World and that can always be stressed, turned against the primacy of the horizon, re-marked as Other of Being . . .

The Absolute has no position – its finitude rules it out. Unlike Being, the One is without ecstasy or existence. *There is* ecstasy, existence, exteriority, but they do not broach or condition the One in return. The One determines them in the form of a unilateral site that no longer has the horizontal form of a plane of immanence, present from all sides at once. The side determined by the Absolute is unrepresentable; it is an immediate given, not an experience-of-consciousness. From this point of view, it is indeed a single side, a uni-laterality. Consciousness or Being is always bi-lateral like the object itself, and experiences itself in the midst of itself and from *all sides*. The One, on the other hand, is experienced without being separated from itself and therefore cannot be thrown towards its horizon, towards any of its sides, towards a universal and continuous side, or even be without sides in the sense that totality would have sublated them. It is not reflected in itself from a side or from its World, or else it would be reflected from all sides at once, or else, more precisely, from all sides-1 as proposed by Difference. But this subtraction of 1 side is not yet authentic finitude. Furthermore, because it is neither a whole nor a continuum of sides, that which it determines cannot be taken from this continuum, cannot be a *partial* and *local* – but still bilateral – place. The induced side remains a side while being, through its essence, finite like the One itself, which prevents it from being a mere mode or a limit in a continuum.

118

If the uni-lateralizing style is different from the positional style, it is equally different from the *transversal* style of some contemporary thinkers. Transversality is laterality ceasing to be finite and becoming universal, side-by-side or relative and continuous laterality, one that reforms a universal plane of immanence. It is to finite laterality what the topological continuum was to metaphysical position – and this is still a bad comparison.

Minoritarian thought, fully asymmetrical and irreversible, thus thinks in those terms of "side" or "laterality" that Hegel the dialectician mocked: "from one side . . ., from the other . . .". But precisely, there are not two sides, a side of departure then *another* side, the side of the Other: it is in this that finite or uni-lateral thought is more originary than the dialectic. The dialectic must immediately presume *two* sides without having elucidated the meaning of this duality, to denounce – surveying and falsifying it – their uni-laterality, without taking into account that laterality, at least if it is real, is necessarily single, as alone as finite solitudes. One side alone and not two: this is what *uni*-laterality means, the laterality that is rooted in the One and thus is not an abstraction of Unity as bi-laterality. One site alone, a single and solitary place: not a continuum of places – the "razor" of finitude rules it out.

As the content of determination in the last instance, uni-laterality can be, at least at first, understood as a specific *operation* of the One. We will first situate it as part of a purely philosophical performativity. With this crucial caveat: we will describe it in what follows as an effect of a "sidelining," [*"mise à l'écart"*] the essential thing being to suggest the difference between the finite em-placement of the World and unitary "being-in-the-world."

Theorem 63. *The content of the phenomenal experience of "unilateralization" is roughly the gesture of "brushing aside with the back of the hand," of becoming indifferent or opposing an "end of non-receiving." The passivity of the finite subject refuses to receive the affection of the World and relegates it far away.*[7]

What is the essence of laterality, its phenomenal content, if it is not a mode of horizontal objectivation or project? Nor a mode of displacement and transversality? It is the operation of setting-aside, of brushing aside. Not in the sense of creating a gap [*creuser un écart*] or making a difference, but of brushing away and setting on the side. Here, setting aside does not mean conserving, economizing, but brushing away by pushing to the side to open a free path and to free

119

oneself. Brushing aside is the most primitive exteriority, the gesture of rendering uni-lateral, before all objectivation or pro-ject, before all jection and movement of transcendence *towards-*. Brushing aside or becoming indifferent to ... is more fundamental than grasping (*begreifen*) and posing (*setzen*), above all for a thought of the real as thoroughgoing passivity.

One brushes aside with the *back of the hand*.[8] The hand is not always a contraction over an interiority, an interiorizing grasp, an appropriation. The originary back, that of the hand as transcendental subjectivity, gives place to another operation, equally fundamental though more concealed or hidden. This operation is precisely a brushing aside, not necessarily always a reversing, a reversion, a reversibility. It is not certain, even at the level of this transcendental performativity, which from our point of view is still marked by interconnected empirical and logical determinations, that the interiorizing grasp and brushing aside *of* a back (immediacy of a gesture of reversal, which proceeds without mediation towards its object) form a performative continuum. It is, in any case, more rigorous to dissociate these two operations and to give to the back its specific content of phenomenal experience. The back [*revers*] is not reversion [*la reversion*], that is, a continuous torsion aimed towards a form of entirely interior unity or towards a plane of immanence that the hand – by creating it – describes. Nor is it forward-momentum, the flight of a jection or transcendence with an intelligent and cunning catch in sight. It is *a way of making place for a thing by setting it aside and making it indifferent*, of recognizing a place as lateral. It is less freeing the front, making a clearing in front of the self – that is a mere effect – than "putting things back in place," in the sense of putting them back in "their" place. And for the finite individual, putting the World in place is necessarily putting it back in "its" place: that is the indisputable experience of the *chora*.

There is a transcendental truth of the hand, of its acting, probably also a finitude of this acting, a finitude of the hand as inalienable subject and above all as an "instrument" of the refusal of alienation. The hand is indistinguishable from what it is in its essence; it is identical to an "activity" that is the immediate symbol of finitude protecting itself. The hand as back rather than as interiorization is the corporeal knowledge (of) itself of finitude.

A similar phenomenon is described by the "end of non-receiving."[9] This admirable expression, no doubt too negative and based in an "opposition" (opposing an end of non-receiving) has the advantage of showing what differentiates uni-lateralization from interruption.

Interruption is a relative-absolute gesture that stops the better to continue. The end of non-receiving is a way of ending, of finishing, but by placing itself still below reception or acceptance. *Reception* is the unitary or transcendent form of passivity, a mixture of passivity and power (receiving is power-to-receive). Yet, sidelining does not even receive, *does not make itself passive* in front of an offering or an activity of the Other. *Passivity is such that it cannot even receive anything*, too passive to be affected from the outside, too finite to be affected by an offering, a presence, or an alterity. The end of non-receiving does not describe the position of putting-in-place, of em-place, but rather its real transcendental condition, which is a passivity without division and which holds the World disengaged at a "distance," that of non-receiving, from which it does not return. It makes it clear that uni-laterality is an em-place (a thing is *in place*) more so than an activity of emplacement. This is also then not a re-jection, a de-ject, a de-jection, but perhaps more a dereliction, a way of *relegating* the World to its place, that is, to *the* only place.

Theorem 64. *Laterality is the primitive phenomenal content of exteriority. It is an outside positively devoid of inside. And it is the ultimate truth of "Occam's razor" as resistance of individuals to unitary philosophy.*

Brushing-to-the-side is a true outside-without-inside, which, moreover, is not the other side of an inside or at best that which fractures it, as is always the case for contemporary thinkers. Radical finitude is not an inside, an interiority, coupled with a correlative exteriority. The interpretation of the structure of determination in the last instance as the coupling of an inside and an outside, of a center and an alterity, of an identity and the Other, would be a complete falsification and misunderstanding of the content of its phenomenal experience. Contemporary unitary thinkers strive to think an outside without an inside, an outside that they are content, for this reason, to couple in a "differential" or "undecidable" manner with an identity, or to remark it as an outside. But what is important here is what uni-lateralizing determination nonetheless precludes: their nature as *indivisible relation* or as *differend*, which makes one of the terms *transcend* towards the other, which inhibits it as its scission, then reciprocally or alternately. The outside is thereby indeed without an inside, but it nevertheless elaborates the inside, at the same time and necessarily, from the outside and from the inside; the outside does not *have* an inside, but it is *also* an inside, to which it is, at least partially, identical.

121

On the other hand, the finite outside, *chora* or laterality, is not an outside *in relation* to finitude, which would make no sense because finitude is not an inside; it is not interior *and* exterior to it. There is a pure exteriority, a nothing-but-exterior and static instance, an object of an immediate experience and one that en-sues irreversibly from finitude. Finally, unreflective finitude does not transcend towards/as the unilateral place, nor does the unilateral place enjoy a recurrence that would make it once more grasp the subject within itself and em-place finitude in turn.

The originary operation, the acting of the One – if they are still operations – are thus not operations for posing the World, for posing itself with it, for de-posing or re-posing it, for op-posing it to the Other in order to overturn it. The finite subject remains in itself and because it remains in itself it induces a finite place, an absolute emplacement. Correspondingly, the lateral is not an Other elaborating [*travaillant*] the finite subject, deconstructing it. Minoritarian thought does not proceed from a gap between a logocentric unity and its Other, it does not settle into its game. It brushes it off (literally but transcendentally) with the back of the hand. Finitude induces an immediate back, an absolute sidelining that refuses to be engaged in an infinite process of displacement and reversal, of reversion. Even if the brushing (-to-the-) side, the primitive and non-thetic effect of finitude, sometimes seems similar to unitary operations of suspending, reduction, doubt, deconstruction, etc., its essence is fundamentally different: it is no longer unitary.

With these experiences, we possess the immediate phenomenal content of "Occam's razor," at least as a real requirement, an immediate given rather than a "principle." It stipulates that the finitude of the subject-without-Object, of man-without-Other, uni-laterally *brushes aside* the World and Authorities, Reason and the Principle of Reason.[10] It does not destroy them, does not negate or deny them, does not even nihilate them: it is in no way a negation, a scission-cut, an analysis, which are unitary operations. Finitude is instead a "principle" of the non-utility of Authorities, of the non-use of the World, at least in what concerns man himself. For the World, without losing any of the properties it has in relation to itself, loses only the illusory claim to extend these properties and these powers to ordinary man. *Determination in the last instance stipulates that it is (really) useless to extend effectivity to the real.*

Theorem 65. *"Human philosophy" is constrained to an irreversible order of experiences (of man, then of the World) imposed by the*

122

finitude of the One or of the subject. There is an "ordinality," an "ordinary" more powerful than the traditional principles of Reason.

Except as an approximation, the real *Krisis*, finite critique, is not a dis-placement, a change of place, but a primitive and definitive putting-in-place. The *chora* is part of the order of immediate givens, but is not itself an ideal order of places, a positional continuum. The only ordinality is the real or transcendental ordinality of immediate givens as they are. From this perspective, there is an *unplaced* [implacé], a forgetting of real place, in both structural and non-structural unitary thought, just as there is an unthought [*impensé*] of the One. But clarifying the content of the phenomenal experience of the *chora* does more than displace the ideal order of places, it also emplaces it; in the absolute sense of the expression, it puts it "in-place."

The real order means first of all that experiences of the em-placement of the World, the State, Authorities, etc. follow upon experiences of the One and are not necessary to the essence of the One. Then, it means that they are identical to the experiences of the absolute remoteness of the World, of its "transcendence" or "beyond." We will not confuse these two experiences, because the *chora*, where the World is em-placed, comes *after* the One from which the World is *also* remote; it is not the remoteness of the World that necessitates that its experience come after that of the One. Irreversibility is not exhausted in the remoteness of the World, but in the order that makes de-distancing [*é-loignement*] come *after* the One, and which is thus no longer a remoteness [*un éloignement*] that is still topological or *in relation to* . . . the One. Absolute remoteness, a way of being of a "qualitative" distant, is of course a form of irreversibility in its own way, but the first is rigorously transcendental or real and protected against any transcendent and physical form of irreversibility.

"Human philosophy" is constrained to an absolute order that ensues immediately from the radical finitude of the subject. It is ordinality that is joined to man as individual and that regulates "individual" experiences. This real order is the "Ordinary" or its real phenomenal content. It is not taken from the World, but the World finds itself taken up in it. The law of continuity only holds for the sphere called "effectivity"; it is itself organized according to this more powerful principle, the *principle of pure or irreversible order*, itself rooted in human finitude, which is the radicalization of the *principle of indiscernables* or of *individual solitudes*. This is a different concept, an "additional" experience of the Ordinary. The Ordinary is the real possibility of all orders: it must be understood in the same

sense in which we speak of a compendium of arguments [*d'un argumentaire*] or a tropary, etc., but which would be determination in the last instance of all possible orders. The Ordinary, in this sense, is more powerful than the traditional principles of Reason and constitutes the criterion or guiding thread for a scientific description of the phenomenal content of Reason.

SECTION III: *Determination in the Last Instance and the (Non-)One*

21. Thinking the (Non-)One

Theorem 66. *Unitary thought has "forgotten" determination in the last instance and its phenomenal content, which is the (non-)One. Thinking the essence of the (non-)One in its truth is a minoritarian task.*

We have just described the primitive phenomenal content of determination in the last instance as a finite topics or a *chora*, which we immediately contrasted to the Unitary Illusion. But we must reflect upon the way we have acquired this *chora* and recover its transcendental truth. We thus start again from the beginning, that is, through the One and the possibility of a determination in the last instance. To highlight what it now at stake, the transcendental truth of uni-laterality, we will speak of the *(non-)One* rather than of a *chora* or a finite place. The (non-)One is the real content of determination in the last instance.

Just as unitary philosophy as a whole, and not only metaphysics, has not thought the essence of the One, it has also not thought the essence of the (non-)One, having reduced it to secondary forms, such as those of Being. We must think the *non* – the finite em-place – as mode or manner of the One, as this *finite-void-of-finitude*, as a nihilation even softer than the difference between Nothingness and Being recognized in the thought of contemporary thinkers. Above all, it cannot be thought according to the World and the authoritarian mixtures, according to Being and as the essence of Being: this would yet again determine it relative to unitary – not only metaphysical – structures, and lose its finite essence, which it takes from the One alone. Perhaps we will later find a special and restricted form of the (non-)One that will sustain something more than occasional and indicative relations with the World. But it is imperative, indeed the One compels us, to stop thinking the phenomenal content of the (non-)One according to transcendence (being and its Being) in order to describe it as the aura of indifference that the finitude of the One immediately induces.

Theorem 67. *The experience of the (non-)One is not metaphysical or ontological, worldly or authoritarian in general. It is an immediate given and its conditions are those of transcendental truth or of the One.*

There is no genetic or effective explanation for the (non-)One. Such an explanation would be vicious and would presume the World as constitutive of the (non-)One, or the One as prone to being alienated: two hypotheses that have been ruled out. None of the content of the World can claim to factually or effectively explain it, nor does the One create it by following the paths of effectivity. Determination in the last instance no doubt "is concluded" from the dual, that is, from the One and the World, from the One and the *non(-One)* as unitary resistance to the One, *but in the sense that it is transcendentally necessitated by the One* and not effectively produced by the World or taken from it.

The *non-* of the (non-)One can no longer be a cut, a primitive scission: this would be to return to the unity-of-contraries. The One does not act through a cut or a scission, the (non-)One is not a mode of ontological transcendence, but rather that which absolutely precedes ontological transcendence: a finite exteriority that neither advances nor withdraws, an absolutely primitive transcendence, so to speak, which no longer takes the form of a universal spatiality, of an open for being and returning from it. It is localizing, but *for* the World in totality, to the extent that the (non-)One or the *chora* neither blooms in the midst of being as the World itself does, nor in-the-midst-of-the-World. It emerges spontaneously "around" the One without forming a periphery, because the One, as we know, is at the center only (of) itself and not of the World. The non-thetic (of) itself One is not encircled by the (non-)One.

The (non-)One, in its essence, is an immediate transcendental given just like the One. Therefore, a "transcendental deduction" of it is possible, so long as any genetic or effective process is excluded. But this "deduction" does not at all proceed in Kant's juridico-rational manner: it just appeals to the irreducible phenomenal content of determination in the last instance as the specific individual causality of the One. Immediate givens are here simultaneously unreflective transcendental experiences: above all, not intuitions, which are by definition always objective.

Theorem 68. *The dual is what allows the necessity of the (non-)One to be thought. It prohibits juxtaposing the One and the World as two transcendently separated entities between which a mediation would then be sought.*

It is therefore necessary to return to the element of the dual.

The dual is the matrix of minoritarian thought. It is as important, at least in its own order of course, as Kant's discovery of *real opposition*, Nietzsche's discovery of *difference*, and Hegel's discovery of *dialectical contradiction*. It is an inalienable form, but one that it is necessary to start thinking, even if it remains unthinkable for unitary thought. The dual is an irreversible order of immediate givens, not a continuous process of disjunctions and synthesis, of scissions and identifications.

There is no One, then the World, and then the (non-)One that emplaces or ex-teriorizes the World. The (non-)One is given – from the One – with the World: this is the order of the real, a transcendental order, and not a temporal or intra-temporal order. It is useless to pose the World only to negate it afterwards by the (non-)One. The real situation does not allow for a unitary and circular generality of this type: on the one hand, the World is not posed (by the One?) *so as to* then be negated; on the other hand, it is only the occasion, for itself, of the (non-)One, and not that which determines it in its essence or would determine its production as One. The (non-)One is a transcendental concept, an object of immediate experience with the subject, not a transcendent concept, like, for example, the Idea of the World. An "unreflective reflection" is necessary to immediately transform all ideal predicates that we might want to forcibly attribute to subjects into what we call irreversible "postdicates."

The World is not separated from the One – a separated place – in a transcendent manner the way the religious Gnostics imagined. The dual is no more the undecidable disjunction of subject *and* object than it is the reciprocal exclusion of Soul and Body, or even of Spirit and Body. Reduced to its transcendental or phenomenal content, the dual is the irreducible core, the essence or affect of dualism, and that which religious mythologies strove to turn towards the glory of transcendence. It is necessary to be done with these anthropological imaginations concerning individuals and the way they live in the World: even the body and the soul are traversed by the dual, structured by it. The dual is the inescapable transcendental that does more than pierce through all conduct. It is not an unconscious: it already affected the World, which reigns in heads, bodies, and unconsciouses.

126

22. The Causality of the "Last Instance" or of Finitude

Theorem 69. The causality of "determination in the last instance" is not that of a present cause, an absent cause, or even an absent-present cause.

Determination in the last instance is a purely transcendental causality, the causality of the real itself. It will thus be a priori different from the four forms of causality known from metaphysics, as well as from the causality of the Other and/or of Difference that contemporary thinkers contrast to them. All these modes of causality are semi-empirical and semi-transcendental. Even the material cause is still, according to a higher turn of thought, an ideal form of causality (any empirical given can be transformed, and in a sense must be transformed, into ideality) that sublates an empirical content. None of these causes is exclusively real or the specific causality of the real.

Determination in the last instance is thus not the efficacy of a "present" cause: the formal, the final, the efficient, and the material are modes of presence, implying the mixture of the real and transcendence. "Last instance" means, among other things, that this cause is not present or does not exist as a mixture: it is the real, it is not effectivity ...

Nor, moreover, is it the efficacy of an "absent cause." Not knowing what to do with the "last instance" because of an unrepentant idealism, and sensing its original (finite rather than circular) character, structuralist Marxism resolved to give a "structural" version of the last instance, characterizing it as "absent" *in relation to* ... the metaphysical (circular and representative) cause. But when it is a question of the real, which does not fall under the "categories" of Being and Nothingness, the negative process is as irrelevant as metaphysics.

Finally, the last instance is not the unity of the two preceding modes: it is not a cause present *in* the World through its absence *from* it. Not being of the World because of its finitude, acting globally on it without being one of its parts, it cannot be a mode of *being-in-the-world* in Heidegger's phenomenologico-existential sense, nor is it yet another way of transcending towards it and as it.

The One is sufficiently finite to not need to be determined by the World and to not be forced to continually act upon it through some universal causal continuity. From its side, the World is not a constitutive part of the One, a limit in a unary continuum, the condensation and fixation of a procession; nor a being receiving the mark of an ideal but exemplary cause. Among other things, "in the last instance" means that the One does not act from itself and through a part of itself that it would alienate in the World and identify with it; and, secondly, that finite acting upon the World is identically and immediately its placing-at-a-distance from the One, the affirmation of its unitary non-confusion with the One. The One acts *only in the last instance* and it acts on the World by determining it to not be the One.

Theorem 70. *Determination in the last instance is the specific causality of the finitude or sufficiency of the One, an "individual" causality rather than an "individuel" causality, which is still universal.*

It is through its immanence, which remains in itself or finite, that the One acts upon the World, uni-lateralizing it. Determination in the last instance means that, in the One, it is its sufficiency or finitude, its indifference, that are the sole phenomenal content of acting. As the real, the One has no reason to leave itself, to go towards an exteriority, to identify with an Other. Therefore, it is its non-directly determining finitude that will be determining in spite of everything, inasmuch as and in whatever form it can continue to be so: with no vis-à-vis. It is *an action without reaction*, one that does not proceed, like other causes, by following the continuous trace of an identification with that upon which it acts, by borrowing the pre-traced continuity of a virtual unity with the determined or the caused. Finite exteriority, absolute em-place, will be – because this, too, is something more positive – this void of all ideal and onto-logical space, of all horizon. It can determine a being without having to receive it beforehand and be constitutively and intimately affected by it: the World is only the occasion or indication of the manifestation (from its own point of view) of this determination in the last instance.

"Last instance" does not designate a first or a last cause in a causal continuum (the famous indefinite progressions and regressions in the conditions of a conditioned), nor does it respond to an additional anxiety to stop the causal chain either by a leap into the totality of conditions of a conditioned, or by a leap into a stop-cause, interruption-cause, or start-cause of the chain. None of these worldly and transcendent avatars of finite and/or infinite causality have any relevance here. *The theory of determination in the last instance does not at all respond to these problems, but rather to their "exclusion," or more precisely, to their uni-lateralization.* The only relevance of a "last instance" relates to the radical and positive finitude of the subject, that is, to the possibility of a specifically "individual" causality, which is the proper acting of the real and must be differentiated from four or five "unitary" causes, which hold for effectivity alone and are mixtures of individuel-and-universal causality.

23. Transcendental Deduction of the (Non-)One or of the "Chora"

Theorem 71. *The (non-)One is what the finitude or sufficiency of the One requires in order to act on the World, Authorities, etc., and in order for its effective non-acting not to be devoid of all efficacy.*

If finitude cannot directly determine through itself by prolonging itself into that which it determines or by forming with it a higher Unity of a universal causality, that is because finitude determines it, in a sense, through what it is not, which no doubt is also finite by its essence but which is a (non-)One rather than a non-Being. Because the determination remains close to itself and even in itself, it affects the determined only in the last instance, that is, in passing through that which is no longer a (unitary) mediation at all, but rather exteriority or the (non-)One. The last instance – the One – thus requires the (non-)One in order to remain last instance or finite while acting on the World. This is the mode by which a last instance can, having given up all mediation, continue in spite of everything to determine. The One is determination through its refusal even of acting, through its passivity with no counter-part, which makes following the paths of continuous or unitary causality useless. Determination in the last instance is the exclusion of genesis, of production, of unreal-real causality; it is the specific acting of non-acting. This is a "transcendental deduction" of the (non-)One, not induced from the World or taken from it, but required by the acting of the One on the World.

That the One requires the (non-)One in its acting on the World should not be understood in a unitary way yet again. The (non-) One could be the manner in which the One would go out from itself, or the manner in which it would be affected by a nothingness, a non-being, or an Other. But if the (non-)One is only understood in its essence through the One, the reverse is not true. The (non-)One is the non-thetic outside-subject, or the outside-subject that is not a departure of the subject outside *of* itself, and the One and only the One is necessary to describe it (later we will find another form of transcendence that will require effectivity or mixtures in addition to the One).

The (non-)One is not the real, it is that which could be called, without once more making a circle out of these two instances, the reality (of) the real, that which accompanies the real as its shadow without the real having to pro-ject and be enclosed in it. The (non-) One is not an independent instance beside the One – between which new relations would have to be woven – it is in a sense the same thing as the One, except that it does not constitute it.

Theorem 72. *The (non-)One is a real "non" that enjoys absolute precedence over any operation or category of negation, over "nihilation" as well, which is a mixed or effective reality. It is an indifference to the World that precedes the World: an a priori indifference.*

We write *(non-)One* to indicate how much this *non*, for having the finite One for its essence, is itself positive and hardly a mode of negation. The (non-)One, the *(non) (-of-the) One*, the *(nothing) (-of-) sufficiency* is, if you will, the "opposite" of the One, but the opposite (of) the One is not at all the opposite of Being. Its essence is the non-thetic or the unreflective itself, absolutely devoid of negativity, and even devoid of this (non-)One that is a consequence, but not an ingredient, of its essence.

This *non* is not merely suspensive and nihilatory, itself neutralized by Being. It is a *non-without-negation*, a non that is real before any negation (always semi-real semi-ideal), the mode through which a positive indifference can determine. We precisely will not believe that the (non-)One is a neutraliztion of the negative; it is not a question of returning from Being-Other to Being-substance, but to the One.

The (non-)One is the indifference of which the passivity that is the essence of the finite individual is capable. Indifference exists *before* that which it indifferences, its phenomenal content is this very precedence: transcendental and no longer transcendent indifference, which thus itself knows (itself) immediately. The *non-* expresses the finite positivity of the One, which thus knows (itself) to be indifferent without being indifferent *to . . .* and which, because of that, does not even need to use repulsion, but rather, as it were, *resists a priori.* Later, we will distinguish this indifference that is not passive but *through passivity* from an indifference that is not active but *through activity*, which will not maintain a mere relation of uncompromising uni-lateralization with effectivity.

SECTION IV: *Real Critique and Philosophical Critique*

24. The Affect of Real Critique

Theorem 73. *Real critique does not consist in passing from consciousness to reality or to the unconscious, but rather in passing from the real to that which is not it or is so only according to the mode of effectivity (Consciousness, Being, the World, etc.)*

We do not discern the reign of the Illusion and its critique through the passage of an "unreflective" or immediate consciousness to a reality of reflection whose secret only we, philosophers, would possess because we would be able to contemplate the truth that experience would not see. It concerns instead a contrary and more-than-contrary passage: from the unreflective real to the scarce reality of the reflective. Real critique is not the passage to the for itself, to a state of knowledge more complete than its abstract or immediate state, which would have integrated the dimension of the possible into a higher and thus finally a "real" synthesis. It is not a question of consciousness but of reality, and at any rate everything occurs in the unreflective. Even the philosophical reflection carried out here is, in its essence, an absolute phenomenal given, and the reflective is still a real essence. No longer taking the form of a reflective knowledge, not even of a mere supplement of reality, of alterity to this knowledge-of-consciousness, it does not oppose the philosophical to the non-philosophical, or conscious knowledge to unconscious knowledge, but rather the order of the real to unitary disorder. For Unity and the World do not sin through an excess of order, but through an excess of disorder: measured against real individuals, against the ordinary as the individual core of every possible order, Authorities are disorder par excellence; this is an inevitable thesis.

   If the dual does not represent a reflective state of the real in opposition to its own unreflective state, this is because the latter does not, properly speaking, have an opposite, except, precisely, through a unitary illusion: unity or opposition of the World and the One . . . The immanent contemplation of the One adds nothing, no real knowledge to the World, no objectivation, no distortion or additional cut: the One is not added to knowledge, it is its absolutely anterior condition.

   The dual is thus not a philosophical montage, one of those "dispositifs" unitary mechanics so adore. It is the primitive structure of the real or of experience, below the unitary distinction of the

131

non-philosophical and the philosophical, for example of the in itself and the for itself. The illusion and its critique undoubtedly only have meaning for and in the dual, but the dual is not an operation external to reality or an abstract construction, an additional knowledge, but rather a real event extending its critical effects within unitary constructions. Critique is a given that is as passive as the real, including the present statements, which, if they seem themselves to gradually constitute a certain real, induce the same hallucinatory illusion.

Theorem 74. *A real critique is utterly different from a philosophical critique: it determines philosophical critique (in the last instance), but not reciprocally. A real critique is a critique of philosophical critique, but a philosophical critique is not a critique of real critique.*

A real critique is possible on two conditions: The first is that there be a sphere of absolute existence, a finite absolute or *an absolute (of) finitude* that uni-lateralizes all Authorities, including philosophical ones, but never allows itself to be delimited by them in return. Ordinary man is this absolute (of) finitude – the real itself – and it is ordinary man who, through his essence alone, his philosophically indeterminable and most immediate existence, carries out this critique. The second condition is that Authorities, affecting finite man in their own way, claim to enclose him completely in their system and to be able to determine him in return.

The encounter of individuals and Authorities – this is the "dual" – in fact gives birth to the Unitary Illusion, the belief that the real or the finite individual is representable and can be inserted under the conditions of logos, of transcendence in general. This belief is a denial of the essence of the real, and minoritarian thought actually begins with this belief, if we assume that minoritarian thought begins beyond the One, which is the condition of all thought but which does not, strictly speaking, philosophize.

However, the encounter of individuals with the Unitary Illusion also gives birth to the possibility of a critique of the Unitary Illusion. Ordinary man does not look upon the World; he is not part of the knot in which the World and its reflection on itself remain forever intertwined. He neither objectivates nor "surjectivates" it: ceasing to hold it at a distance and identify with it, he determines it in the last instance, or uni-lateralizes it in a finite place, which puts an end to all unitary projects of identification of the subject with the World. We are not in fact critiquing a mixture or a unity as is, the way they are critiqued unitarily, starting from themselves and through negation, but rather starting from an instance of a truth that is not unitary, which, without ceasing to be a determination, is no longer a more or less negative limitation, but rather the real itself, that is, a determination in the last instance. This is a minoritarian axiom: the critique of Authorities or Unities can no longer be a unitary thought, for example an auto/hetero-limitation: it is a real dualysis, a dualization of Authorities, a freeing of the real phenomenal content of the dual. It does not consist of reflecting or of doubling reflection, but of creating a void, of inscribing philosophy in a chora determined by "individual" finitude. Knowing how "to forget," a non-philosophical forgetting, a forgetting of philosophy by the real, one that requires no supplement of the will. Abandonment always already abandoned, effectuated, or actual. It is no longer a question of interpreting or transforming the World, or even of displacing and deferring it. It is a question of arranging it according to "ordinary" man, that is, according to an irreversible order: of contemplating it from the immanence of the One, then, possibly, of making it into an object of practice proper to this human essence.

Critique, when it is joined directly to the real and blends with the causality proper to the individual, proper to his finite essence, deprived of future, history, world, etc., it can no longer be a tendency, a goal, a project, or a process. The minoritarian thinker simply describes the order of immediate givens – the real and that which irreversibly ensues from it – and in this order he finds a moment of *Krisis*. As soon as it is only real or finite, critique ceases to be a wholly philosophical operation, that is, paradoxically, a half-philosophical and half-real operation. Contrary to this philo-centrism, ordinary man knows (himself) immediately as the real in which philosophy does not co-operate, and which philosophy merely reproduces through its processes drawn from effectivity. For ordinary man, it is an immediate given that the World drifts at the center of an absolute remoteness, in an insurmountable strangeness: this is the affect of critique, not a "thesis," but rather the most ordinary experience of the real, the experience of the dual that has already suspended the operations of cutting, of synthesis, of difference – the entire philosophical technology.

This is why the critical procedures proper to unitary thought are here replaced by descriptions of two sorts of experiences (the "mystical" and the "pragmatic"), which together form the irreducible phenomenal content of critique. To dualyze is first of all to contemplate the World and Authorities in a uni-lateralizing way, and then to "analyze" them pragmatically. The first moment recognizes that the real is outside-mixture; the second recognizes that it is possible to extract, under less absolute conditions (because they presume the existence of the mixture) its other ingredient: a special, non-thetic transcendence (as we know, the terms will be less separated from each other than they will be from the form of the already-mixed).

Theorem 75. *The dual, which is the place of the Illusion and its critique in its two aspects, mystical and pragmatic, seems first to be indistinguishable from resistance or the non(-One). But it is not a philosophical artifact, a construction external to the real or a scaffold attached to a building.*

The non(-One), the resistance of effectivity to the real, seems to be born of or with it, while the dual, inversely, seems to be born from the affection of man by the World, from that which man feels of this affection. This is because the conditions of this affection are such that the World immediately negates the One, explicitly or not, as soon as it attempts to *represent* it, which it does just as immediately. This instantaneous defensive reaction explains why, at least at first, the dual seems to be indistinguishable from the non(-One) and why its reality seems as . . . unreal as its own.

Nevertheless, the reality of the dual is more profound than that of the Illusion, otherwise it would be a mere philosophical artifact and could not enable the critique of the Illusion. The forgetting of the One, the Illusion, takes its meaning from the dual; it even becomes indistinguishable from it because before the dual is reduced to its core of practical validity, it rests entirely on the non(-One): the reality of the dual, which is not that of a symptom, is first of all that of an illusion or a hallucination. On the one hand, the real essence of the dual is the One, even though, for its part, the One does not need the dual. On the other hand, the dual is a requirement born of effectivity itself, from that contingent affection that touches man and will not cease, that will prolong itself beyond the *topical* critique of the Illusion: from this perspective, the dual and the Illusion share a core of effective reality that pragmatic critique alone will be able to uncover. The dual, which begins in the unitary hallucination, is thus not itself wholly a hallucination. In and through ordinary pragmatics, it will reveal a core of reality, the irreducible function of the World as a "signal" of practice and one that will partially legitimize unitary resistance, but no longer in the initial form under which it appears here, as non(-One). Even as an unreal hallucination, the Unitary Illusion is real as effective, as it will soon demonstrate.

But we have to understand that the Unitary Illusion has a stock of effective reality. The dual is motivated by the resistance of the World and, for example, of unitary philosophy, but it is not limited to being a philosophical construction. The latter might be its authoritarian occasion, but it does not exhaust its essence, which is identical to the real order of experiences and does not allow itself to be unitarily broken down into unary reality *and* into effectivity. We acknowledged it previously: the dual is not the external or arbitrary encounter of the One and the World as previously "separated" and "in themselves." The dual is the transcendental order of uni-laterality, even if the affection of the World remains for the One contingent. This affection is its indication or occasion, but not its essential cause. It thus possesses an absolute reality below all the external reconstructions starting from separated and transcendent terms. The dual is a transcendental experience, not the transcendent concept of philosophical "dualism," which is an abstract reconstruction. Even if the dual is motivated by the World, even if in the end it has no critical significance except for the World, it is not reduced to a philosophical artifact. Critique begins with this resistance of the non(-One), but this contingency is integrated into the real situation, and does not empirically or externally condition an abstract operation of thought.

The dual is therefore not an additional construction, a philosophical addition to the One. The World always denied the One: this is not only an "effective" situation but a real or transcendental one. The dual is motivated by effectivity, but beyond that it is still the relation of effectivity to the One, a defense mechanism that has an essential or "transcendental" cause. If the One did not exist, resistance would have no reality as a worldly event. The non(-One) is always actual, even when it is not actually thematic; and it is necessary to distinguish actuality, that is, immediate givenness, and thematization, which is not constitutive of the real itself. We settle for describing a real situation in which the authoritarian resistance of the World is indeed a contingent fact through its effective cause but not through its real essence, which, as transcendental, has already touched the World: if the World claims to hold for the real, it is because the real affects the World or announces itself to the World, and because the essential cause of the illusion is real or transcendental. This is what accounts for the illusion being *over* the real or *as to* the real and for the very fact that *there is* an illusion.

Theorem 76. *The transcendental point of view of the dual avoids a disastrous "dualist" disjunction, its unitary reduction sometimes to the One alone, sometimes to the World alone.*

Real critique is carried out by means of the One, but not for the One, because the One does not need it. Is real critique then carried out for the World and Authorities? No: in the sense that, given over to themselves, they are incapable of conducting this type of critique, and settle for a philosophical critique that preserves the unitary illusion. Yes: for them, provided that from now on we think them as inserted into the "ordinary" order of thoughts. It is indeed Authorities who must be freed of an illusion, but insofar as – and this is the same thing as real critique – they cease being thought as the absolute or the real, abandon their unitary abstraction, and are reinserted into the order of immediate givens.

In reality, minorities and Authorities do not maintain transcendent relations of exclusion or separation. It is an error to pose the problem: critique for whom? while naming sometimes the One and sometimes the World. Doubtless, neither the One nor ordinary man needs this critique, but critique is the work of this man, and concerns him in this one capacity, as soon as the real situation – which is not the One in its sufficiency, but rather the dual that includes the affection of the World – is reestablished. Critique is only necessary because Authorities also emerge beyond the One in a way distinct from that of the One. No critique is possible without the One, but its occasional cause is the World. The point of view of critique is therefore the dual that "includes" the World.

For example, in a sense, it is the One that makes its unitary forgetting, the Authoritarian Illusion, possible: but this is so in the sense that it is the hallucinated object of this forgetting, not in the sense that it would be its "effective" cause. We will say that its intentional and reflective introduction is necessary to provoke the resistance of the non(-One), and that the Unitary Illusion is only discovered when the One is taken to be the guiding thread of all experience: the One alone, or ordinary man, knows that Authorities or the World suffer from this illusion and are its seat, even though they themselves do not know this. The "presence" of the One is in fact necessary. But it is an immediate given, not an external operation or an arbitrary encounter hoped for only by the philosopher. Furthermore, the non(-One) is locatable in the dual and even *as* the dual, without the dual "completely" creating resistance, even if it reveals it.

In general, we cannot contrast the World as the seat of the illusion to the dual as the seat of truth and critique. Nor can we contrast the point of view of the World *in itself* to the minoritarian point of view of the dual. In a sense, the World remains in itself in the dual; the World, which denies the One in the dual, has always denied it. The real situation is the dual itself, which is not a philosophical artifact and does not modify the World for the ends of knowledge: the One tolerates it, does not nullify it, but merely emplaces it while maintaining its "in itself" character. We cannot distinguish between the World in itself or outside-dual, nor even in relation with the One, and the World "in" the dual. This is an obvious distinction: in the dual, the World remains in itself because it is not ob-jectivated and because its finite em-placement is not an "objective reality." And in any case, the dual is not added to the One and to the World, it is born with the non(-One) of the World and has the One for its essence. By contrast, the World does not know that it is already taken up by the dual, and this ignorance (of) itself is identical to the Illusion itself. The point of view of thought has never been anything but that of the dual insofar as it has the One for essence and the World for occasion. It is neither reduced to the point of view "separated" from the World (the Illusion, precisely enclosed in itself), nor to the point of view of the One. It is the element of minoritarian thought that finds its occasion (beyond the One . . .) in the World, in its Authorities, their totalitarian demands, but insofar as they are received by finite man, who here "becomes," so to speak, the ultimate "point of view" of the World on itself.

The point of view of the dual finally allows us to evaluate the Illusion: it is not a flaw in the One, but a flaw *in* the World. However, here again we must clarify: it is not a flaw from the point of view of the World and according to its mode of existence (this claim to autonomy is the Illusion itself). But it is a flaw that affects the World from the point of view of the One and for the One, that is, for whoever thinks the World, Authorities, etc. non-philosophically by simply following the real and nothing else. This illusion does not take anything away from the One or even from the World, which is assumed to be isolated and unable to see the One such as it is: it is only denounced as an illusion as such in the dual and on this basis, which is that of the real, of minoritarian thought.

25. The Positivity of Real Critique

Theorem 77. *Critique is not a reduction, a nihilation, a general destruction of the World. The World continues to affect man according to the mode proper to it, an affection as indestructible as the World.*

The dual allows us to contemplate the Unitary Illusion in its stubbornness without destroying it but rather by "putting it back in its place." The finite subject contemplates the Unitary Illusion uni-laterally without objectivating it; it even grants it an additional posi-tivity, that of its em-place. Just as the illusion that comes from the non(-One) is not a symptom, its critique is not a process of circular displacement. It is an absolute contingency or exteriority, more or less motionless, without degree, but which has the benefit of leaving it as is and enabling a rigorous science of it.

There is no dissolution or liquidation of unitary mixtures. Their em-placement is neither a destruction nor a negation, neither their division without remainder nor their decomposition into two sides. The (non-)One is as positive in relation to non-being as the One is in relation to Being. It is a "nihil-uniting" . . . rather than a nihil-being.[11] The dualysis of mixtures is also different from their unitary analysis, from their *unilateral division* that would allow them to remain as one of the sides of division. Rather than a nullification, it is a "unary" or "ordinary" contingency of the World, of the State, etc. Of course, they are *not* for the One, but this *not* is not a way for the One to refuse itself to them. The One itself does not need them, but it gives itself to them in the last instance or allows them to exist in this mode of uni-laterality. It affects them with its finitude, but not as an Other penetrates the World, distorting Authorities, the Polis, etc., excluding and including them. It localizes them through its indifference, through the acting of its passivity, which remains in itself before proceeding to any operation of position, negation, deposition, overposition, etc. The finite individual feels himself, finds himself affected by the World, but only from the primitive site that lends its contingency to that affection. The finite individual is thus affected by mixtures as such, by the always empirico-ideal *facta*, particularly by the World, the most encompassing factum of all. However, this affection by which the World or the mixture affect themselves or one of their parts is imme-diately "dismissed" or affected in turn by man as finite, lateralized or "remote" in the *chora* by the subject who is always distinguished from it, and who em-places everything up to his own body insofar as he is affected by the World as one of its parts. For the finite subject, the World is only "Theworld" and the already-mixed is only lived as "Themixture" rather than as play or differend. And the finite em-place in question is obviously not an experience that is thinkable from the inside of the mixture, from its empirico-ideal components. It is an immediate given, the phenomenal content of contemplation with which ordinary man combines his essence. The *chora* is an absolute situation in finite exteriority because the One is not a pure and simple power of dissolution of the mixture of the World, of the general amphibology that affects us and in which we are effectively inserted by something other than a mere illusion.

It is within this uni-lateralization of the World, of the State, of Philosophy, from this site in which they are suspended, that they will constitute a sort of final resistance or trigger signal for the practice or the pragmatics to come. The pragmatic dimension of the ordinary existent will unfold inside this contemplative suspension or mystical "relation to" the World, and will enable the extraction of a Non-Reflective-Transcendence outside of the mixture in which it is enclosed. But the mixture will not be dissolved there either, because this operation will be carried out after the fact and will assume the givenness of the World: an a posteriori extraction, it will not be able to destroy, properly speaking, the mixture that it will continue to posit. No doubt it will not take from the mixture a part homogeneous with the whole, but rather one of its two ingredients: this will not be a sufficient reason to speak of a dissolution. For the moment, at least, individual finitude simply em-places mixtures uni-laterally, affects them with an absolute contingency without yet practically *dualyzing* them.

Theorem 78. *If all phenomeno-logy is unitary and belongs to the World (no longer in a restricted or Greco-phenomenological sense), then phenomenology, which is the forgetting of real phenomenality, must be de-logicized. This is the condition for an absolutely positive critique of the World.*

Struggle, destruction, subtraction: this is not the content of the (non-) One, of its mystical acting upon the non(-One). Nor is its content a suspension or a reduction: the phenomenal generosity and positivity of the One cannot allow these phenomeno-logical restrictions, these operations that are still too negative for the purely passive or real acting of the One.

This contemplation of the World "in" the One in which we see all things, this acting of absolute passivity, is an efficacy even less direct or continuous, even less transcendent – entirely immanent – than the contemplation of the World by the Phenomenological Ego. Even Husserl does no more than make or deepen the difference with the World. He still undertakes an operation, an activity that must make a unitary compromise with the World: distinguishing itself from it without being able to distinguish itself from it, a relative-absolute distinction, that famous *nothing* of the parallelity that Husserl places between the Transcendental Ego and psychism. But finite man breaks this final parallelism of the transcendent and the transcendental. He no longer has anything in common with the World, which is why he can situate or contemplate it without having to extract himself from it, without having to go beyond its margins . . .

Dual contemplation is the acting of the One through which it recognizes the absolute validity of the World by localizing it without destroying its *in itself*. Only a dual thought – rather than any more or less religious dualism given externally – that is, a thought that begins with the One and not with the World, which moves from the One to the World and not in the opposite direction, can love and legitimate the World, can end the eternal game of unitary resentment by which philosophy departs from the World, distances itself from it and "turns around" *towards* and *against* it. By identifying the Whole and the Absolute, unitary thought is condemned to affect the Whole with an immanent and permanent doubt, with an indelible anxiety that immediately begins philosophizing. The necessary condition for recognizing the absoluteness of the World and Authorities, their ungenerable nature, is the precedence of the One over the World, of minorities over Authorities: de-realizing the World so as to stop negating it, or de-logicizing it to better re-phenomenalize it. Above all, "dual" dualism is not the negation of the World or an attenuated form of that negation, but only the declaration of its non-pertinence to the One and, simultaneously, its affirmation *as it is*: what we call "Theworld" and its absolute character as emplaced. The World must be de-absolutized from the point of view of the One and re-absolutized from the point of view of its uni-laterality.

Theorem 79. *The Unitary Illusion is not destroyed at its effective root, but only in the belief of the World that it holds for the real. It is reduced to the state of a hallucination and is contemplated as such (as it is).*

The dual, because of its unary foundation and the acting of the One, which is not a negation or a suspension but a "mere" uni-lateralization of Authorities, leaves Authorities more or less intact. The problem of a science of the World that would be an integral part of its object and would modify it is no longer posed. "Theworld," we know, is neither an object nor an objectivity, and the dual is not an even higher or extraordinary form of objectivation.

The non(-One) thus remains non(-One); it even gains an immediate positivity across the dual "distance," the longest and strangest distance. The illusion is contemplated in the finite site as being in itself, as strange and irreducible as the mixture – its cause – without being affected by an alterity or a cracked closure. As a mode of the World, the illusion is no more annullable than the World itself, but rather is suspended in the primitive place and thus ceases to count for ordinary man in that which it affirms or denies of him or of the One. The uni-lateralization of the World – above all not its neutrality, the *neither the one nor the other of two*, that is, Difference, which is the neuter par excellence or the higher form of neutralization – allows it to subsist without once more unitarily altering it, analyzing it, etc. the way philosophical critiques do. Because the last instance remains in itself, it has the power to legitimate the illusion in its effectivity without still claiming – this, precisely, is the height of the unitary illusion – to destroy it at its root and eradicate it. The illusion is challenged in its claim upon the One, but it is legitimated in its effective cause. It is no longer constitutive of the real, but rather subsists *as it is* with the World through absolute remoteness and irreversibility. The World is not sup-pressed, and in a way philosophy continues to exercise its unitary tricks, though they cease to be taken for the real and are recognized as never having been the real and as being nothing more than a halluci-nation. What has always and actually been suspended is the claim to reciprocally determine individuals and also the hallucinatory necessity of a philosophical operation of suspending. The illusion, understood properly, is not *in itself* completely a hallucination, a phantasm, a mirage. What is destroyed is only the World's ignorance (of) itself, an ignorance that is a hallucination of the real and that is only destroyed by something other than an additional consciousness: by the finite real of the distancing chora, and first of all by ordinary man who knows (himself), in an unreflective way, to be not enclosed in the World, and who knows that the World has not known him.

Theorem 80. *Real critique is not the analysis of a symptom and does not posit the conflictual unity of the One and the World. This unity – the symptom – is precisely the content of the Illusion itself: the symptom as such is not just semi-illusory, but entirely an illusion, at least from the point of view of the real or of individuals.*

This produces a form of critique that is utterly different from philo-sophical critique and from the analysis of the unconscious, as well as from their intersection, emerging, however, in its own way as a new type of the old critique: "deconstruction." All these modes dis-place or de-limit defenses and symptoms. But it is not clear whether the Unitary Illusion is a symptom, or whether it is only a symptom unitarily. Nor, moreover, is it clear whether real critique is another mode of ana-lysis and dis-placement, or whether it is so only unitarily.

Resistance, not the unitary resistance that we are describing, but the resistance Unity conceives of itself – when Unity is capable of going as far as resistance, that is, as far as an outline of dualism as in "psychoanalysis" or "deconstruction" – possesses the knowledge that is not known, a self-denying knowledge. This is the symptom itself, globally considered or uni-lateralized, which is unreflective ignorance (of) itself; only a *real*, not a supplement of consciousness or even of the unconscious, can carry out its "critique."

But if the non(-One) is not a real resistance to the One, it is a real resistance to that which we call Non-thetic Transcendence, which is the specific object of ordinary pragmatics. At the current level of the dual's exposition, we can not yet see the reality of the Illusion, its kernel of truth and legitimacy. In reference to the One, it is only a mere hallucination, based on a representation of the One that is in reality without object, that is, deprived of the One. The One does not fall under representation: it is the sphere of the Invisible.

Theorem 81. *Based on the finitude of man, real or "dual" critique is the only means of eradicating the resentment and hatred of the World innate to unitary or philosophical critique.*

The dual and duality are not renunciations of critique, but rather ways of fulfilling it by transposing it from unitary or philosophical terrain to the terrain of the real or of ordinary man. This changes the style and pathos, the habits and affects of critique. Critique was only an elaborate mode of the unitary refusal and denial of the real, an elaborate mode of the spirit of vengeance and negation that always ensues from Unity. Now it derives from the real and turns "against" Unity.

As a unitary project, philosophy has always taken up the World's hatred of itself. When the World sees itself it is stirred up by disgust and carried beyond itself by hatred: unitary philosophy is the expression of this malaise, which is extended by "critique" as though by an additional form of the natural authoritarian denial of the real. Unitary or philosophical forms of critique thus contain significant fear, refusal, fascination, and auto-destruction. It merely varies their forms and means, stretching or intensifying them while respecting the old ideal of continuity. In the guise of positivity, it makes do with relations of neighborliness or proximity, with an entire topology that claims to be "friendly," but which can do little more than displace or differently distribute existing relations, that is, existence in the mode of relation – this circular economy of the close by *and* the faraway, an economy of bad faith in which philosophers recognize each other but do not recognize real individuals.

In particular, the World or a part of the World has always been criticized in the name of a higher – or else a particularly certain and self-assured – form of knowledge. Critique was logo-theoretical, based on the ob-*jectivating* or sur-*jectivating* form of knowledge, on its core of transcendence in general. This essential, higher knowledge is here rejected from the side of the World and critiqued in the name of the real, which is still a "knowledge," but no longer a knowledge *of* itself, objective or surjective, or implementing a form of transcendence.

Critique must cease to be an instrument of vengeance against the World. Critique swaps ends and means, becoming positive and ceasing to be a mode of negation by giving its entire extension to the World, by returning this unitary resentment to it, by confusing it with philosophy itself, which claimed to abstract or detach itself relatively from it. Finite individuals experience the World at the most extreme distance, a distance from which one does not return. This remoteness, this indifference with no counterpart that nothing will balance, cannot enter into any relation or economy whatsoever (exchange, debt, statistical distributions, etc.). The individual is not a part adjacent to the machine of the World. He does not refuse the World within a wanting or a desiring-the-World; he does not de-limit the World from within his identification with it, or as a means of this identification. He disregards these games of infinite bad faith and makes the World positive, but in a finite way. Unitary thought and unitary critique themselves are also made positive, precisely because the individual does not redouble them, does not reflect them, does not elevate them to the nth power, but maintains himself in a finite distinction with the World and Unity, untainted by any resentment, that is, by any repression. If he still represses anything, though in a completely positive manner, it is the authoritarian repression of ordinary man. Far from working and operating against the World and producing resentment, he is protected from this danger because the critique he carries out is joined directly to its very reality and merges with its acting.

Ordinary man substitutes dualyzing finitude for negation. We know how much contemporary philosophers strive to attenuate negation, to render it finite and make it escape from Being, to experience it as a mere "nihilation." But the One (rather than games of Being and of the Other) and radical finitude (rather than Nothingness and the Other) were needed to displace critique outside the terrain of the World (of philosophical games, textual games, language games, etc.) and return it to its real or "individual" element.

Theorem 82. *The real is not at stake in critique, and real critique is not a mode of unitary conflict. Ordinary man determines conflict in the last instance, but does not essentially or constitutively participate in that conflict.*

A real critique does not have the same "stakes" as philosophical critique. This means that it does not have "stakes" in general, stakes par excellence, that is, philosophy itself, as stakes . . . *The real is not a stake*, except for unitary philosophy. For ordinary man, it is nothing of the sort: it is him, this finite man, that is this real, who knows (himself) as never having been a piece of the authoritarian machine, as never having had any care, concern, interest *of* his own.

The real is given before, not with, the World, and this immediate givenness, which does not need to be extracted from the World, suffices to make critique stop being a struggle, a conflict around the real (Science, Technology, the Proletariat, the Unconscious, etc.). Critique ensues irreversibly from the real for Authorities; it is not – at least in its essence – a battle of Authorities with themselves. The real is given in essentially passive experiences, and cannot ground a metaphysical and political activism or voluntarism. Even the pragmatics it will make possible will not be the sort of activity philosophy imagined. The real is not a vague instance, the jewel of ideology; it is "individual" experiences. And, in any case, even philosophical critiques are made in the name of the real, but a real unitarily confused at worst with knowledge and at best with transcendence in general (Physics, Language, Being, Time, Work, Desire, the Other, etc.) – in the name of an amphibology that is the object of the new critique.

What is the use of real critique if it is not useful to the One and to individuals "against" Authorities? It is useful to Authorities, to keep them from succumbing to the illusion of believing that they are the real, to the hallucinatory magic of their action upon individuals. But it is also useful indirectly if not to protect the essence of individuals, then at least to protect them from the magical belief with which the World haunts the individuals – that they are no more than one of its parts; to assert the "dual" against the unitary hallucinations with which Authorities overwhelm and charm ordinary man.

SECTION V: *The Science of the World and of Authorities*

26. The Reality of an Absolutely Subjective Science of the World

Theorem 83. *Determination in the last instance establishes the reality of an absolute science of the World and Authorities in general (of the State, Language, Sexuality, etc.); it is part of the transcendental science of man.*

The entire undertaking, or rather its necessity, of thinking beyond the One is based on the contingent affection of man by Authorities, then on the resistance of Authorities to the individuals thus affected, whom they resist because of a finitude that is incomprehensible for the authoritarian manner. The resistance of subjects to this denial of their reality is "determination in the last instance." If this denial is its occasional reason, the finitude of subjects is its essence, its real foundation. The non(-One) is no more than the occasion of the (non-) One, at the very least its manifestation, and even then only for one who grasps it from the World and its denial. Moreover, the (non-)One is an immediate effect (of) the One, and indicates nothing more than the autonomy of the One, its indifference to the World. This is why determination in the last instance was introduced as early as the first chapter. Although it is not a constitutive characteristic of the essence of the One, it ensues immediately from the One, even if it only actually emerges with the non(-One) and thus, in a sense, *for it*. We know that this is the property of the dual, and it does not preclude – quite to the contrary – the immanence of the One, forever un-forgettable. Nevertheless, the rigorous order of experiences requires that determination in the last instance not be dealt with until Authorities are introduced, and the content of individual causality not be explored until the forms of individuel causality, that is, of still necessarily universal causality, are announced. The capacity of individual causality to establish an absolute science of Authorities, of the World, of the State, etc., thus remains to be dealt with.[12]

The science of man is in general an *absolute science*. Such a science is not the science that we, as philosophers, could claim to have of the Absolute. It is the science that the Absolute, that is, ordinary man rather than the philosopher, has of himself and of the World. The Absolute is not the "object" of this science, nor even its subject and object at once, their infinite circle. The Absolute is only the subject of this radically subjective science – it is this science – and in contrast it is forms of effectivity (which are utterly distinct from the Absolute), mixtures or totalities – World, State, Authorities, Language, Power, Sex, Economy, etc. – that now form its "object": as a result – we will have to put this to the test – something other than *ob-jects*. Absolute science is too subjective to have ob-jects – only unitary philosophy has those, and it is thus not a genuinely absolute science – which is not to say that absolute science has no "object" and is a science of clouds.

Given its identity with the finite subjectivity of ordinary man, this absolute science is not the product or correlate of a system of transcendent operations of cutting up, of setting adjacent or adjoining, of analysis and recomposition, of negation or suspension, etc. It is straightaway actual, completed, and can only be described in its indisputable phenomenal content: that of determination in the last instance, which is the element of the absolute knowledge (of) the World with which individuals otherwise confuse if not their essence, then at least their status as existents.

Determination in the last instance is the foundation of this absolute transcendental science. Because it is completely subjective and without vis-à-vis, only it can respect its object, which is to say, can refuse to objectivate it once more on an even "higher" mode. It does not add itself to the real, to that which is, through a partially autonomous philosophical operation. It coincides with the absolute or finite experience we call the real. On the one hand, uni-laterality is not an extrinsic property of "finite" things of "determinations of the understanding"; we no longer regard it from the outside as a relation or a lesser relation: it is a knowledge (of) itself, an unreflective transcendental experience, and not at all an empirico-materialist concept. On the other hand, this absolute of subjectivity or finitude is not what deprives it of any "object," separating it abstractly and idealistically from the World. On the contrary, its positive indifference and finitude ground its capacity to determine the World in the last instance, to obtain a knowledge of the World utterly different from that of the empirical sciences and that of philosophy, because it will take the form neither of a knowledge of an ob-ject nor of a knowledge of the objectivity of the ob-ject. The sort of "transcendental deduction" carried out above in relation to the (non-)One or to determination in the last instance guarantees the possibility or rather the reality of this science.

Theorem 84. *The subject (of) absolute science has no ob-ject as vis-à-vis or as correlate.*

146

The subject (of) absolute science *is* immediately this science and for this reason is not the ob-ject (or one of its parts) of which it is the science. It is not a part of an ob-ject, nor even the collection of the *relative* (-absolute) conditions of objectivity. The finite individual induces a place (an *as it is*) of which it is neither a part nor a limit, which the subject in an ideal continuum would still be. The thread that traditionally binds the subject and ob-ject, whether or not it takes the form of an intentionality, the function of an intentional continuum, is broken here. The finite subject has no intentionality *towards* the pure place, which it no doubt induces, but to which it does not refer as to a pure index of objectivity or a kernel of meaning. Transcendence or exteriority is itself finite, not continuous and synthetic, and does not turn back upon the subject where it is nevertheless based. It has been explained at great length that the finite subject does not transcend *towards* or *as* this finite place, but rather that this finite place arises simultaneously with the finite subject, which is not alienated in it.

Philosophy is unitary because it remains in a *relation* with its ob-ject. At worst, it is objectivation, at best, surjectivation or relation of difference (undivided distance, topology). Philosophy institutes knowledge as a blend, an equivalence between itself and its ob-ject; sometimes a relation of non-equivalence as higher equivalence, etc. The philosophical science belongs to the corpus of its ob-ject, or, more precisely, main-tains a relation of neighborliness with it. Thus, what should be an *absolute science* is nothing but *the absolute form of an empirical science*, a topology sublated by philosophy, for example.

If it does not want to be taken for a "religious" and "metaphysical" regression, which the unitary gaze will no doubt take it for neverthe-less, absolute science must be an *Ante*-Copernican science in a particu-larly rigorous sense of the term. It is only a science by being the subject (of) science, that is, a subject without vis-à-vis: *absolute precedence over any objectivity and revolution*. Subjectivity, finite or without ob-ject, means that its essential "object" and the knowledge of that object are not the *same*, do not form a relation of difference. The object is not an integral or constitutive part of this knowledge, and this knowledge is not the object that possesses knowledge about itself. It is in this that knowledge as well as its content "as it is" are finite: they do not re-form the more or less tightened, more or less split or extended, circle of unitary knowing [*connaissance*]. No higher subject to refex-ively hold the subject (of) phenomenal experience together with this experience, no higher yoke or Unity able to accumulate existence and essence, the object and the knowledge of that object.

An absolute science does not propose to do fully what philosophy, as always, could only do partially: find a rule for dividing up, an egalitarian economy, a rational decision between subject and object. It provides nothing of the sort and does not complete philosophy there where it fails. The decision it raises between the finite subject and the World, between minorities and Authorities, is strictly finite, more-than-undecidable, transcendentally identical to the subject itself. It is indistinguishable from the existence of ordinary man who *is* this absolute science. Unlike the philosophical form of science, which refuses to make the decision between "subject" and "object," it makes or *is* this decision. But this decision does not pose the finite em-place; it *is* immediately that place, and is thus "undecidable" in its own way and does not depend upon philosophical will.

Theorem 85. *A unitary philosophy cannot be an absolute science, only a relative-absolute science. In an absolute science, the subject (of) knowledge is neither part of, nor transforms, its object.*

The project of an absolute science is a philosophical project. This means that, even as the project par excellence of philosophy, it remains ... a project. No past or future philosophy will be enough to fulfill and actualize it; that is, they demonstrate by their very existence, by their very claims to fulfill the project, that a project is destined to remain a project. An absolute science cannot have the same phenomenal content when it washes up on the shore of a unitary philosophy as a mere "project" or an intention to be fulfilled, and when it becomes actual in the real and merges, if we know where to grasp it, with the existence of finite individuals. Minoritarian thought does not complete or accomplish the old project: it frees absolute science from its form as project, always semi-real, semi-possible, and always problematic.

A traditional unitary philosophy cannot be an absolute science. It is always a system of operations *upon* the real (thus relative to it), but which then identify with it (thus absolute): a merely relative-absolute knowledge for which the real is *at once* subject and ob-ject, and not only the finite subject. By virtue of this circle in which the subject is alienated in a reality to be known, any philosophy must both include itself among its ob-jects (the subject of knowledge is simultaneously one of its ob-jects) and deduct itself from them to be their *absolute* science. Now, a genuinely absolute science should not be an integral part of the corpus of the ob-ject: but the unitary circle, deeper and more extensive than the circle of "theories of knowing," by definition prohibits the object to be known from being determined once and for all – as it ought to be – outside the act of its knowing, from being positive in its order independently of its determination by its knowing, a determination that ought not alter it or add to it predicates that would be the predicates of knowledge or knowing. Knowing knows something – this is its intentionality – but its knowing of the object is not added to this object as a specific predicate. To know is not to transform the object practically or determine it by adding additional determinations, by overdetermining. Absolute science is indeed a determination of its object, the World, but *only in the last instance*. It is a contemplation of this object, but one that does not transform it at the same time or is not a part of its concept.

Theorem 86. *Absolute science has no ob-jects (empirical sciences may not, either): it is the contemplation of the World "in itself," of Authorities "in themselves," etc.*

Because the subject is neither thrown towards exteriority nor alien-ates itself *as* exteriority, it can determine an actual and finite form of exteriority and thus make possible an absolute science in the element of this exteriority. Because the non-thetic subject (of) science – the absolute or subjective science is also the subject (of) science – is neither a higher ob-ject nor the form par excellence of the subject, because it is not of this World or a higher Authority, because there is an *unconditioned finitude*, the World can finally be seen "in" the One, that is, "in" this science rather than "by" it or by a series of opera-tions, hypotheses, or constructions which are the lot of other sciences, above all philosophy.

Indeed, if absolute science is not a science of ob-jects, it is also not a science of objectivity, a science of universal essences or realities – a philosophy. Determination in the last instance has as correlate a space, or, more precisely, a chora, a place, but always finite or indi-vidual, never a space of universal ideas or a space that is itself ideal. The *As It Is* is thus not an operation on an ob-ject. It preserves the World, which it does not negate but merely em-places. More gener-ously than phenomenological bracketing, unilaterality respects the World without objectivating or altering it; it preserves it as "in itself," with the difference that here the in itself is no longer redoubled in the form of an ostensibly absolute *autonomy* of the World, in relation to the One, of course. Even the natural attitude is preserved in finite em-placement, even logocentrism, etc.: they take part, respectively, in suspension or erasure, all of which together is em-placed. The finite As It Is is more powerful – that is, more contemplative and respectful of its object – than doubt, bracketing, sublation, difference, etc. These are not all equivalent, but they are all operations, whereas unilaterality is no longer an operation upon the worldliness or the logocentrism, etc. of philosophy. The World presumed to be "in itself" or absolute and the World inscribed in transcendentally grounded exteriority are exactly the same World. Its em-placement is neither a transformation nor an alteration, but rather a contemplation of this "as it is," which is the phenomenal given forming the content of absolute science.

Even more than unitary intentionality, the dual and unilaterality rigorously realize the "transcendence in immanence" that is the cross of traditional philosophy: the transcendence proper to the World (the "in itself" of the unitary type) is inscribed without remainder in this absolutely primitive transcendence of finite topics, which is itself immediately derived from transcendental immanence and no longer forms with it an unstable mixture, an impossible amphibology as is the case with both the unitary intentionality of consciousness and the unitary ontological intentionality.

Theorem 87. *Absolute science excludes temporality in its access to the World. Finite individuals do not maintain a historical relation to History as Authority.*

In its philosophical form, absolute science has always confronted the problem of the flux of the object affected by time (Plato, Kant, Husserl). It is not enough to explicitly pose the insertion of the subject and its operation of knowing in the ob-ject, or the inverse, because this insertion is temporality itself. On the basis of this unitary presupposition, two opposite solutions are possible. Either, with Nietzsche, we reduce this object to becoming itself, once more suppressing the problem in the affirmation of its impossibility, elevating its aporia to the state of a solution; or, with Heidegger, we affirm the non-subjective finitude of knowledge thus related to the Other as to that which is at once internal to objects and external to them: finite knowledge, no doubt, but radically temporal once again. In both cases, we transform the problem into its solution, which is the unitary vice, instead of showing that the problem, while not a "false" problem, is a transcendent problem that ought to be critiqued in a real or transcendental way.

An absolute science is a theoretical or contemplative science in the rigorous and justified sense of the term. It is not a science that transforms its object and introduces into it and itself the dimension of historicity and of "stakes." The inevitable effect of the reality of this science is the positive exclusion of time, at least in the form of worldly unitary time that is based on transcendence, and thus of temporalization as originary transcendence. Temporality is a generality mediating between science and its object, the unitary element of their synthesis or their analysis. Moreover, its banishment outside of any constitutive function is – like that of language – the effect of a non-worldly, purely phenomenal, science of the World, of the State, of Authorities

Finite individuals no more maintain an originary temporal or historical relation to the World, and, for example, to History itself, than they maintain a linguistic relation to language. History, in all its forms, from the most reified to the most "temporalizing," is one of those Authorities that oppresses them, certainly the greatest Greco-unitary fetish that ever concealed minorities and attempted to capture the finite essence of ordinary man.

27. The Absolute Science of Mixtures or of "Postdicates"

Theorem 88. *The As It Is is the "empirical" in its transcendental truth, that is, as radically determined, but without transformation, by the One, and no longer determining the One in return. The empirico-transcendental parallelism is broken by the dual, which is no longer a correlation.*

The *As Such* or *As Is* [*Le* Comme tel *ou* l'En Tant que tel] is the content of the ontological project, of the most universal a priori horizon of meaning into which an ob-ject can come to be inserted. The phenomenal content of the As Such is meaning, but as Unity, or at best as unitary difference. In contrast, the content of determination in the last instance, which is no longer a project at all but rather a uni-laterality we call the *As It Is* [*le* Tel quel], to suggest that absolute science, which relates the World to its em-place, respects its object "in itself" more than a project, which alters it, would, and a fortiori more than an analysis, which identifies its object under the law of Unity, or a synthesis, which objectivates it. The As It Is is even more positive vis-à-vis the World and Authorities than the As Such, which nevertheless says what a thing is. But Being is at least a *throwing*, a transcendence of being, and hence already a transformation or a production of being.

Unilaterality is the originary appearance of things in a form that is not that of the ob-ject: the As It Is, as the content of unilaterality, is the correlate neither of an objectivation nor of a surjectivation, but of a determination in the last instance. If the As Such is the circular meaning-of-being that belongs to a being and blooms in the midst of being, the As It Is is no longer a meaning but a real essence, the unreflective but unilateralizing content of essence with which science affects the World and any mixture whatsoever.

The As It Is is a matrix that gathers mixtures, Totalities, or Authorities not by totalizing them once more, surtotalizing them, detotalizing them, etc., but by finitizing them in an exteriority devoid of any horizon, any synthetic unfolding (continuous surface, plane of immanence, etc.). It strips them of their unitary hallucinations. It is the real phenomenal content to which their determination, as unilateral, reduces them by grounding them in the immanence of the finite subject and knowledge. It is more than and different from a "secondarity," it is an irreversibility, irreversible twice over: first because unilateral exteriority is based in the finite subject upon which it depends the way the (non-)One depends on the One; second because this place marks the absolutely derived and conditioned character of the instance that occupies it in relation to the subject that thus finitizes in a mode other than its own, that of exteriority, the World.

Theorem 89. *Through the (non-)One as finite place, the One abandons the World, rendering it useless and contingent, making it into a surplus or a too-much. For finite individuals, the World is too-much.*

The subject enjoys an irreversible precedence over its works. They do not extend it, and the subject does not alienate itself in them. This means that in reality, the subject is not its own work, nor does it have works in the World. Its only work is its "non-acting" and the (non-) One that ensues.

Theworld, the As It Is, is clearly no longer the objective correlate of a subject alienating itself in it. The finite subject does not produce objectivity, it induces an exteriority, which is more primitive than the exteriority of the ob-ject, and one from which the latter draws its own phenomenality, that is, its paucity of reality. The One does not bind Being originarily, or, as the Other, does not obligate it, numb it with responsibility: it imposes upon it an absolute em-placement through which the World ceases to be a neighbor of the One. For Being, the State, and all those great authoritarian universals, this is a sort of pre-alienation, an absolute finitude that precedes Being's self-alienation, but also this quasi-alienation, this finitude through the Other, which contemporary thinkers have tried to place in Being. *Before* Being alienates itself *as* Other or *through* the Other, it is localized by a place that is not its own, which is utterly different from its own topology, and which is therefore no longer that of which it is ultimately capable: an affection, an alteration, an alienation.

Rather than a negation, the (non-)One is a call to an absolute or finite existence, identical to a radical contingency. It is no longer onto-logical because it is precisely the finite or absolute existence of Being, but an existence of which Being on its own is no longer capable, an existence that never passed through the Other but that comes to it directly from finite man rather than from the Other. The (non-)One is this contingency that a priori precedes any contingent thing in the World and thus counts globally for the World; it is an absolute outside that does not affect from inside and outside at once.

Exteriority without transcendence, without even an indivisible dis-tance. Indivisible distance is Difference, but the (non-)One is instead the nothing as absolute surplus, as *too-much*. The World, Authorities, are too-much through the strength or weakness of the One. The World is not affected by insufficiency, by alterity; it is not neutralized or enclosed/cracked – the Other has not yet appeared – but rendered globally useless for the One. This contingency, this uselessness, is a new way for it to exist. A *surplus* character comes to it that is not foreseeable or programmed in the principles that make the World.

Contingency or too-much is not an empirical but a transcendental affect conditioned by the sufficiency of the One that is its essence. The *surplus*, the *there is* of the finite place, are henceforth reduced to their content of phenomenal experience, and are different from any mode of worldly or unitary transcendence, from any process of scission and synthesis – from *supplementarity*, for example.

The (non-)One thus expresses the abandonment of the World by the One, the absolutely abandoned by the One, the dereliction of Authorities in the grip of minoritarian finitude, which has already grasped them from beyond their nevertheless unlimited sphere of domination. This abandonment is irreversibility itself. It is the subject who, far from having to abandon himself once more to Being, aban-dons Being to its destiny. There is a shadow (of) the One rather than a sun of Reason, and the shadow of the One is stronger than the sun of Reason.

Theorem 90. *The One is not the pre-predicative. But the World, Language, Authorities in general themselves cease to be predicates of the One, of the real, and become mere "postdicates."*

Of course, the finite em-place, the exteriority of the chora, is a manner of relating to the One in the sense that it is based in the

One or depends on it as on its essence. But this is not a relation in the sense in which the thing relating to the One would constitute the One in return through this relation. Transcendental relation *in*-the-world, the fundamental concept of all unitary thoughts, is broken: there is indeed a transcendental relation, but unreflective and irreversible, and now it is a relation of the World to the One. However, this *to* no longer has at all the same circular meaning as the "*to*-the-World."[13]

Because the One is a finite subject, an essence without predicates determining it, or without vis-à-vis, the World in its *as it is* or as *Theworld* in turn definitively ceases to be a predicate, the universal predicate of the subject. A predicate is generally that which "puts itself forward" in a mode of saying, the vainglory or conceit of logos staging itself. The (non-)One transforms the predicate into a *postdicate*. Thus em-placed, Authorities, Language for example, the State and its games of power, the Polis, and History, are no longer attributes of the One but rather postdicates that find their real and sufficient essence in the One. Inversely, the One is no longer their support, their subject gliding underneath, though the finite place can appear, itself, as a radicalization of the support *for* the postdicates, but a support that would no longer be determined by them in return. These attributes no longer say themselves from the One, or even from the (non-)One, they only say themselves from themselves or from their wholeness by virtue of their circularity.

Language in particular, to return to it, is perhaps the predicate par excellence, that which wants to say itself in an absolute manner, and which puts itself forward to the point of concealing or hiding the real. The finite subject em-places language-in-totality, which becomes a mere postdicate. That which says itself, the World, things, but also language itself, says itself after the real subject, in an irreversible order. Furthermore, the subject does not say itself, but only shows itself. Also, that which says itself, that which generally lets itself say itself, comes definitively after the subject or phenomenality, which does not say itself (in a constitutive manner). The true pre-predicative is the finite subject, the individual, so much so that its correlate is no longer the predicative, at the risk of this redoubling, which the proponents of the pre-predicative have hardly noticed – but the *post-dicative*. Because the One does not say itself constitutively, even as retraction or subtraction of saying, rigor demands that we even renounce all ante-predicativity. There is the One, then the postdicative. Saying is always by definition posterior: this is dual irreversibility.

154

Theorem 91. *Absolute science is the specific science of mixtures, philosophy included. It is not a philosophical science in the unitary sense, but the science of unitary philosophy beside linguistic, historical, worldly, statist, sexual, etc. mixtures.*

Philosophy, precisely when it aims to be unitary, is never an absolute science of the totality of objects (of the World), of Totalities-As-They-Are, of Mixtures-As-They-Are, but only a science of objects other than itself, and thus a knowledge of-itself-as-Other. A totalizing knowledge cannot be an absolute knowledge of Totalities – only a finite knowledge is the knowledge of Totalities – but only the knowledge of objects other than this knowledge itself, and thus also a knowledge of itself by means of this alienation. A unitary philosophy is thus a relative science of Totalities *as such* (the relativity of knowledge and the "as such" content of this knowledge go together), whereas the finite science is the absolute science of Totalities *as they are*, that is, of Totalities-as-such (unitary philosophies) *as-they-are*.

The meaning of absolute science expands if we locate in it and on its human foundation the only possible science of mixtures (the World, Authorities in general). Traditional – unitary – philosophy is a mixture and therefore not an absolute science of mixtures and of itself. Only a science that does not have the mixture as its essence can be sufficiently absolute to be the science of mixtures, Totalities, and Unities. This real or finite science of mixtures, established on its "individual" foundations, is that which replaces, in a different place, unitary philosophy.

To summarize: absolute science is the science of empirico-ideal mixtures *as mixtures*, or, more precisely, of mixtures *as they are*, of the essence-of-mixture (of the World, Language, History, Sex, etc.); philosophy is the science of mixtures *as such*, and therefore is itself a mixture that frees itself from others and from itself, including itself with them and deducting itself from them; finally, empirical sciences are sciences not of mixtures themselves, but of the things taken from mixtures in the forgetting or the refusal – the non-need, perhaps? – of the mixture-form essential to the World, to History, to Language, to Sexuality, etc.

Theorem 92. *Certain appearances notwithstanding, the Absolute Anti-Copernican Science is more remote from unitary philosophy than from the empirical sciences. It is a rigorously singular science of universals (a finite science of the infinite, a minoritarian science of Authorities, etc.).*

Someone will object that this is an absolute – "archaic" and non-relativist – conception of science.

It may be that the relativity of the physical or life sciences is not the banality that unitary philosophy invents and attributes to these sciences in order to better claim for itself the absolute conclusion of their knowledges. The radicalization of the transcendental instance presumed by an absolute science has an additional effect (in the sense of the "dual") of a radicalization and an autonomization of the empirical instance of the sciences, at least in relation to unitary philosophy. Though we cannot demonstrate it here, it may be that tearing the real in its transcendental truth away from the spells of unitary philosophy makes it possible and necessary to also subtract from them the empirical, the object of the sciences, this form of effectivity that no longer falls under philosophical legislation and that is the specific "object" of the empirical sciences. For the time being, it is clear that because it is no longer a "philosophical" science, this absolute science *seems* to distance itself from the empirical sciences more than philosophy itself, while returning to an archaic form of knowledge. Nevertheless, even from this point of view, it is this science that allows us to denounce an objective mythology within unitary philosophy, a mere counter-mythology, even an over-mythology, which attempts to fill the gap between the empirical sciences and absolute science, denying the true proximity of the two: *non-topological proximity*, to return to this theme.

Then the *absolute of science* in question is precisely no longer the absolute for which unitary philosophy settles, which is never more than semi-absolute, a shameful forcing of the "relativity" of the physical sciences, a unitary abuse committed against them. Under the name of "absolute," it is a question of the real: the real *is* this absolute science of the World, of effectivity – there is nothing metaphysical about it, and it may well be that this conception was closer to true science than to the image ordinarily given of it.

Finally, it is a question of a new science, but non-historical, not achieved through a revolution or a continuous cut, the way a *continent* or an *episteme* would be, which are always knowledges in the form, despite everything, of totality, merely deferred, amputated, reduced, etc. On the one hand, this science is *absolute and thus non-totalitarian*: this amphibology must be dissolved to do justice to reality. An absolute knowledge is a non-universal knowledge, always finite or singular: mixtures or totalities cease to be given over to themselves, that is, to their unitary delirium, they are torn from their desire for mastery and have no knowledge *of* themselves.

156

On the other hand, if an absolute science is only absolute and not relative-absolute, it necessarily is non-positional (of) its "object." It traverses no universal epistemic surface and establishes no laws or regularities, but only "theorems." As the science proper to ordinary man rather than to the philosopher, it is the science of universals not *as* singulars – these are concrete or singular universals – but rather *as they are or from a point of view that is radically singular in the last instance.* Perhaps there is no science except of the universal, but the question is actually of knowing whether this science is itself universal in turn, at least in the way its object is. This is the definition of absolute science when it exceeds its individual foundation: it is the singular or finite science of universals.

As a finite science, absolute science is in fact radically subjective or individual; the subject (of) science is never in turn a universal, because this would be to return to the unitary circle. But as a finite science of universals, it is also completely original: if an empirical science presupposes universals and uses them hypothetically, and if philosophy is the science of universals as such or if it relates them to themselves and prohibits them from being taken as an "object" of an absolute science, then absolute science is the only science that has universals-as-such (unitary philosophy) for "object," and that will not merely presume them (like empirical sciences) or constitute them (like unitary philosophy). It is the first time that the World, Authorities, mixtures as-such cease to be yet again related to themselves, and instead are related to an absolute or finite knowledge completely foreign to their own constitution. This, therefore, is the absolutely singular or individual science of universals. Even (transcendental) phenomenology did not manage to "reduce" the World in this way, to radically exclude it from the Transcendental Ego so as to establish it as a mere "object," the knowledge of which would be this naiveté without self-reflection. The Absolute alone can still act "upon" totalities and mixtures. Because it is the most singular, it can exercise a determination upon universals – but only "in the last instance."

Theorem 93. *Given its radical subjectivity, absolute science does not belong to philosophers, who have never been able to realize it because they only wanted to realize it and turn it against individuals. It belongs to any man as a finite or ordinary subject, who, not needing philosophy, has never entered philosophy and does not intend to leave it.*

The finite individual, "minoritarian" man, *states* nothing determinate regarding the essence of Authorities, Language, History, the World. He, and only he, *is* immediately, according to a mode of phenomenal monstration that displays itself before any statement, that which is absolutely determined in the World and outside the World. He *is* straightaway, by the very fact that he is an *existent*, the most concrete essence of the World and of History. The existent is man insofar as he determines Authorities in the last instance, insofar as he *is* the (finite, but never totalizing) absolute knowledge of these authoritarian universals in the turnstile where Greco-unitary philosophers have trapped themselves. He is the proof in action, not of the powerlessness of philosophy, but of its derived character, contemporary of the World rather than of man.

It thus is not for philosophical, religious, ethical, or political reasons that we stop giving philosophy responsibility for the highest "ends" of humanity, for the essence of man, in the hope of passing it on to that which philosophy itself, making the first move, was careful to designate as "communal consciousness," "healthy understanding," "good sense," "common sense," "commonplace," "everydayness," "gregariousness," "people," and also, "ordinary." Such a transfer of the functions of philosophy to non-philosophers is here out of the question. The ordinary or finite subject is none of these fetishes of non-philosophy, of the missing-from-philosophy, of the pre-philosophical, etc.; this also includes the philosopher, but as finite man *before* philosophy. Ordinary man is not an originary and pre-philosophical instance: he is the point of view (of) the real that determines the philosophical in the last instance and makes it understood that the philosopher, in claiming to pronounce something concerning the World, states nothing at all determinate and is even in himself not at all determinate. He is only a shadow, a mythology that haunts the World and hides finite man from himself.

Radically finite thought is not the expression of the final prejudice typical of the philosopher, who is ready to accuse philosophy of powerlessness or limit its power, as contemporary thinkers do, rather than give up philosophy. *Rather philosophize about non-philosophy, about the limitation of philosophy, than not philosophize at all*, this is the last maxim of the desire-to-philosophize and of its survival. Ordinary man does not recognize such a maxim; he does not give up Greco-unitary philosophy; he does not limit or delimit it, or even exit from it, such an "exit" being the final absurdity with which he could be honored: he never entered Greco-unitary philosophy – he always already determined it by rendering it definitively "unilateral."

158

28. Critique of the Unitary Transcendental Deduction

Theorem 94. *The fundamental operation of the "Transcendental Deduction," carried out to dispel the mysteries of representation, is itself, in its unitary form, a mere supposition of the real whose essence remains unelucidated and a mystery.*

The Transcendental Deduction should not be interpreted superficially as a juridical operation proper to the *Critique of Pure Reason*, but rather should be reduced to its phenomenal content. From this point of view, it is definitely the fundamental operation of a unitary philosophy, whether explicit or, as is most often the case, implicit. It is the operation of which this real (or transcendental) logic that is unitary philosophy in general is capable. It consists in auto-positing, the requirement of the *unity* of logos and the real. Transcendental or real logic is its own requirement, and this requirement is the logical form (in all the senses of this word) of the *veritas transcendentalis*, of the truth that de-limits the metaphysical illusion.

What belongs to such a unity of logos and the real, a unity that can take the analytical form of an auto-position, the synthetic form of a "finite" deduction as in Kant or Heidegger, or the form of an absolute, rational-positive deduction, as in Hegel, or "differential," as in Nietzsche? The logico-real unity presupposes and requires itself, but more profoundly such a unity requires or posits the real, not only the empirical real that is one of its terms, but the "higher" real or the "truly real," which it is itself as Unity. Transcendental logic or the unitary paradigm assumes that the reality for which it is the logic, the reality that allows it to enter with it into the form of the "already-mixed," exhausts the whole of the reality or the essence of the real. But if the Transcendental Deductions, thus brought back to their phenomenal content, are such positings by itself of an already logicized real, it must be acknowledged that measured against the finite experience of "individual" structures, they rest upon void and nothingness. These are mere expressions of the missing-from-the-real that affects the logico-real mixture. Transcendental Unity is only a "real possibility," a presumed real that is based on a lack of elucidation of the positive essence of the real.

Instead of being examined in its proper essence, the real is actually merely presumed: either as an empirical datum, or as a factum of science; either as an Other at once internal *and* external to logos; or as an Other *re-marked* as external to logos, etc. The "Deduction" is the transcendental relation of logos to the real, a relation that redoubles the real in a higher form.[14] It is a synthesis inscribed in the essence of the already-mixed, as mysterious and contingent as the already-mixed and Unity in general. Carried out to dispel the mysteries of representation, it is nothing more than the philosophical or higher form of these mysteries, which it merely registers, transforming the problem yet again into its solution, making the solution the extension of the problem. Unity is the mystery and the bad philosophical mysticism [le mauvais mysticisme philosophique], the obscure point of Reason that "ordinary mysticism" [le "mystique ordinaire"] must suppress or confine to the World. The solution is in the suppression of the problem of representation (of its agreement with the object, pre-established harmony or not; of its conditioning, genetic or not, of the object) as a problem that is not real, but one that is wholly enveloped in the veil of the Unitary Illusion.

Theorem 95. *The real critique of the Transcendental Deduction frees its kernel of truth and reality from its unitary context and thus completes the critique of the philosophical form of absolute science.*

There are three stages to invalidating the fundamental unitary operation:

1. The real is no doubt given, but its type of givenness prohibits it from also being required or presumed, from being blended with the possible or with ideality, or from being a mere tendency or even an actual infinite becoming. The real is finite in the radical sense of this word, which is the immediate givenness (to) itself – non-positional (of) itself – of indivision. The One is its own mode of givenness (to) itself; its finitude is the immanent or transcendental criteria of the real. This mode of the givenness of the real bars from the real the participation of possible and thus transcendent modes of givenness, be they empirical (sensation, impression) or pure (ideal essence). Thought begins with the *veritas transcendentalis*, which is its inalienable element rather than an inner end simultaneously given and posited. This is why minoritarian thought does not know the Transcendental Deduction, at least in its form as a unitary operation in which the One is replaced by Unity, by the logico-real mixture, and in which it only exists as a mode of presupposition and self-positing, a mode of veritative process rather than of actual truth.

The central problem of "minoritarian" thought is not the problem of its *real possibility*, that is, of the manner in which thought will attain the real in a valid or veritative form, in which the equation logos = real, thought = real will be actualized or resolved. The finite essence of thought does not generally take the form of an equation (of a formal identity, or a synthetic and "real" identity, or even of a difference, etc.) but of a full and finite passivity. Thought is straightaway finite or real; it is not problematic or aporetic and does not need philosophy to contaminate a wound that does not exist.

As for the rest, that is, in the World, the form of the already-mixed, the metaphysical equation thinking = being or logos = real, resolves the pr\oblem or is the solution laid out by this problem. In reality, the Transcendental Deduction is an operation that is always already carried out; it is the essence of unitary thought and cannot give the impression of being an invention, a solution, etc., except when the general problem of representation is laid out in a restricted form, a juridico-rational one, for example (Kant). The problem of a Deduction thus does not appear as such, as a solution to be created, except when we begin by reducing the real, making it the mere unity of the equation thinking = real in its empirical and sensible form. Outside of this occasional empiricist cause and this anti-empiricist strategy, it is the fundamental operation by which and for which unitary thought, which is limited to revolving endlessly in this circle, exists.

Thus, the Unitary Transcendental Deductions do not actually attain the real because they are limited to presupposing it, to attaining it only under this form of presupposition/positing. Furthermore, this operation is linked with a doubling of the real into a lower empirical form and a higher form, that of "real possibility"; the entire deduction consists merely in circling within this gap or this difference. For all these reasons, they are circular, vicious operations twice over: they repeat the structure of the already-mixed, and once installed in it they move circularly in accordance with the law of the mixture.

2. The second way to invalidate the operation of the Transcendental Deduction in its unitary form is an effect of the first. Not only is logos as possibility or transcendence excluded from the essence of the real, but the real (that is, unreflective thought, not a brute or transcendent real) de-rives logos irreversibly, determines it in the last instance or em-places it in a topics, orders it radically according to itself. Logos – or what philosophy always understood by logos once it equated it with the real, saying that thinking and being are the same – is given contingently for finite subjects, but this contingency is also what is responsible for its surplus possibility.

3. Finally, pragmatics in its finite form will constitute a model of additional givenness of the real, a completely new mode of the real

that is thereby given as a "correlate" of practice. "Ordinary" pragmatics is that which reserves the access to the real as *Originary Other* or as *Non-thetic Transcendence*: the real no longer as truth but as meaning (cf. the following chapter). After the One and the "mystical," the pragmatic, which gives the form of the real as "Other," is thus the measure or criterion of the claim of logos (of that which will turn out to be the non-thetic core of logos, *meaning*) to the real, and, equally, to the World and to effectivity. It will allow us to situate meaning between the One and the World, truth and effectivity.

In a way, it is pragmatics that completes the "destruction" of the Unitary Deduction. Pragmatics is not content to de-rive it unilaterally, but goes back over the unitary problem and gives it the only rigorous and non illusory form possible. It frees its kernel of truth by posing the authentic relation of meaning to the real and to effectivity by dually dissociating the circular complementarity of two unitary uses of the real (empirical and higher or "truly real"), and by transcendentally validating, rigorously and actually, this double relation of non-thetic meaning or logos to the One and to the World. Pragmatics will be the key to the Transcendental Deduction; it will dispel its unitary mystery by displaying its true right as Deduction, that is, its *own* degree of necessity and reality *as a Deduction*. The right of the Transcendental Deduction is certainly a problem that is more "real" than the rather illusory problem of right for which it was invented on the unitary terrain. The mystical and the pragmatic are this operation's phenomenal content, which tears it from its unitary context, which here is idealism (sometimes subjective, sometimes absolute). With this *real critique* of the Deduction as *philosophical critique*, the critique of the unitary paradigm – that is, of transcendental logics evaluated in their claim to "attain" the real – will be complete. This will be the final move to tear absolute science, the science of the real, from the philosopher and give it to the one who does not ask for it: ordinary man.

— IV —

ORDINARY PRAGMATICS

SECTION I: *Critique of Pragmatic Reason*

29. Pragmatics as Real Critique of Philosophy

Theorem 96. *Pragmatics cannot be a real critique of philosophy unless its concept ceases to be a by-product of unitary philosophy and is elucidated in its reality and finitude.*

In the order of experiences, we now find the experience of pragmatics, of "ordinary" acting as "use" (of signs, but also of bodies, objects, techniques, etc.). We will explain why it is a question of pragmatics, and why in this precise place, when we examine its real essence (Section II). We must first take stock of the "stakes" and carry out a brief critique of *philosophical*, that is actual, forms of pragmatics.

The real critique of unitary philosophy is above all not its becoming-real, which is only the becoming-philosophical of the real. It is its practical or pragmatic "abolition." But this abolition comes after its strongest uni-lateralization, of a mystical nature, and is thus based on the unreflective character of the real. Real pragmatics is thus not a process, but the second concrete transcendental experience, the second immediate given that displaces or derives unitary philosophy among Authorities, but in a mode that recognizes in it, as in the World, a certain reality. It is likely that it thereby makes conceivable a new philosophical practice that makes philosophy a mode of pragmatics rather than pragmatics a mode of philosophy.

Non-philosophical primitiveness is impossible as long as it remains a project or an ideal, a philosophical ideal without actuality, a unitary obsession, a thorn in the flesh. Such simplicity must be radical or finite and be realized as a duality of the pragmatic and the philosophical. We are doomed to sever this Greek knot of the pragmatic and the philosophical, to no longer settle for untying the knots of the real and reason in order to slide along a continuous thread, but instead to give pragmatics the unreflective essence of finitude, which knows neither knot nor chiasmus, to give it a nearly absolute precedence over the philosophical. The unreflective is the essence or the real in its non-unitary simplicity: there have never been any knots in the real. The principal knot, the Unity of Contraries, is the philosophical diversion, the unitary enchantment of individuals in the snares of reason and language, in the aporias of philosophy. The "ordinary" coincides with the simplicity of the *veritas transcendentalis*: this "theorem" can be extended to pragmatics and its theoretical description, and ought to be if pragmatics wants to cease being the sub-philosophical product it is at present and be elucidated in its real content [*sa teneur en réalité*]. "Use" is a form of the simple or the unreflective, not a simplification . . .

When unitary philosophy wants to give itself up – and how could it not? – it finds "use," the "ordinary," "practice," "existence," the "game," etc., which for it are the bad angels of nihilism, the forms of unitary powerlessness and hypocrisy. Thus, what is opposed to philosophy are language games, an existence, and a practice that are still philosophical, whose concept retains the essential part of logo-unitary determinations, instead of "opposing" to it a real and finite acting. The refusal of transcendent hierarchies, structures, schemas, and models is not enough: never has an indetermination made a reality, never has a negation made a determination, never has an *Un-wesen* made a *Wesen*. The culture of indetermination and under-determination is the unitary nihil that wants to bring the real down with it. All possible transcendence should be excluded. Philosophers are never sufficiently demanding in the critique of philosophy: they do not want to switch instruments and set themselves overly limited goals – those of "auto" or "hetero" critique. The philosophy that imagined itself to be fighting in favor of the real was until now no more than a closed circuit battle against itself.

An example of this law is the "therapeutic" ideal of philosophy, dating from well before Wittgenstein, but which he recalled in a linguistic form audible to contemporary ears. This ideal is only an ideal or a project, and is destined to remain so. It is too easy or too insufficient to believe that insoluble philosophical problems arise from the unusual or fortuitous intersection between different uses of the same symbols ("language games"). Unitary philosophy still survives inside language games, when they are correct: it survives there not as an accidental element, but as their essence or real concept, because the famous "games" are no more than the ordinary projected by philosophy, an unconscious projection, however, because philosophy has been made into such a narrow and barely Greek concept. Conversely, the intersections between games, correct or not, are not philosophical errors but the very *essence* of unitary philosophy. Unitary philosophy is homologous to language games; it has the same general grammar, and is not an illusion, but is identical to the very cause of illusion. The aporetic essence of philosophy is merely actualized in the aporias in action that the games are. Functioning correctly, language games would themselves need a "therapeutics": but precisely not a philosophical one . . .

Theorem 97. *The philosophical use of pragmatics reduced it to a discipline of substitution, the symptom of unitary nihilism.*

The philosophical or hypo-philosophical pragmatics of contemporary thinkers since Wittgenstein has the heaviest burden to bear: of the philosophy it no longer wants but cannot discard. From this, three essential features:

(1) Pragmatics – use and conduct – will have been the great hope of tired philosophers who call upon practice as an unhoped-for resource. All of Anglo-Saxon philosophy is marked by this context of failure and resentment, by this use of practice as the spare wheel for impossible philosophy. Hence the hesitations between a pragmatics devalued by logic and philosophy and a pragmatics overvalued by philosophy when logic is devalued in turn. This see-saw, catastrophic in the long run because of the anti-philosophical nausea it provokes, is only philosophy itself in its unitary circle.

(2) That pragmatics is "ordinarily" a discipline for intellectuals or shameful philosophers explains its syncretistic and fabricated character, its nature as a product of synthesis or as a linguistic ersatz for philosophy, that is, for logos in its broadest phenomenal content. It is an undertaking of philosophical and linguistic tailoring intended to return to philosophers a work of substitution demobilized by the last avatars of philosophy. By tailoring we also understand what Bergson meant when he said that Greco-traditional philosophy is a garment too large for the singularity and precision of its object. The logico-linguistic context is mismatched to the real needs of "use" and of "users" as finite subjects, and "pragmatics" as a doctrine is ill-suited

165

to real practice; its fantastical and imaginary character must be endlessly corrected, rectified, made good, etc.

(3) Pragmatics was always the vague terrain of philosophy, a space
of concentration and marginalization for failing philosophers. This
is what it still is in Wittgenstein: a fallback, a last resort, and a hope,
not yet this actual and complete experience, absolute in its order,
this immediate given of use that is neither a surrogate for logic nor a
logico-positivist substitute for classical rationalist philosophy nor a
rocky and rough ground rather than a smooth and slippery surface
... Pragmatics must be a precise experience – not the only mode
of experience, which would constitute the unitary ideal of vague
synthesis – and be inserted into the order of immediate givens that
form the life of the finite or ordinary existent.

The pragmatic cannot in general be a substitute for the foundation
and the ideal, still idealist, of *Realgrund*. The distinction between *Real*
and *Grund* is as important as the distinction between *Idealgrund* and
Realgrund that grounds Kantian critique. *Grund* remains somewhat
universal, and missing from finitude or from the real. Individual causality, the real, is certainly not logical, but in the sense that it excludes
all logos, all logico-real mixtures. The pragmatic of philosophy was
never simply real and finite, but always more akin to a surrogate and
a remainder: in the Greco-unitary context, the pragmatic only has
a residual, secondary, and substitutive reality. It has never escaped
this original Greek defect, a logical rather than theoretical defect of
practice. But if use or the pragmatic is not a remainder, it is also not,
or not only, a mere requisite of logos: we do not *go back*, we do not
return here to pragmatics as to a solid ground, a certain foundation
...

Theorem 98. *The Greco-occidental agon or the Unity-of-Contraries
is the unitary capture and falsification of real pragmatics, of the
acting of ordinary man.*

Pragmatics is the real core of the unitary or mytho-philosophical
agon, which is a distortion of pragmatics. The game (game of Being,
game of the World, language game, etc.), the struggle, the conflict (of
Being, of interpretations, etc.) represent the authoritarian capture of
the pragmatic element for the benefit of the Unity-of-Contraries and
of Difference. There, the pragmatic loses its finite individual essence
in order to come under the law of Unity in which it is reflected: in
the Greco-unitary *agon*, it is struggle that reigns and judges. Even
when the *agon* is purified in the form of Heraclitean or Nietzschean

"Difference" and becomes a duel without judge, it still remains a semi-transcendent judge, a third who sur-veys the adversaries: this is the duel itself, the victor over all adversaries. The *agon* is thus the loss of the real essence of terms, their becoming-adversaries under the law of Unity or of War for the glory of which they fight. The clear distinction of ordinary experience and of the philosophical concept of the pragmatic is an urgent task and presumes the expulsion of all transcendence from the experience of use and not only from all "logic."

Theorem 99. *A real critique of Pragmatic Reason is not a circular or philosophical critique but the dissociation of the mixture of pragmatics and Reason – their duality. Unitary philosophy is the forgetting of the real essence of pragmatics.*

It is not enough to invoke pragmatics against philosophy, and eventually to invoke it to rescue philosophy, which is decidedly too cunning for its adversary. Pragmatics itself needs a real and non-philosophical critique. *Real critique of pragmatic reason,* this is the first task that must be opposed to those who use it in a frantic and suicidal manner, entirely permeated by philosophical resentment. A real critique of pragmatic reason is not a circular auto-critique – the unitary vice – but a critique of the logico-pragmatic mixture, of the blend of pragmatics and reason, of the logical but also *infra-logical* interpretation of "use" and of the "ordinary." It is first and foremost the dissociation of this mixture, the elaboration of a nothing-but-real essence of pragmatics, its foundation in the finite essence of the subject. What we seek here is the ultimate individual structures of pragmatics, against its unbridled, unitary, and violent logico-positivist uses as all-purpose arguments.

The philosophy of pragmatics is its authoritarian interpretation, based on the forgetting of the real essence of use, a forgetting consummated in superficial and naive affirmations of the pragmatics of language. Even if this essence is un-forgettable *in reality*, all of contemporary pragmatics is based on its arrogant denial. The birth of a *New Pragmatic Spirit* must be greeted properly: if this was nothing but the sanctuary of philosophical powerlessness and ignorance . . . but it is first and foremost the refuge of unitary prejudices against the real or radical subjectivity. Practice and subsequently pragmatics enjoy a natural prestige, justified in a sense, but all the more dangerous, against *theory* and *logic*. This is why they must be carefully examined and validated: on the one hand, organized according to the real, that is, according to the "mystical" experience of the finite individual and, on the other hand, freed of the forms of unitary transcendence that still obstruct them in their naively anti-philosophical use.

Theorem 100. *A real critique of Pragmatic Reason cannot repeat the prejudices of the Greco-linguistic image of pragmatics. The latter posits a reciprocal determination of use and its object, while the former shows that finite use has no ob-ject.*

Any philosophical interpretation of pragmatics is rooted in a certain number of Greco-unitary presuppositions, most of which are linguistic. Concerning the case of *pragmateia*, we can demonstrate these presuppositions, the primary of which is the idea of a reciprocal correlation between use and its ob-ject.

Pragmateia, care or concern for everyday affairs, states the transcendence of the World to which it is necessarily related and the plurality of affairs for which man cares. This is no doubt a first reduction of pragmatics to its real content: the immanence of everyday life, concerned and worried, busy and gregarious. But this is an etymo-*logical* vision, already philosophical and Greek, of pragmatics and its phenomenal content, reduced to the sphere of vital, signifying, and transcendent activities. There is nothing there besides the old Greek collection of the unitary hallucination of acting, in which philosophy will have sought safety and from which it will have from the outset drawn its concept of use. Worried everydayness, concern reified and statistical, this slurry of tropisms, unfinished activities, and roughly sketched conducts – these are the muddy collections of stupidity in which philosophy gazes at its own reflection, in search of its Other: at once that which it loathes and that to which it aspires, fascinated, to escape itself – the double function of any alienation.

This endless crushing, this universal functioning, thick yet fragmented, does indeed form a sphere of immanence, even in a sense a true pragmatic apriori, that of everydayness. But this immanence remains the ideal immanence of a totality or of a transcendence: the World, to which everyday acting is supposed to relate in an essential or constitutive way, precisely through the oscillation of repulsion and attraction. Acting is thus a con-duct, a relation, or a synthetic behavior of the World, but relative to it – to Language, to History, to Techniques, etc. Philosophy is this play of the relative and the absolute in the capture and elaboration of the Greco-linguistic collection of use.

In contrast, we will simply describe accurately pragmatic experience, its rigorous individual givens, which – even more than "existentials" (Heidegger) based on the real as Other rather than as intrinsically finite – distinguish themselves from this unitary image. A real description of pragmatics is not foreign to the everydayness that haunts the World, but it cannot be reduced to it since we know that ordinary man or the finite individual is *really* distinct from the World. Pragmatics is thus also really distinct from the register of concern, worry, or care with which Heidegger and Wittgenstein confused it.

Care and concern, interest and worry, are modes that have become transcendent, of finite use proper to individuals. They deny and extend beyond individuals the way the World and Authorities claim to extend beyond them. They are fundamentally obscure intentionalities that alienate and go out of themselves, an unconscious pragmatics where use does not get its light from itself, but only from an other to which it is relative. These uses are reciprocally determined by their *ob-jects* that are taken from the World. Perhaps what was said of the finite subject should be repeated in relation to finite use: it has no ob-ject upon which it bears and it does not ob-jectivate the World on its behalf. Here again a real critique of practical reason involves releasing practice from its ob-jective and sur-jective context and practice ceasing to be a *jection*, a transcendence in general. *Acting has no ob-ject* in the sense that it does not ob-jectivate it: it is a finite subject, devoid of the ontologico-unitary structure of objectivation and sur-jectivation. However, this is not an undifferentiated or unthinkable structure. Its essence is the simplest one there is, even though, unlike the One, it presumes an occasional material, which is the World, but upon which it depends only partially and not in its essence.

30. Use as an Apriori of Pragmatics

Theorem 101. *As an apriori of pragmatics, use must receive a real – finite or individual – content instead of a merely philosophical or logico-real content, which would make it a possibility and not a reality.*

The notion of *use* lies at the intersection of several contemporary requirements: the ordinary rather than the philosophical; the multiple rather than logical unity; the immanence of the human and the signifier rather than transcendent rules; the functional and the relative rather than the metaphysical and its "absolutist" customs. But all this merely designates effects or motivations. The true philosophical significance of use lies elsewhere, with the cause of these effects. *Pragmatics needs an immanent apriori and use is this concrete apriori of pragmatics. This is the phenomenal content of the use of "use."* This requirement is not present in all its theorists, though it is in any event prescribed by the Greco-philosophical tradition of *pragmateia*. The proof of this is immediate: use exceeds, extends beyond the opposition of syntax and semantics, its rules determine formal syntactical organization but also the production of meaning. It points, beyond disjunctions, towards transcendental unity and reality, those of language, for example. Hence, these generalized concepts of "grammar" (Wittgenstein) and "syntax" (Heidegger, Merleau-Ponty), which are the *difference* of the formal and the semantic, which are *practice itself as the unity of this disjunction,* as concrete or real experience identical to the rule in its essence. The rule in its phenomenal content is actually the synthesis of the universal and the singular, of the rule and the case, a transcendental or philosophical relation. Use is thus the real or the concrete, which means that the real is here still a synthesis of opposites or a process of concretion, a relation of the universal to the singular. *The ordinary, in its phenomenal content, which is here still logico-real, is this higher rule that governs philosophy itself; it is the universal apriori that creates both philosophical illusions and their philosophical therapy.* Everyday use is the principle that subjects the act of speaking to a set of syntactical and semantic rules. Understood in this way, with its unitary phenomenal content laid out, the ordinary is in reality the *factum* of the analysis-of-language. This is why, in human and signifying activities, the ordinary and the pragmatic are the same thing.

Against empiricist or crude interpretations of use, it is necessary nevertheless to uphold this philosophical, that is, transcendental, meaning and truth. Or, at least, its requirement of transcendental truth: because remaining a philosophical concept prevents it from really reaching this truth. The philosophical, that is, *logico-real*, elaboration of a concept is an absolute requirement to dismiss *infra-philosophical* forms of empiricism, and to not confuse under any circumstances these philosophically or unitarily degraded forms of experience with the authentic real, which is also, but in a completely different way, no longer – really no longer – philosophical. But this requirement is only a requirement: it is not yet the authentic transcendental experience that must be that of use.

Use is indeed an apriori, but in its philosophical or logico-real interpretation it remains permeated with transcendence. To be nothing but immanent it must be ordered according to truth, that is, according to transcendental finitude. The immanence of use must be specified, distinguished from the immanence of the symbolic, of logic, and finally, among other things, of a strategic calculation according to rules – of a *game*. The game is a mere pluralization of logos and returns to unitary calculating reason. As a pragmatic apriori, the finite use we seek will be devoid not only of ob-jects, but also of syntax and semantics, of rules in general. A use-without-rules is of course inconceivable for philosophy, which cannot see what can subsist as a remainder once all these "reductions" are carried out. Nonetheless, there is indeed a pragmatics endowed with an absolute precedence over rules and over any form of transcendent order. The experience of use cannot stop at the experience of a continuous formality, be it transcendent (rules of synthesis, laws, codes, formal syntax) or immanent: it is absolutely prior to all formality, logical or otherwise (and hence still logical). If use must be a *concrete apriori*, it does not have to be taken from the continuous fabric of ideality or interpreted *functionally*. If it shows or is its own reality, its *how* does not have to be a mere *possibility*, yet another way use remains in Being, is inserted into it or functions within it. The *how* of *reality* is no longer a mere philosophical *possibility*, invariably logico-real. The *finite or real how* shows itself absolutely without passing through the transcendence of language and of reason.

Theorem 102. *The game and use as game remain variations on the unitary paradigm. They do not overcome logicity itself in its essence, but only the lesser – formal and fixed – forms of logic.*

Like the other heterogeneous elements manipulated by the philosophical pragmatics of language, the notion of the rule is, for the most part, used arbitrarily, in a spirit of functional savagery.

Inside unitary thought, the true reduction of logic would consist of saying that a use represents the real for another use. Mired in linguistic and grammatical, psychological and vital transcendence, theorists of pragmatics cannot even maintain this thesis, too deficient as philosophers to complete that which nonetheless remains a mere reduction, a philosophical operation required by the entire Greek tradition. In the best of cases, the regularity of rules will merely be interpreted according to their application rather than their logicity: there are rules *of* use, but also the use of rules, the chiasmus of use *and* of rule, immanence of the game superior to the immanence of use empirically considered. But in the end, this interpretation of the regularity of rules according to their application remains equally abstract. Their constitutive or transcendental application is merely logico-real, which from the finite or individual point of view is not a significant progress over the logical-formal.

171

In play or use understood philosophically, a sign represents the real for another sign; from one to the other there is a tauto-logy of difference. It is a logico-real mixture without being a pure ideality, and this is enough to prohibit any true surpassing from the unitary point of view. Undoubtedly, there no longer is a mere parallelism between intention and the sign-tool, but rather a continuum of identities and alterations in which any given tool represents the use of another, a word the use of another word. This nevertheless remains a possible use, not a nothing-but real and actual use. But if a rule, be it a rule of use rather than a logical rule, can never become nothing-but-real, and remains permeated by the logicity proper to the onto-logical sphere, where does the illusion of having overcome logic come from? It comes from the fact that there is an additional degree of fusion or knotting of the rule and use (= real), a becoming-immanent of the rule that is the suppression of the most reified forms of its transcendence, a suppression that passes, in unitary thought, for a sufficient positive determination of the essence of use.

Here is the height of the unitary illusion: when the exclusion of a certain form of regularity is identified with real content, with the positive essence of use, when the impossibility of a rule is confused with the real of use. This is the logico-real illusion, and it is transcendental in its own way. It returns to situating use as an intermediate level between pure logic and positive experience – two dogmatic extremes – making it function as an interface between the signifying subject and the World. We know that it is immediately excluded from this function by the finite subject that is not itself localized in an inter-face or a difference, but rather who determines a *uni-face* (the lateral finite place, then transcendence or the Non-thetic Other, the non-logical meaning that is the correlate of pragmatics). It is thus a philosophically barbaric error to say that Wittgenstein, for example, abandons logicism in favor of language games. In truth, he only abandons certain inferior and conspicuous forms of logicism, forms that are anti-empiricist, overwhelmingly idealizing or Platonizing – but he does this only to become, like Nietzsche in his own way, the most unbridled of logicians. He *saves* logos by detaching language from formal logic.

Ultimately, use is still subjected to rules, games, forms, repeatable procedures, ("family") resemblances. Games always develop in a universal milieu: when this is not the univocal meaning of Being or the identity of a repetition of the dissimilar (Nietzsche), it is analogical "family resemblances" (Wittgenstein). Derived though it may be, the universal is still constitutive of essence and the real. It is not enough to take up pieces of activity, fragments of language and life, to knot them up and make them represent each other through and for the other: these are indeterminate generalities or vague universals that reconstitute a *continuum of uses*. The fluidity of uses is not the suppression of unitary presuppositions, but their fulfillment: the pluralization of unity is the ultimate unitary ruse. Use remains a manner-of-signifying, an ontological how, a real-as-manner, all determinations that presume the transcendent element of Being. The "ordinary" seems to refuse logical univocity, but it is only a matter of the constituted discipline of logic; as for the rest, it naively entrusts itself to analogy or onto*logical* univocity.

Theorem 103. *The unitary philosophy of use posits the reality of use without elucidating its essence, which is individual finitude.*

In the best unitary cases, there is a *surjective* rather than objective structure from the rule to its application. The rule does not hang over its application, but forms a continuous process with it. Not a meta-rule or an auto-objectivating meta-regulation, but a sur-regulation, a surjective calculation of rules in general. But use understood in this way remains an intentionality "towards transcendence" and merely substitutes a surlogicity for a reified logicity yet again. The relation of surjectivation is in fact the indivisible or *immediate relation*, the relation *to* . . . (being-in-the-world).[15] Even indivisible and reduced to the real content of this indivision, even devoid of a metarule likely to dominate it, by itself it remains on the order of a regularity. When surjective use appears from itself without passing through the constraint of an external foundation or a global or specific rule, it must posit reality, its own, under the form of an unlimited process of games, under the form of an infinite time presumed to be quasi-actual. Use is thus a synthetic force, a synthesis through itself that extends up to the Other and the infinity of time. As game, it makes its undecidability radiate around itself, rendering it unlimited, but its illimitation is not yet its reality, which should instead be finite.

Because use is its own reduction of logic and its own norm, a certain meaning of immanence is acquired. But this is a transcendent or ideal use of use, of the criterion of immanence, that is still entrusted to language instead of to individual finitude. Pragmatics could have found in this the occasion to question itself about an even more concrete immanence than that of the "game." But philosophical pragmatics posits this undecidable unity of the game and the rule without elucidating it. And as the essence of this unity is use itself in

173

its essence, it is indeed the essence of use that it allows to float in an exteriority of non-thought. The accumulation of entirely universal and thus under-determined determinations is an aporetic procedure and turns into an infinite regress that replaces real experience.

Theorem 104. *Use ought to be described in its finitude, that is, in its real autonomy in relation to its ostensible rules and to all the transcendent apparatuses that unitary philosophy adds to it for the purpose of the production of meaning, which it does not necessarily need.*

The unitary paradigm does not imagine that the immanence of use could be finite and consistent through its inherence (to) itself, devoid of the support of transcendence or exteriority. It believes itself to be obligated to give it a transcendent content of rules, acts, and games that negate its immanent phenomenal givens. This is how use, and with it pragmatics as a whole, is generally interpreted starting from rules that are less the actual rules of use than the rules of the production, the construction, and the calculation of a logical and transcendent meaning, rules of operation that are themselves transcendent.

The empirico-transcendental mixture of use and its rules is what the minoritarian thought of pragmatics proposes to separate. Use does indeed produce meaning, but the production of meaning, at least of finite meaning, which is utterly different from logico-linguistic signification, is not necessarily subject to rules or to an entire apparatus of activation and inhibition, of combination and analysis, of "structuration" and "machination." For traditional philosophical reasons of which they are often unaware, the theorists of the pragmatics of language constrain the experience of use with normally transcendent restrictions, with paradigms that are linguistic or logical, or taken from common experience and turned into the conditions of existence of acting. But nothing about these codes is really necessary: their only purpose is to reproduce the unitary or authoritarian form of experience. By contrast, in a transcendental pragmatics, the exclusion of rules of combination, formal and even general syntaxes, metaphysical models ("game," "machine," "difference," etc.), logico-linguistic schemes, etc. is a categorical obligation.

Nevertheless, on the condition that a rigorous interpretation of this exclusion is given. In general, the mere exclusion of transcendent (logico-metaphysical) codes or models is confused with a sufficient determination of the real essence of the game, of the unity-of-surjectivation of use. But this unitary process leaves the essence undetermined. Exclusion never does justice to the real as finite phenomenality; instead it is a mere effect that ensues from an immediate determination, that is, from a finitude that precedes it without return. This special autonomy of the real, minoritarian or finite rather than rational and authoritarian, ought to serve as the guiding principle in the description of use.

Theorem 105. As use, the "ordinary" cannot be a philosophical double of experience, an empirico-philosophical mixture, but rather must receive a finite transcendental legitimation. In the end, there are three senses of the word "ordinary" in the expression "ordinary man."

At stake is the "ordinary" in the philosophical sense as "use." It is confused with a subtraction philosophy and logic carry out upon themselves in the name of experience. It is not elucidated in its individual essence or in its finitude. It also remains below its positivity and its "pre"-philosophical or unilateralizing power and receives a most heterogeneous content, made up of bits and pieces haphazardly taken from real experience, a whole bric-a-brac that marks the unitary genius in general, and that of Wittgenstein, the analysts of language, and the "theorists of pragmatics" in particular (grammatical rules, signs, objects, signifying activities, forms of life, etc.).

These obviously form a system, but the elements of that system themselves remain unelucidated in their own essence. Their relations are supposed to provide for or render unnecessary the examination of their supposedly well-known constitution. This "ordinary" is an untraceable concept, a "family resemblance" whose essence is likewise not elucidated, a mere list of uses: sometimes simplified or elementary forms of language learning, sometimes their everyday or de facto uses, sometimes particular linguistic systems in which language fulfills performative or else constative roles, etc.

This conception of the ordinary and of pragmatics must be demolished. A finite test of use, an insertion of pragmatics into the transcendental "relation" of the finite individual to the World, disallows them from being empirically taken from the World and reintroduces into these concepts their irreducible phenomenal content. In order to be only a real = finite experience and no longer a logico-real one, the ordinary ceases to be a syntax or a grammar, even a "general" one, ceases to differentiate the unity of syntax and semantics. As formal, syntax precedes the most empirical experience: as real, it is identical to experience; but more deeply there is an "ordinary" experience (of) use as prior – through its finitude – to any general syntax, that is, to any generality, syntactical or not. The individual test of pragmatics conquers the ordinary (and use) as the pre-philosophical concrete that unilateralizes philosophy and even the unitary retraction undertaken by philosophy in a "use" that is a half measure. All of these concepts have received a transcendent meaning within dominant philosophy, whether that philosophy is logico-positivist or not. Neither Wittgenstein and his followers nor Heidegger take far enough the "reduction" of this transcendence of the "ordinary" or of "use," and, correspondingly, of the "everyday." The suspension of logic is insufficient, as we have suggested, because it remains a suspension and because logic still prevails in all that is not real causality, that is, determination in the last instance.

A rigorously grounded concept of the ordinary is therefore necessary, one that is acquired through a transcendental deduction without this making it a logical entity. Logic is unitary, but the fear of logic is just as unitary and almost as dangerous as logic because of the illusion it gives of having defeated logic. These indeterminate and vague concepts that philosophy (Anglo-Saxon or otherwise) proposes of the ordinary, the everyday, banality, learning, etc., have no reality or phenomenal content other than unitary mixtures in their logico-empirical form. The elaboration of the phenomenal *truth* of the ordinary and of use would have been the first task of a thought of pragmatics, except that it is a task that is properly speaking no longer "philosophical," nor for that matter a mere falling back onto "experience": rather, it is a rigorous description of immediate finite givens. Above all, the ordinary is not the "everyday" in its philosophical but still empiricist meaning, nor even in its existential elaboration by Heidegger, which is simply copied from existentiell everydayness, excepting the Other, and insufficiently critiqued in what remains in it of transcendence. The ordinary is *existence* in the sense of acting or of the (non-)One of which the *existent* is itself capable on the World when its resistance is taken into account. This is the authentic "transcendental deduction" of the ordinary and of use. Of course, the structures of ordinary pragmatics remain to be described: this is the object of Section II.

Nevertheless, we can as of now, for additional clarity, anticipate the results to come and state that the experience of the ordinary passes through three linked stages or follows an irreversible order that enriches its concept. These are the three experiences of the ordinary that must be understood in the expression "ordinary man," which are completely different from the unitary extraction of heterogeneous pieces from experience, or from the infra-philosophical meaning of the word.

1. the finite individual in its real essence. The ordinary here means that a philosophical operation is not necessary to define the ("individual" ["*individual*"] rather than individuel [*individuel*]) individual [*l'individu*];

2. the finite existent who determines the World in the last instance and, through the finite em-place it imposes upon it, institutes an absolute order for all possible logico-worldly or rational orders: this is the ordinary as *finite order for* the authoritarian forms of order, "ordinary mysticism";

3. "pragmatic" existence or the relation of use the existent has from the World. This meaning of the ordinary approaches without touching the unitary meanings of the word (all of which are logico-everyday mixtures), completing rather than displacing them.

31. Philosophical Pragmatics and Real Pragmatics

Theorem 106. *Pragmatic finitude means that the subject is not determined by the World and authoritarian procedures when it acts upon them: acting is really different from the World upon which it nevertheless acts.*

Pragmatics must be elaborated in its finitude: the existent gets its life and its acting, that is, its existence, from itself. That existence is finite means that there is no meta-existence or over-existence, no meta- or over-pragmatics. The unitary style combines a pragmatics with a surjective essence in an over-pragmatics that unfolds in unlimited games. From the start, it forgoes the possibility of a *simple* or *ordinary* (unreflective) essence of existence and acting.

Neither transcendent rules (their transcendence is attenuated, not suppressed, in the process of their application), nor psycho-socio-polito-etc.-logical data, nor symbolic data. Deprived of these crutches, acting does not cease to be real and actual. The immediate actuality of use must be recovered prior to all the linguistic or other projections in which unitary thinkers, that is, intellectuals, engage. There is a dimension of unreflective transcendental experience in any pragmatic acting.

177

Everything in "worldly" or "authoritarian" existence can be re-inserted into textual, linguistic, political, or technological games – into their semi-immanence. But there is a real inalienable core of acting that cannot be inserted into the World and its universal flows. Between nothing-but-human pragmatics and the World, even though the former affects the latter, there is a "real distinction" in the rigorous (that is, dual) meaning of these words, and an enduringly individual causality in use. Individual: simply singular and that does not pass through universal and worldly (linguistic, logical, mechanical, technological) processes. The fundamental object of a critique of Pragmatic Reason is the elaboration of the rigorous concept of "pragmatic causality" (cf. Section II: *The Essence of Pragmatic Causality*) and its real difference from the unitary forms of causality – linguistic, physical, and meta-physical.

The only criterion to be followed is real immanence. It demands that the *pragmatic apriori* be radically de-logicized, purged even of the demi-solution of "games" and "difference," and that use take its reality (from) itself or be identical to its finitude. This is to say that the forms of technical transformation no less than the calculation-following-the rules or the form of the game and/or of difference are expelled from it. Once all these transcendent models are determined unilaterally, an essential "remainder" of pragmatics, with a specificity and a consistency, survives. It will not be reconstructed from heterogeneous bits and pieces taken from the World, debris and waste, traces abandoned by Authorities. The pragmatic "relation" to the World is not composed or synthetic in general, and even less traced from the circular relation of the World to itself, of Language to itself, of the Text to itself, etc. Acting in the pragmatic mode places the World in a new unilaterality in relation to the finite subject and lets it be understood that, because of their very universality, worldly authoritarian forms of use are too narrow for the pragmatic subject and only form its material and the signal of its activity – we will return to these points. Thus de-rived a second time, the universal and transcendent modes of causality will be deprived of the power to reflect themselves in individual causality and to pretend to legislate on the pragmatics of the ordinary existent.

Ordinary acting produces transcendence – we will examine how – but does not itself need transcendence. It does not "function," does not unfold towards/as the World of which the finite subject will always be deprived. It is not obedience to rules, learning of behaviors and signs, symbolic games. It is entirely consumed in itself, acting *on* the World without being alienated in it or following authoritarian paths, and also without, like force in its transcendental-unitary sense does, drawing *all* its effects or its final consequences. Certainly, acting is "everything" ["*tout*"] (Nietzsche), but only in the sense in which there is no subject behind the act and the act is a subject that is finite or non-thetic (of) itself, but precisely not in the sense in which the act would immediately be the whole [*le tout*], the singular immediately a universal, as is still the case in Nietzsche.

Acting is not necessarily splitting, opening perspectives, tracing openings, delimiting horizons, projecting indivisible spaces, introducing angles and fractures. Unitary philosophy was never able to think in any other way than in fantasies of a sublime geometry, a spiritual spatiality, oscillating from the depths of the soul to the horizons of Being, from smooth surfaces to rocky grounds, from metaphysical centrism to the "square" angularity of writing. But the existent traverses nothing of the sort and is not carried towards the World when it "acts": the essence of acting is completely different from the transcendence of the World, even if that transcendence is part of that upon which it acts.

Theorem 107. *The real critique of Practical Reason must recognize the radical or finite, non-Copernican, subjectivity of acting; it does not extend contemporary philosophical gains.*

Here we no doubt register, once and for all, the progress in the destruction of *unity* realized by Nietzsche, Heidegger, Wittgenstein. The continuous multiplication of use and even of language games is a gain against the primacy of the classical dogmatic use of logic, and, for example, against the postulate of atomicity. But the One is not an ultra-Unity: the minoritarian or the finite are not the ultra-unitary. We do not propose to add to these various deconstructions of the logical parergon, to refine these very moderate appeals made to it, to refine this half-measure, which remains unitary and which, as a result, preserves the essentials of logicity. Rather, we propose to draw the consequences, for this historico-systematic formation of philosophical pragmatics, of a radical, finite ordeal of use and of acting, which will involve an entirely different economy – something different from an economy – of the subject, of use, and of meaning. That the unitary illusion, which takes refuge in the ideal of the pluralization of uses and games or in the deconstruction of logos in general, protests and resents this final invalidation of its existence as a still "metaphysical" enterprise, an attempt to recreate a transcendent parergon – this is inevitable, and this is unitary logic itself. We can only respond to

179

it through the actuality of *real* critique (Section II): it concerns a misunderstanding – we are not speaking about the same thing, in the sense that the unitary ideal speaks and does nothing but speak, and that minoritarian practice surrenders itself to an ordeal that situates language *absolutely* and affects it with an indisputable finitude.

The finite One is not a new universal, superior even to the plurality of uses or linguistic multiplicities. If it fulfills common functions, it is in relation to those that still perceive it as a universal. But its essence is not universal: this is what allows it to claim to have never been prisoner to the logicity of logos in general, and never believe it was able to "escape" from it, but rather to emplace or situate the economy of logos in totality in an a-logical order, which is the irreversible order of the real. The contemporary gains in the "deconstructions" of the archaic primacy of logos (and not only of logic) can be intensified, totalized, accumulated, dis-placed, but the real problem is in fact to irreversibly or finitely emplace them in a pragmatic mode that follows the mystical mode.

The logical – that is, logico-real or philosophical-unitary – Ideal has not been eradicated from pragmatics. The logic presumed to be its own master has been replaced by the *use of logic*, by the ordinary care or concern for logic. Philosophical pragmatics ends in this transfer: formal logic and real logic (the unitary philosophical element) cease to be the essence of language or life in order to become the principal predicate of use and of its subject. This transfer is conservative. The task of finite pragmatics is instead to carry use into the absolute immanence to which it is disposed as soon as it receives for essence the finite subjectivity of ordinary man. The subject-without-predicate persists through use-without-predicate; the subject-without-object through use-without-object and devoid of vis-à-vis: it also, though with less rigor, transforms the World into a "postdicate." Finite pragmatics is no longer a pragmatic reason, and the World *does not revolve* around human acting; the World and its objects are no longer anything more than its occasional material, but by no means what it produces. It is useless to balance Anglo-Saxon pragmatics through the Copernican Revolution or the philosophical critique of practical reason: the finite practical subject is no longer "Copernican." If unitary pragmatics still expresses a mixed point of view on use, if it confuses the subjective finite essence of use with its worldly conditions of existence or its transcendent operating conditions [*conditions d'exercice*] and conceives of it as a universal and "objective" plane of universal immanence, it is indeed because the *user* has not been elucidated in its essence, not as consumer of the products of use (consumption of meaning: comprehension, etc.), but as immanent and finite subject of use that is not alienated in logico-linguistic forms of meaning.

Theorem 108. *The real critique of Pragmatic Reason does not merely extend the concept of performativity beyond its linguistic and metaphysical limits. It makes this extension into not the condition but the effect of the return of performativity to its finite essence.*

To make pragmatics co-extensive with existence and turn it into a fundamental experience of ordinary man, its concept must be extended, unfolded without limitations from the side of the World. A critique of pragmatic reason, that is to say of the rational limitation of pragmatics, begins with posing an a priori unlimited inventory of performative acts (identified, as we will see, with use). This is the equivalent of a "metaphysical deduction" of the a priori structures of expanded performativity. It would not have any meaning if this inventory did not break all linguistic, psychological, and metaphysical limitations.

(1) The limitation of performative acts to language games and to the list Wittgenstein gives of them (to affirm, to interrogate, to command, to describe objects, to measure them, etc.) must be eliminated. The definition of pragmatics as linguistic and within the sole context of language, indeed of enunciation, is a vicious operation, a very narrow mixture, as is that of philosophy as "philosophy of language." As for unitary philosophy itself, it is already an overly narrow and reified circle. Pragmatics must be *general* to be philosophical and extend beyond its linguistic limitations. It is below syntax and semantics, but also below both language and the World in their unitary opposition. For example, to take up once more its philosophical concept, it is at least the sphere of activities that are transcendental or constituent of the World and of the ontologies secreted by uses and games (not the empirical, but the "higher," real). Use is an intentionality that animates things, corporeal possibilities, and not only signs: extending performativity beyond language is an absolute requirement, a requirement that Nietzsche and Heidegger, the two greatest thinkers of pragmatics, imposed on themselves by extending ordinary use beyond enunciation. Of course, from our point of view, this is, in the end, a unitary mixture that disallows any real critique of language and philosophy.

(2) Then there is this other limitation, philosophically more limited, that opposes the *performative* and the *constative*. This opposition,

metaphysically very derivative and copied from a superficial and transcendent concept of activity and passivity as opposed and complementary, must be abandoned, and the concept of performativity generalized to all acts, to all possible operativity, even one that apparently refers to receptions, to passive or "theoretical" phenomena, to descriptions. In the last instance, the finite essence of performativity will probably be passivity, but not the passivity that is liable to be coupled with activity, rather the passivity of radical finitude. Performativity is thus liberated from its side and can no longer be limited in extension by supposedly passive phenomena. The sphere of acting in a pragmatic mode includes all *existence*, which is defined below the opposition – superficial on this level and without real foundation – of activity and passivity.

(3) A third limitation must be lifted, the one metaphysics placed on performativity by distinguishing between ontological or essential operations and (common, ordinary, everyday) pre-philosophical operations. Essential operativity, that of Being, is articulated around *position* (*Setzung, thesis*): this ontological limitation will have been partially lifted by contemporary deconstructions of metaphysics, as different than they are, which knew how to distinguish themselves from *position* and embellish their variations on this invariant: deposition, over-position, differe(a)nce, etc.

From this point of view, there is an elementary performativity of philosophy as a transcendental logic; a logico-real pragmatics; mixed operations, deeper than categories and acts. Contemporary philosophy, especially, has its own way of being empiricist: finding the irreducible meaning, the core of truth of the simplest acts. Not only posing (classical metaphysics or ontology); but throwing [*jeter*], objecting, sur-jecting (Heidegger), over-posing (Nietzsche); suspending (Husserl); turning (Heidegger); slitting (Lacan); twisting (Bergson); cracking, differing (Derrida); reversing and producing difference (Deleuze). Even more than reading and writing, speaking and hearing, which are complex and derivative – essentially linguistic – operations, these are elementary operations of thought. We could keep a running list of such fundamental operations, veritable philosophical "catastrophes" more or less irreducible to each other (this would be a point to examine), like the list of categories in the old days. But these are more primitive gestures than the gesture of categorization, of the position of a predicate on a support lying in the background, which is a derived mode of position. It perhaps concerns the deepest depths of unitary philosophy, that is the operations of transcendental logic, a whole variety of "catastrophes," and a whole elementary performativity, too, that philosophy has explored locally but not systematically. These are perhaps also uses of thought, a veritable transcendental pragmatics and not only an empirical pragmatics. It defines the ontological level as well as the deconstructor-of-the-ontological, thus the essence of unitary thought, and enjoys a degree of universality higher than linguistic pragmatics.

Nietzsche and Heidegger in particular extended practice beyond essential conceptuality, beyond fundamental ontological gestures, which thereby cease to be their own reference. They suspended it towards the Other [à l'Autre], whatever the particular way each experienced that Other. They thus made essential philosophical practice circulate between logos and language, language and everyday empiria, Ideas and the sensible world, etc. – between all the contraries, with pragmatics becoming along with them co-extensive with the more or less decentered circle of all possible activities. In particular, the tight, logico-metaphysical circle of language and philosophy to which so many theorists of pragmatics confine themselves is loosened by them, brought to mere topological proximity. There is a topology of use as neighborliness with things, with the World itself, and it is called "thinking."

(4) But this extension remains fundamentally philosophical and unitary, even when, under the pressure of the Other of Being, it seeks (for example in language understood as signifying textuality) an extension of the performativity that philosophy is capable of enacting – that is to say, still, of tolerating under its "authority." This is a mere displacement of limitation, or at best a re-limitation. Use is thus the mask for the anonymous power of the Other; it is no doubt extracted from infinite metaphysical subjectivity, but through a finitude that is partially in exteriority. It is not brought back into its individual conditions, into the heart of authentically finite subjectivity. The philosopher remains a master of use, and pragmatics continues as a philosophical game, whereas essential finitude would allow it to be returned to its real bearer: ordinary man. The extension of performativity by its passage, topological or otherwise, under the law of the Other still remains a final unitary limitation of pragmatics.

What is the essence, more generally, of this philosophical performativity? These are mixed or transcendent operations, necessarily real and logical in diverse proportions in accordance with the type of transcendental logic, that is, of philosophy, that fills them with Being instead of with the Other, giving them their truth. Whatever the proportions, the only thing that matters here is the requirement to combine the real (Being or Other) and logic and, consequently, to be a worldly and authoritarian performativity; still a mixture predominantly made up of transcendent activity and claiming to constitute the essence of the real and of thought. This performativity does not reach the essence of the real, which is passive through and through and therefore cannot be even an elementary activity (the essence of activity is not active), a transcendent operativity, and which is not, in the end, and by definition, a mixture. The essence of the One, and even of "acting," which seems to ensue from it under the title of "determination in the last instance," is not at all like a "performance." Finite emplacement is a real experience, that is, passive through and through, not a production of place or a voluntary fixing of the World or any given thing onto a place; not a genesis or an occupation of place.

In what, then, does the critique of Pragmatic *Reason* consist? It cannot reside in the third extension/limitation, which is obviously already such a critique, but which remains within the final *limits* of philosophy or language folding back on themselves and surveying themselves. Moreover, it amounts to accepting a content for pragmatics that is still logico-real, even if that content includes the Other in itself.

Under the condition of this quadruple "extension" – but is it still a question of this process? – beyond acts of language, beyond the most superficially active acts, beyond essential, ontological, and even philosophical acts, and beyond, finally, the Other and its diverse contemporary uses – there is a performativity co-extensive with existence that innervates from the inside everything that is given, from the World or Authorities, as conducts, projects, wills, desires, powers, thoughts, etc. It is "unlimited" as a matter of principle, but in the precise sense that its finitude distinguishes it from any worldly or authoritarian illimitation/limitation. Not only does it merge, if it is viewed from the World, with all the verbs language is capable of inventing, but it has an essence that implies its real distinction from the World. This is its authentic "extension" – something quite different from an extension or an illimitation proceeding through strokes of limitations and interiorizing them. Put differently, there is indeed a performative manifold, a multiplicity of the ordinary that forms the deployed content of Pragmatic Reason. But this deployment remains strictly intra-philosophical or unitary and must not be the condition of the return of acting to its finite essence but rather its effect: this is the *real* critique of Pragmatic Reason, a pragmatic critique of Reason rather than a rational critique of pragmatics.

184

SECTION II: *The Essence of Pragmatic Causality*

32. From the Mystical to the Pragmatic

Theorem 109. *Pragmatics or "use" forms a specific and autonomous sphere of reality that must be elucidated a priori in its immanent phenomenal givens, starting from the finite acting subject rather than from the World.*

Mysticism and pragmatics are the two means man has for escaping from unitary – philosophical and linguistic – enchantment.

There is a pragmatic causality, an "ordinary" acting that has been constantly requisitioned by linguistic and philosophical pragmatics without being elucidated in its essence. Philosophy used this motif piecemeal, remaking it from elements abstractly taken from experience such as it imagined or fantasized it. As we have seen, up until now it has always been a question of disgraceful philosophical interpretations under the name of "pragmatics," of "use," of "ordinary."

A single question deserves to be posed: is there a specifically pragmatic causality, a pragmatic mode of this acting of which the finite subject is capable, which we call in general individual causality or determination in the last instance, whose first mode we examined? Practice has rarely been thought according to finite subjectivity, and rarely has its essence been distinguished from its operating conditions, which are not at all its conditions of existence. This individual, inalienable subjectivity is what we make use of here as a criterion or guiding thread for describing the immediate givens of "use." It is this real essence of pragmatics that we must now lay out in its phenomenality, after having, as an initial stage, extracted it in its finite, ordinary concept from its philosophical interpretations. Reduced to its content of indisputable experience and therefore subordinated to the mystical moment, the pragmatics of ordinary man can cease to be this unitary fetish and become the radical, unrepentant critique of philosophy.

Pragmatics is a sphere of "autonomous" reality that must be acquired through an experience of its real essence rather than through an abstraction of the "conducts" of an indeterminate subject. It must be transcendentally deduced from the finite subject as that which actually extends the mystical form of determination in the last instance, which we have characterized as a specifically human causality on the World. It will thus have certain essential characteristics of that

185

causality. Ordinary use can thus be elaborated in its individual structures and receive a radical interpretation as a sphere of immanence
distinct from the structures of effectivity but also from topical determination in the last instance. For example, we here forego cutting
up and taking a transcendental field of uses, conducts, and projects
from common and unitary "experience." It is not a question of abandoning the transcendental experience of use, but, on the contrary,
of liberating it by abandoning the idea of a unitary field or plane of
immanence. Following the One and finite topics, use is indeed the concrete "ground" of existence, but it must be detached from its unitary
context (Nietzschean or Heideggerian, for example) and not only
from its limitations, that is, its logico-linguistic universalizations. The
concrete of use cannot be *acquired* through the refusal or subtraction
of these determinations, a philosophical refusal of philosophy, but
must be *experienced* as an immediate given in line with the immanence of the One. Use thought from itself, which means: not from
logic, against it and thus complementary – indeed, supplementary – to
it, but from its real essence.

Theorem 110. *Pragmatics coincides with the sphere of existence. The
succession of experiences is the following: essence, existent, existence.
Essence precedes the existent, and the existent precedes existence.*

We distinguish the One or the *real essence* of the finite individual from
the *existent* or the finite individual insofar as it determines Authorities
in the last instance, and finally, from *existence*, which is the practical
sphere of the existent when the latter acts "pragmatically" and not
only "mystically" upon the World. Whence the following theorems:
1. real essence precedes the existent; 2. the existent precedes existence; 3. "individual" or minoritarian thought is a thought of order as
precedence or irreversibility . . .
    The existent precedes existence? – What does this mean? This
formula is ambiguous.

(1) Under "existence" in the unitary sense (which is a universal
whether it is concrete or singular) it is a question of recovering the
existent, the concrete that unilateralizes the universal itself. The existent does not need universal existence in order to be determined,
though it precedes it in the sense that it renders it unilateral in its very
universality. The existent precedes existence: it determines it in the
last instance. It does not precede it the way in unitary metaphysics
essence precedes existence, or the inverse. This precedence is absolute

or one-way, and neither essence nor existence insofar as they are liable to be coupled are capable of such a precedence. Unitary existence therefore is not the most concrete. The *esse*, the *how*, the *quod*, the *Weise* or *way* of being, etc. are still thought in their unity with ideality, and existence is in turn an "essence," but of a higher degree: effectivity. It crushes man under a new universal, under a "concrete" totality: it is a philosopher's means . . .

(2) However, the finite existent, in its turn, makes possible a new experience of existence, which it opposes to that of the philosopher: it is co-extensive with pragmatics. The existent in its "mystical" truth here precedes existence as well, though in a more originary way. Under the name of pragmatics, we will examine the immanent phenomenal givens of existence. Of course, this experience of existence is the only one the finite subject, as distinct from the World, can receive as its own and as human. The passage from the mystical to the pragmatic is the same as from the existent to existence, and it allows us to recognize, in a rigorous way, the non-unitary phenomenal content of existence.

Theorem 111. *Pragmatics expresses the generosity of the One or of finite man that recognizes in the World the reality the World continues to claim beyond its unilaterality.*

Existence, that is, acting in a pragmatic mode, is inscribed within acting in a mystical mode. It involves it but provides it with a specific and original determination. It appears with the World (or Authorities, the State, History, Language, etc.), which is announced as unilaterally em-placed. It assumes finite topics so as to be able to act upon the World, but it can only act upon it in a different way, namely in the "practice" of which ordinary man is capable.

Even more than ordinary mysticism, pragmatics takes the World and authoritarian universals seriously. It is conditioned – we will have to see how – by the contingency of their intervention and their resistance. The World is em-placed or determined with no counter-part by the One, but pragmatics determines it by recognizing an autonomy in what was no more than a mere function of indication or manifestation. Unlike the existent, existence recognizes a certain reality or truth in the resistance of the World or the *non(-One)*: it is even existence that partially legitimates the World and the unitary amphibology. From this point of view, the significance of pragmatics in the life of man is twofold:

187

(1) It recognizes the irreducible in the non(-One), which the One had no reason to recognize. The One, being finite, was too strong for the World; finite topics or the existent was already the taking into consideration of the World, but not of worldly resistance and the Unitary Illusion, which it in a sense reduced to nothingness *from the point of view of the One*. On the other hand, existence manages to take them into consideration. The affection of the subject by the World is a contingent fact that is straightaway unilateralized. But as illusory as it is in relation to the One, it interests us because, as minoritarian philosophers, we find our starting point in this Illusion or resistance, in the point of view of the World and not only in the One. We have acknowledged, beyond the One from which we have not, however, "exited" because it is not a Unity, this contingent affection; we have begun with it as though it unleashed a minoritarian thought: through pragmatics, we recognize this departure in spite of its unilaterality, we do justice to this World that posits the finite subject, whether the finite subject wants it or not, and even if it is mistaken about it. The One tolerates us taking into consideration this call of the World, it makes pragmatics *possible* – insofar as it does not prohibit it – and renders it *real* in its essence beyond its effective cause in the World. Generally speaking, the One and unilateral determination are not unitary interiorizations, idealist processes, raising, interiorizing, and suppressing the World. The World subsists with its non(-One), they exist together, at least from their point of view, which is not suppressed but only "seen" *in* the One (and this is not a *unity* of the One and the World). It is the One that motivates pragmatics, which itself is a struggle or the real phenomenal core of any struggle, of any *agon*, with the World.

(2) Pragmatics not only confirms the transcendentally contingent fact of worldly affection by taking up its point of view "beyond" its unilaterality, but it also as a result assigns it a certain reality, releasing the core of truth hidden in the non(-One) and thus partially legitimating the Unitary Illusion. *In the end, pragmatics is the generosity of the One or of ordinary mysticism recognizing the right of the World, recognizing in it a certain reality from the point of view even of the One, which is in no way diminished or affected by this recognition.*
Ordinary pragmatics completes the process of the One's progressive recognition of the reality of the World. The One has none of the repulsive and negative characteristics of Unity. It is a sufficiency that does not reach itself through the mediation of a negation, even an immediate one, of the World. Philosophical radicality, which is the

spirit of negation and vengeance, must be distinguished from real radicality, which is finite or intrinsic and does not need to reduce the World to nothingness. The phenomenal generosity of the One, which neither dissolves nor alters mixtures, retains the possibility of not annihilating the World in the critique of worldly illusion of which it is the seat. This is what is expressed by the pragmatic moment, which solves the paradox of being inscribed within the mystical suspension of Authorities while recognizing their possession of the reality they claim.

Theorem 112. *The structures of pragmatics must be elaborated according to finitude and really distinguished from the corresponding unitary structures.*

Of the four traditional sides of any practice – scission, continuous unfolding or mode of action, a thing worked or acted upon, effect – the first is radically excluded in ordinary or human acting and replaced by the essence of the real, inalienable or finite. The second remains, but must be transformed in its own constitution: because its essence is no longer scission, it will itself no longer take either the form of a universal or of a continuum (cause, power, technical processes) spreading out. The third remains, but as mere occasional material (we will explain this function) rather than raw material. Finally the fourth, the finite product or the effect, remains only as transformed: this is what we have already referred to as *Non-thetic Other or Non-thetic Transcendence*, as a-logical Meaning rigorously distinct from linguistic signification and the logical form of meaning.

The phenomenal givens of finite human pragmatics are made up of these four elements. We will only describe (paragraphs 34 to 36) the final three because we already possess the first, the finite essence of the real or of individual subjectivity, which serves us as the guiding thread of this description.

33. The Finitude of Pragmatics

Theorem 113. *Finitude is not the idealist "auto-nomy" of the Unitary Absolute or the Unitary Subject, but the real essence of this very autonomy. The science of man is based not on autonomy but on real finitude. There is no meta-pragmatics or over-pragmatics.*

Contemporary philosophy has passed from the theory of knowing to the logic of meaning and, in some cases, from the metaphysical

189

meaning of Being to the truth and then the locality – the topology – of Being. This means remaining in the primacy of pure logic or, more precisely, logic that is finite in exteriority. The ideal that guides it is thus the ideal of immanence understood in the unitary-idealist manner of autonomy (*Selbständigkeit*), in the form, for example, of surjectivation, which is a unitary half-measure whose phenomenal content remains permeated with logicity because of its finitude that is only in exteriority.

Of course, the finitude of the existent is no longer that of a *causa sui*, otherwise it would be simultaneously a *meta*-existent. The ordinary existent of contemporary thinkers takes its essence from itself but also from outside of itself, for example from Being as from its Other. Its essence and its life happen to it from within and from without, from a *plane* of immanence or from a transcendental field, that is, from a universal that does not pose itself, but simply over-poses itself.

Nevertheless, absolute autonomy or even autonomy rendered finite by an Other remains an *ideal* rather than a real ordeal, and authoritarian, like all ideals. The apriori of use, its ultimate phenomenal content, is not surjectivation, but individual subjectivity. The latter is a real immanence more radical than autonomy. *Selbständigkeit*, autonomy as auto-position, even altered by the real-Other, is not the essence of individuals. Finitude is intrinsic: present from the very beginning, it determines everything irreversibly, not circularly like an ideal. Just as there is an individual *before* any process of individuation, there is a finitude prior to any process of finitization. Unitary philosophy believed it had found in finitude a delimitation of itself, but it preserved the essential core of its pretensions by reducing finitude to an experience of the Other and a temporalization. Finitude must spring up from the very essence of ordinary man and irrigate its existence from there without having to affect it again from the outside, and, for example, from the World, which does not know real finitude, only the mixture of the finite and the infinite.

Therefore, it is not enough to expand pragmatics beyond utterance and signification, beyond these metaphysical limitations. We must still go "beyond" this final limitation, which is its deconstruction or its opening-to-the-Other, a "beyond" that we know is instead a unilateralization from the One. Unitarily, the procedure consists in alienating use in its occasional operating conditions (language, games of power, signification, techniques and machines, etc.), then of balancing this alienation with the tendency to autonomy or revolution, to return, reversion, etc. of the subject to its essence, sometimes across the greatest distance, that of the Other that tolerates one final proximity. Autonomy, it hardly matters whether finite or infinite, is the reflected, unitary image of the individual finitude that is the essence of man.

Use is an unreflective, a non-thetic (of) itself acting, which neither poses nor overposes itself in order to be itself and reach itself. The individual phenomenality of use explains that there is no need for meta-pragmatics or even for over-pragmatics (those, for example, of Nietzsche, Heidegger, and Wittgenstein). The force of ordinary use is that it draws its truth from itself and does not receive it from the materials, ends, and techniques of the World. Only the individual finitude of use can tear pragmatics from its unitary context. Use is fulfilled in itself or remains itself without being alienated or semi-alienated in linguistic or technological relations. We must understand – experience in its rigorous phenomenal content – a *simple* or unreflective activity devoid of the structure of "towards [à] transcendence," that of auto-position or surjectivation. Pragmatics has generally made do with the unitary equation: activity = reflected activity, not just activity = self-consciousness of activity but activity = overposition (of) activity. Unitary acting is always a concept, a theory, a reflection or an overposition of acting: always a use reflected in logos. The authentic ordinary pragmatics intends to substitute action for the representation of action, to split the mixture of theory and practice, the first finding its real core of *absolute science*, mystical or contemplative, and the second its real core of *absolute practice* or without-logos, without-representation-of-the-World. Ordinary acting is an immediate finite given; the World can be its material but not one of its constitutive ingredients.

Theorem 114. *The immediate imbrication, identical to the test of its essence, of pragmatics, and of individual finitude, allows not only for use to be extracted from its unitary context, but also for practice to be inscribed in the real itself, thus rendering it sterile from the point of view of effectivity.*

Individual finitude is the authentic "reduction," the one that would itself be "reduced" to its transcendental truth and rendered useless in its transcendence by actual finitude. It is this essential finitude of really ordinary use that we oppose to philosophico-linguistic hubris. Use is thus intrinsically finite, through a non-thetic inherence (to) itself. A transcendental pragmatics reconciles – without remainder and without mutual excess – the real and human character of use with the finitude that makes ordinary man, stripped of philosophy, politics, authority in general, the sole "bearer" of acting.

It is the ordinary individual himself who, through his mere existence, acts or uses the World by displacing it absolutely, non-reciprocally, and no more topologically than its "mystical" unilateralization. The subject absolutely precedes use but use does not extend beyond the subject. The World is not the Other finitizing use from the outside, and use, which by no means exhausts the essence of the subject, does not extend beyond it. The World is not necessary to the essence of pragmatics, and pragmatics is not necessary to the essence of the ordinary individual. These are all "active" phenomena of transcendence between man and the World, which are thus excluded from ordinary practice.

For example, acts or activities, linguistic or otherwise, are not necessarily mixtures of activity and passivity. Pragmatic acting is an "activity" that is not posed as such in opposition to a passivity. It has no counter-part precisely because its essence is passivity or the real. A passive use or acting should be no more of a surprise than the "passive syntheses" in which Husserl sought the secret of the constitution of the sensible. But it is something different from this mixture: activity is passive through and through, and yet it is nevertheless an activity, though devoid of transcendence in the World, which renders such an affirmation actually unintelligible. This immanent constitution of practice, its real passive content, renders acting as static and uncreated as anything that touches the real or individuals. The effect of practice must be considered as passively inscribed in the real, in the relations of the real and the effective World.

Use, therefore, is not an operation of transformation *on* a raw material, a change of forms. In virtue of its finitude or its passive essence, it *is* straightaway identical to a new sort of unilaterality – which is its "effect" – of the World and of Authorities. It is real use that passes on its finitude, their dearth of finitude, to "games." Finitude does not come to use from games and their logico-linguistic Authorities, which are merely worldly *data* or the occasional, worldly conditions of use, but not that which determines use in return.

Therefore, pragmatics will indeed produce something – meaning – but without effectively transforming the World. As *absolute science* with a mystical foundation, *absolute practice* remains as passive as the real itself and is not a mode of inter-vention into the World, of which it would otherwise be a relative part. Minoritarian or finite acting is not an effective transformation of effectivity: it is neither a nature nor an industry nor their synthesis. Just as there is no absolute science that is not sterile when measured against the criteria of a transcendent knowledge, and above all of philosophical knowledge, there is no ordinary practice that is not itself also sterile when it comes to the World. The production of the Non-thetic Other or Non-thetic Meaning has "effective" sterility for its absolute condition.

Theorem 115. *Finite pragmatics breaks the originally Greco-linguistic parallellism pragmateia/pragmata in which philosophers of pragmatics have remained trapped.*

Along with Wittgenstein, the two great philosophers of pragmatics are Nietzsche and Heidegger. The first for his critique, his trans-valuation of vital pragmatism, his reduction of use to its authentic or real phenomenal content, which nevertheless remains the sort of logico-real immanence proper to the play of differences of force and to the Will to Power. The second for his description of the immanent phenomeno-*logical* givens of workhood and of the continuum of reference tools, but also for his de-limitation, from this phenom-enological point of view, of an unlimited and rational pragmatics through the accentuation of the phenomena of failure, breakdown, and catastrophe erupting into use. These two solutions – even that of Heidegger, who still relates use to its Other or to a non-metaphysical transcendence more radically than Nietzsche – remain within the limits of the unitary paradigm and merely copy, excepting the Other, the correlation *pragmateia-pragmata* conveyed by the Greco-unitary model of the relations of being to Being, or of relations of force, in both cases a model of an ob-jective or at least (this is a part of their originality) "sur-jective" *relation*.

In relation to such a schema, characteristic of contemporary decon-structive thought, we must introduce a double modification:

(1) Use is no longer con-duct, synthetic behavior (*verhalten*). This remains a mode of ontological grasping (*begreifen*), a *jection* that is no longer merely conceptual but which is already finitized by its object. In all of these cases, behavior is detained [*la tenue est dé-tenue*] by that which it possesses and which possesses it. The con-duct described by existential phenomenology is an attenuation and a transcendent finitization of grasping, but which does not entirely remove from use its voluntaristic allure, which its pluralization in "games" no longer manages to hide. A game is the immediate combination of the finite and the infinite, their difference; its finitude remains partially external to it and the game is only related to the real as to the Other.

It is now no longer a question of finitizing a grasping from the outside, or even from the inside *and* from the outside (= Other), but of experiencing acting in its radical subjective finitude.

(2) A finite, non-Copernican pragmatics cannot but break the mixture of *pragmateia* and *pragmata*, its intentional correlative or relational nature where, as indivisble as it is, the two terms involved still determine each other reciprocally. This determination is excluded by the individual or of-the-last-instance essence of the acting subject. The most immanent givens of use reveal nothing like this correlation, which is merely a Greco-linguistic necessity.

By ordinary pragmatics, in the rigorously transcendental sense of this word, we understand the non-thetic (of) itself knowledge of use and its immanent givens. Use must be understood in a broad sense, as use of symbols, of bodies, of things, etc. But these objects are taken from the World itself and from Authorities, of which they are the ultimate structure; this is a still worldly unitary extension of use. Instead, we seek its finite essence. This is no longer use co-determined by its linguistic ob-ject or any other ob-ject or ob-jective rules, but use that has for simple material rather than for ob-ject the World or mixtures, possibly the things of the World or authoritarian phenomena considered under the angle of their constitution as "mixtures," which, as we know, are no longer – for the finite subject – ob-jects. The relation of acting *in*-the-World [au-*Monde*] is thus no longer what we seek in finite practice. Ordinary acting is perhaps not a relation to [*rapport à*] ... or a transcendence towards/as the World.

What, then, does acting reveal, if not ob-jects? It is a revelation of the Other, of Transcendence, but as it is or non-thetic; a manifestation that does not proceed through an aim that is itself transcendent. Philosophy confuses the material of acting (the World) with its transcendental correlate, the Other, which precedes any logical and even linguistic economy of pragmatics. Acting has no essential reference, in the sense in which reference implies a transcendence towards/as ... The parallelism *pragmateia/pragmata* is here broken.

Theorem 116. *The operating conditions or the worldly data of pragmatics must be excluded from its essence: on its own, pragmatics is neither a transformation, nor one of the four forms of causality, nor a signifying and continuous intentionality.*

For use to be finite means that it does not transcend towards its worldly operating conditions, that acting is not a way for the subject to spread itself out or surpass itself – to alienate itself as well – *as* the World and beyond ob-jects. Ordinary acting is not a transcendence in general: in the midst of transcendence it is necessary to place the material and technical transformation of matter and nature. We do not eliminate production of the ontological type, through *eidos* or *telos*, from the essence of acting so as to conserve in it the efficient cause in one form or another. Matter, produced objects, techniques, all the material-and-ideal elements of a transformation or a production, belong to the *data* of pragmatics but are not the ingredients of its essence, towards which, for example, acting would spread out and in which it would provisionally or definitively alienate itself (according to philosophy, which would interpret the phenomenon and thus deny its indisputable real givens).

The final reason is that the subject does not alienate itself in its use or its transcendent conditions: in an instrument, a linguistic symbol, a machine, a material, etc. Ordinary pragmatics precisely means that the existent does not lose itself in the World *upon* which it works and which it manipulates. Ordinary man aims at the World while remaining in himself: *and he can aim at it pragmatically because he remains in himself and is not constituted through an identification with the World*. Pragmatic finitude prohibits identifying the subject with the World. To speak, for example, one does not need to identify oneself with language. "Language games" still presume a partial identification with the comprehension or understanding of phrases and significations: a philosophical inhibition of language.

The distinction between mechanical causality and causality through motivation, characteristic of human activities of signification and understanding, is of no use here. Ordinary acting in the pragmatic mode is perhaps a practical intentionality, but lacking an end or a motive, which are always transcendent and taken from the World and Authorities. In human signifying activities, symbolic or not, use is animated by an intention that links or synthesizes the set of inert givens (signs or symbols, objects, rules, qualitatively determined intentional acts, etc.) upon which it imprints a unity at once structural and intentional. Therefore, at least in its unitary essence or phenomenal content, beyond any variations in its qualities and data, intention is an ideal continuum, an intentional continuity, that is, an ideal immanence capable of transcending or surpassing itself as an intention of . . . Elaborated by phenomenological techniques or left to the arbitrariness of anti-philosophical empiricism and anti-logical savagery, either way acting is reduced to an ideal or logico-real intention; use is understood as a combination or a mixture which Husserl gave its definitive – but entirely traditional – formula: *transcendence in immanence*.

It is in relation to this formula of the composition of use in the unitary regime that we must describe ordinary or human acting. Not only reaching its internal essence beyond the heterogeneity of bits and pieces taken from the givens of experience and out of which it is claimed to be reconstituted in a voluntaristic and unitary manner, but also distinguishing its real essence from its philosophical images or interpretations, as we set out to do in the preceding section. And, in particular, avoiding giving it yet again an analogical or even univocal, which is to say a universal or unitary, structure.

Theorem 117. *The operativity of use is not obscure or unconscious, except for the unitary ideal. It is an unreflective knowledge (of) itself whose unitary negative is the "Unconscious."*

Philosophy is ignorant of the specificity of practice and the positivity of acting, not only of technical operativity but of operativity in general. It appeals to practice, of course, but only under difficult conditions, as to a last instance that allows it to escape the ordinary aporias of logos or of theory. Or it wants to honor practice, reducing it to practical *reason*, to representation or logos in the broad sense in which we have understood this word, in a sense reducing it to theory in its transcendent form, for example to intuition (sometimes intellectual, sometimes more sensible), even to consciousness and all the unitary ontological presuppositions. Or else it foregoes this sublimation of practice and makes it into an obscure and crude activity, permeated by the unconscious – sometimes an imagination that is formative but secret and "hidden in the depths of the human soul," sometimes a primary or unconscious process.

One of the most profound unitary prejudices about use and operativity in general is thus that it is either semi-obscure, a limit of consciousness, or fundamentally obscure, an unconscious or an Other of representation. This prejudice is part and parcel of the transcendent interpretation of use, with a limited test of its immanence, acquired through the subtractions of the most external forms of transcendence. This ostensibly constitutive or real capacity is only a residual opacity, the correlate of a philosophical operation of "reduction" of logic, powerless by definition as to the real.

Here again the same unitary argumentation must be denounced, the argumentation that would rather falsify and denigrate the real than give up the only image its powerlessness can give of it. It consists of transforming the unitary or logico-real incapacity to think the unreflective essence of activity into an obscurity of activity, which is opposed to the transcendent phenomenality of Consciousness or of Being as a fundamental unintelligibility. But the alleged obscurity of acting, its irrationality, its nature as a primary process or, if need be, its intuitiveness, are only the logical negative of an essential "obscurity," of a non-thetic but perfectly positive essence of thought. The phenomenality of acting is of the same sort as the phenomenality of the mystical, which is its essence; it is prior to the disjunction of visibility and invisibility, each inherent (to) the other. It is, so to speak, a finite parousia that can be formulated in terms of night and invisibility, but only if the opposite of unitary or transcendent phenomenality is not projected into them: transparent night, without distance from itself, devoid of the distant light of Being. Acting is knowledge or experience (of) itself, non-thetic experience, completely devoid of the fascinating brutality of the primary process or the mute efficacy of technical operativity.

It is perfectly accessible, if not to the philosopher then at least to ordinary man, who by his very existence is straightaway or immediately this practice. The subject is not given exclusively in the experience of acting; it is already given (to) itself in its non-positional inherence (of) itself prior to any acting. But it is indeed the subject and nothing but the subject in its existence, not an "unconscious" fragment of the World surreptitiously included in the subject, which is given (to) itself in the pragmatic experience.

Although occasionally induced by the World, pragmatics remains ordinary or individual: it does not exceed the subject, just as the subject does not alienate itself in it. The drive of acting is an additional determination to the essence of the subject strictly speaking, and this is existence. But neither existence nor the existent are anything but modes of this essence and do not transform it. The (non-)One, which they elucidate and of which they are concrete modes, has the One for essence, and the former introduces no alienation into the latter. The subject experiences itself actually in topics as well as in pragmatics, which it imposes upon Authorities: between the two there is only the growing taking into account of the autonomy of the World and the specificity of the unitary claim. Use is a concrete apriori because it is finite, identical to the unreflective experience of use.

34. The Essence of Pragmatics: (1) The Finite Drive

Theorem 118. *Ordinary pragmatics is an acting that must reach the World without transcending or surpassing itself towards it.*

The conditions for resolving the problem are extremely limiting: how to conceive of an acting that indeed relates to the World, but does so not as to a global *ob-ject towards* which it would surpass itself and *as* which it would alienate itself in order to realize and return to itself? On the one hand, practice must confirm the existence of the World, without which it would have no necessity because topical causality is here insufficient. On the other hand, practice must not alienate or go out of itself, but rather must reach the World without any self-scission or self-cutting, which are precisely worldly processes. The causality that specifically addresses the World as it is or as a finite totality cannot be taken from the World; this is an unavoidable requirement. Such a causality remains finite or in itself but nevertheless can act upon the World.

The only way to resolve this paradox is to suspend traditional or philosophical-unitary interpretations of practice as metaphysical causality or "practical reason." Generally, "practical reason," with its content laid out, means that acting is structured like a unifying scission, the unity of contraries, or transcendence. Sometimes self-scission is the essential condition of acting, sometimes it is immediately identical to acting itself, and not only the condition of a continuous causality *on* the thing. But whatever the degree of exclusion of the generalities (consciousness, being, economy, relations of production, etc.) that mediate the unity of scission and of the unfolding over . . ., the power over . . ., the unitary paradigm posits the unity of action and of scission.

Real givens of action, however, do not contain any sort of scission or cut. Therefore, action, for its part, is also not a universal unfolding, a continuous flux, a power-over . . . extending itself continuously into the acted-upon thing.

Theorem 119. *The subjective-finite side of pragmatics is a drive, a drive on the World but inherent (to) itself.*

What is acting, and what does the subject who can say *Agito* rather than *Cogito* do? Reduced to its indisputable phenomenal content, acting is pushing. Action is first of all a drive before it is a transformation or a production.

The minimal active core is the pushing that is indivisible, but a lived indivision received immediately through itself. The drive is the only displacement, the only movement the subject can make without going out of itself. At least here, the drive is not yet a transcendence: it is the immediate given of movement before its universal inscription – for example geometric, but also psychological, psychic, etc. – in the World; a rigorous immediate given inasmuch as it is not dissimulated and does not require a practice or a method of philosophical analysis and cutting up, as is still the case for the immediate givens of the Bergsonian "duration." Ordinary acting, before any constitutive philosophical intervention, is a completely original kind of intentionality, not an *intentional continuity*, but a pushing that does not leave itself. Acting on the World, the subject does not split itself, does not become a part of the World, a part of its machine. It reaches the World in a movement without extension or continuation, in a mere pushing rather than a power-over . . .

The affection of the World by this drive would only appear unintelligible if we project worldly forms of causality onto it instead of transcendentally legitimating it from the (non-)One and the World as is. This legitimation is enough to impose this drive and its specific intentionality *on* . . . the World; to guarantee that the finite subject reaches the World in a real experience and through a mode that no longer borrows the means of traditional causality.

The drive is drive on [*sur*] . . . the World. The *on* indicates an intentionality, but devoid of any transcendence and positionality. Acting is not posing action, not a position or a mode of the position altered into de-position or over-position and rendered absolute as auto-position. The Finite drive is devoid of negativity and even of nihilation. The (non-)One is thus a positive pushing, and acting is real without needing all the mediating generalities (relations of power, of force, or of production; desire; Being; etc.) The non-thetic or non-positional (of) itself action is what is denied by practical reason, though it is nevertheless its requisite.

Thus the *on* . . . of acting on . . . must be preserved, but finitized: it no longer expresses this continuation of action that passes from acting to the acted upon and is proper to power that continues (to) act on . . . The *on* . . . is the finite drive itself that affects or touches the World but into which it does not persist. Action is not a whole or even a universal flux that traverses the World and takes it as one of its parts or limits. Rather, there is no drive that does not bear on the World "in totality" or as it is, and that does not define for the World a second mode of the As It Is – as occasional material or signal of pragmatics.

Theorem 120. *The drive acts immediately on the World without spreading itself out as a continuous universal element: there is no mediation between the World and acting, no transcendence in general.*

What distinguishes the phenomenal truth proper to the drive from the truth proper to power, desire, and the will (the three traditional forms of activity in the unitary sense) is its inherence (to) itself, without which there would be no transcendental pushing but only a miraculous transfer, an exchange that would remain incomprehensible without a mediating milieu or continuous conductive element between cause and effect. "Between" the finite subject and the World, there can only be a drive, that is, an act with neither distance nor a neutral, third-party generality, without a universal conductor of action from the subject to the acted-upon thing. The drive is the positive experience that renders *actio in distans* useless. The unitary theory of causality and practice is a permanent miracle that is resolved or suppressed only by the mediation of the universal-continuous element that serves as vehicle or support for action, an element that extends the miracle by giving to action the infinite as condition of existence. Between the individual subject (and) the World, there is nothing: not even a gap or a difference, which are still unitary and would serve as the final residual mediation for acting.

Here as elsewhere, the unitary paradigm merely requisitions and functionalizes activity, placing it in the service of reason, of the will, of Authorities, assuming that the *undivided, undecidable unity* that *is* the transfer of action on the acted-upon thing is an absolute, positive, and actual given. In reality, this transfer, this continuum of action *on* ... presumes in turn an absolute and actual experience, that of this indivision itself "as it is," that is, of the driving moment that is enclosed in the continuity or continuation of acting, but which is not reduced to it.

Freed from its representations based in its operating conditions, the drive is only the irreducible transcendental remainder of all activity, that is, of any passage, any transition from one term to another. Philosophers know that the most fundamental Greco-occidental matrix, that of the Unity-of-Contraries, is the *practical* essence par excellence of thought, and that the ultimate core of any thought is an acting (an acting of becoming or of passage from one contrary to another, historial acting of Being, practical essence of Pure Reason, primary process of the unconscious, etc.). But they stop the analysis too soon, before they have reached this ultimate transcendental energy of finite acting, the individual drive that comes to affect the World without having to displace itself, either in relation to transcendent benchmarks that do not exist, or in relation to itself since it is inherent (to) itself.

Theorem 121. *The unreflective drive was distorted into the unconscious and games by unitary philosophy, which transforms its unreflective nature into obscurity and unintelligibility.*

The transcendental topics is followed by a transcendental energetics, as finite as the first, but more primitive and more real than the philosophies of Practical Reason and of pragmatics.

The true experience of acting is the finite drive. It has been captured twice: first by philosophy and its agonistic Greek ideal; a second time by psychoanalysis, which diverted the drive and made it an obscure or unconscious activity towards transcendence: the forgetting of the essence of the drive. Philosophy discovers practice only in order to immediately sink it into the matrix of reason, or else of difference ("mechanical production"), or else of relations of production. Psychoanalysis discovers drive only in order to immediately sink it into the "primary process" or the unconscious, to make it into an unconscious activity. The two agree to separate drive not from what it can do but from its finite essence, in order to confuse it with precisely a power or a possibility-of-being, a presumed-drive, which is the inconsistent bedrock of psychoanalysis.

Finitude renders the drive autonomous, extracts it from the unconscious chain. Its multiplicity is that of individual finitude, no longer that of the Unity-of-Contraries. A unitary drive rests on an unconscious edge or a cut, on a scission in general, and unfolds as a universal flux so as to come to lose itself in an other, to ideally identify itself with it and form a driving concatenation that is the habitual fabric of the unconscious – or of the "game," game of Being and language game . . . An intrinsically finite drive, by contrast, does not rest on an anterior drive that is obscure for it: practice is not a "game" or an "unconscious." Being finite and remaining in itself, the real drive does not need such a support. This is to say that it also does not unfold the way a universal does, but rather that, remaining inherent (to) itself, its sort of singularity allows it to take universals themselves head on in an ungraspable laterality.

Even disfigured by philosophy and psychoanalysis, made unconscious and deprived of its individual essence, the drive preserves this immediacy of acting, which does not leave itself and remains as close as possible to itself, and which, for this reason, is doomed to the most complete exteriority, that of the unconscious, when it is in spite of everything conceived of as scission and transcendence. For philosophy, acting is a sort of enigmatic experience, an absolute of proximity and immediacy it does not know how to think in its essence, but which it regularly needs in order to escape from its aporias. *The immediate givens of action*, which are completely thinkable, are thus reflected in the unitary mirror, giving them a rational image as a false transcendent immediate or an unconscious image as an unthinkable primary process. These images, which make acting into an obscure and finally brutal absolute, are the unitary caricature of the real finitude of acting, the philosophical mimesis of the real absolute.

Theorem 122. The drive that immediately reaches the World is not a transcendent causality or a transformation of the World.

We must repeat in relation to the drive what was already said of acting in general. The fact that drive affects the World "as it is" entails the exclusion of the empirico-ideal modes of causality inventoried by metaphysics. As a causality that bears *on* the World rather than on one of its objects or sectors, it cannot be applied through physical contact, or through the exemplary efficiency of the Ideal Form, or by the End, etc.

The drive *on* . . . is therefore not, strictly speaking, a "transformation" of the World. We transform that which has a form – ob-ject form in general – be it raw material or an already completed product. The modes of transformation are the modes of the four causes. To them, it is necessary to add the inter-material modes of transformation practiced by the sciences, whose philosophical conceptualization is not yet achieved, least of all by the theory of the four causes. On the other hand, to this must be added the causality of the Other, be it simple (Nietzsche), or re-marked and quasi-autonomous as a kind of second principle (Heidegger, Derrida), or absolute like the ethical Other [*Autrui*] binding me and taking me hostage (Levinas). All these modes of causality are still unitary, except *perhaps?* for the scientific causalities and the ethical causality of the Other.

Transformation or production involve the *continuous* penetration of activity into raw material, the insertion of the latter into the universal flux of acting, but also the identification of acting with the raw material itself. This identification, however, is what is absolutely forbidden by the finite and inalienable structure of the drive. The latter does indeed touch the World, affecting it with a certain unilaterality that has a new content, but it cannot continue itself in the World, *as* it, cannot form a *body* with it. Unitary acting always makes a body, which it produces and which accompanies it (theoretical problematic, scientific continent, archeological episteme, desiring body without organs, eternal return of the Same, single substance of attributes, etc.). Acting, raw material, processes, and product reform a vast immanence that is transformed by relations of proximity or positions of relative functions: an entire topology of functions in the productive whole. When it is partialized or partial, when totality is only immediately reduced, such an immanence remains if not global or total, then at least unitary. Finite immanence, by contrast, that of the drive that remains in itself, does not penetrate into the World and does not reform a higher unity with it. Even if the product of ordinary acting also has finitude for essence, the World has its specific essence (the already-mixed), uncreatable by the One and thus non-transformable by the (non-)One through unitary causality. The finite subject does not alienate itself in its acting, but finite acting is not a transformation of the World the way there is a transformation of nature.

Theorem 123. *There is an absolute difference in nature between the acting subject and the World. This is what makes ordinary man subject (of) an absolute practice just as he was subject (of) an absolute science.*

We understand the pragmatics we are describing in a particularly broad sense. But it is above all its essence that is original because, as unreflective, it is incommensurate with the universal itself. The use in question cannot be the one that is invested in the causality of a matter, of an Idea or Form, or of an efficient cause, etc., but rather the sole causality capable of acting on these four causes *as they are*. Not on a particular being – this is Being or the World – but rather on the World in person or on Being as it is, on mixtures in general. Ordinary man is not definable by philosophical operations or properties: this is what makes him the bearer of absolute practice just as he was the bearer of absolute science: practice without ob-ject because it has the World itself and all the authoritarian universals as an "object," that is to say – we will explain this problem – as *occasional material*.

Instead of leaving practice in the World and defining it circularly once again, as the circle of its raw material, of its action unfolding universally, of its effect – here we experience a practice that has the World itself as an object or "raw material" and that is thus really distinct from the World. Absolute practice has the same conditions as absolute science, with one qualification: its object cannot be – the way "raw material" still is in spite of everything – a part of itself or of the practical subject. Otherwise the practical subject would transform it, but through a completely relative practice, affecting no more than a part of the World devoid of its unitary properties and alienating itself in its acting. To the contrary, we seek a practice that bears on the final unitary structures themselves, on the World or Authorities, one that bears not on a given social, political, or physical – that is, empirico-ideal – phenomenon, to the exclusion of empirico-ideal difference, but on that difference itself.

More generally, finite man is the key to an acting capable of affecting the highest Greco-occidental experience of acting, the Unity-of-Contraries, the unitary amphibology in general. An absolute practice is non-Copernican or non-worldly, it bears on the World as it is, on Revolution, etc. Ordinary man is not "stronger," more "powerful" than Revolution, whatever that word might mean. Through his finitude, he is really distinct from any Revolution, and thus is able to act upon it, instead of allowing himself be compromised, seduced, carried away by its fluxes and whirlwinds. The relation of the individual to the World is not a matter of different degrees of power, of intensity, but of *absolute difference of nature* in their respective constitutions.

This is what grounds a practice of "transformation" that is unique because it bears on *unitary mixtures* "as such," on Authorities, that is, on the aprioris of political phenomena rather than on the phenomena themselves; on the State as polito-logical difference itself rather than particularly and exclusively on such and such a phenomenon that would be one of its modes, but whose practical transformation would leave its essence intact.

With finite topics and then finite pragmatics, ordinary man possesses a science and a practice of worldly and authoritarian *essences* "as they are." Not only of the highest experiences philosophy could imagine – from which it would have to deduct itself, in this way failing to be their absolute science and practice – but also of this deduction or withdrawal itself. Non philosophical, absolute science of this relative-absolute science that philosophy will have been.

35. The Essence of Pragmatics:
(2) The Immediate Givenness of the Other

Theorem 124. *The correlate of the drive, that which corresponds to its effect or to pragmata as their real phenomenal content, is an Other, but non-positional, a Non-thetic Transcendence (of) itself (NTT).*

Having freed the finite core of all *pragmateia*, we must now free the core of its other side, the one that corresponds to *pragmata*, the effect or "finite product" of acting. What exactly does ordinary man produce when he is busy with his affairs in general, and when he transforms neither nature nor produces use values, consumable objects in general? What is the finite transcendental remainder of what we call in mechanics, as in metaphysics, an "effect"? The effect must here be distinguished from *effectivity*, which is the mixture; it is extracted from effectivity under the drive of acting and therefore no longer has the essence of mixture, but rather that of finitude. What is present in the mixture and can be extracted from it that is not the One itself or acting? Just as the One corresponds to Unity, but as not included in the already-mixed, and only corresponds to it in this form of mixture (which is the whole "second principle" and its autonomy, its uncreatable essence), it is *Non-thetic* Transcendence or the *Non-thetic* Other (=NTT) that correspond to the thetic form of the Other present in the mixture of the World. This is what acting extracts from it, but here too it only corresponds to it in the form of the almost already-mixed. Ordinary pragmatics only produces one thing: transcendence, but liberated from the form of the already-mixed; a non-positional Other, an alterity devoid of the positionality in whose service in general it is unitarily put, and from which it receives a certain benefit, metaphysical comfort, to be specific.

Theorem 125. *The Other, the immanent phenomenal givens of NTT, has a real essence, though it is regularly denied by unitary thought, which settles for fashioning an Other from common experience and requisitioning it against metaphysics.*

More and more uneasy in its unitary reduction, Western philosophy seeks in the Other – differently re-marked upon from Nietzsche to Heidegger – a resource that would allow it to appeal to the game without abandoning it. In doing so, it forgets – this is the real "forgetting" – to wonder about the mode of originary givenness of this Other, and takes it from the metaphysical game, which it must then disrupt, defer, appeal, etc. Therefore it is not only metaphysics but also its contemporary deconstructions, based on a specific, more or less accented, experience of the Other, that give themselves the Other by *assuming* it, the same way they gave themselves the rest: Unity, the Same, Difference, Being, etc., without elucidating its essence. It cannot be repeated enough, at least from the point of view of the finite subject, that unitary thoughts that appeal to the Other still engage in a simple, originally "metaphysical" technique, from which they only hope to reap the benefits or surplus values, without having first elucidated it in its real essence, but only, and after the fact, in its mere possibility.

The essence of the Other? Yes, like the rest, the Other does indeed have an essence, and that essence – a real essence – is the One. Instead of manipulating the Other and requisitioning it against any narrowly understood – that is to say, metaphysically understood – doctrine of essence, we would have had to ask ourselves what real primitive experience the finite subject can have of the Other, and how does the finite subject *really* reach it before the philosopher, with his customary brutality and shamelessness, seizes it and places it in the service of his problems and obsessions.

Instead of this scientific description of the Other in its immanent phenomenal givens, unitary thought, through mere abstraction, takes its concept of the Other from an experience that is in reality already very derived from transcendence and the transcendent, that is, from their blend, of which it merely takes photographic images that repeat the structure of worldly effectivity, whereas it should be a question of describing the real transcendental experience. Instead of the real specific essence of a concept to be legitimated transcendentally from the One as an immanent criterion, completely relative pieces of sedimented or worldly experience are abstracted as absolute, out of which an edifice is attempted to be remade, where the good architectural genie of Unity as synthesis-of-contraries, that is, the philosopher *ex machina*, is supposed to hold everything together. *Unity*, even a rational unity, when measured by the generosity of the One, is syncretism and violence, and reason is simply a process of always forced rationalization of the real confused with effectivity.

We will also invert the unitary process: instead of requisitioning it for anti-metaphysical tasks whose phenomenal givens are unelucidated, instead of simply taking it from metaphysics and only pondering its essence through its functions to the point of fatally giving up on acknowledging its essence – we will first examine how, for the ordinary subject, for finite man, an experience (of) transcendence, or rather of the Other, becomes not only possible but *real*. If this Other, thus acquired, is liable to receive determinate uses, their examination can only come afterwards. This approach, which is not functional, not "pragmatic" in the unitary sense of the word, but rather simply scientific, and above all the idea of an immediate givenness of the Other, will of course appear to unitary philosophy to be a contradiction in terms: unitary philosophy, which has always resorted to the Other, given in a mediated way, to crack, impair, trouble an immediate fetish, intentionally pre-fabricated by unitary metaphysics in the forgetting of that which could be a real experience (of) the immediate. How could it see only the problem?

206

Theorem 126. *Ordinary man makes the primitive experience of the Other from the World, but as irreducible to it. The immanence of real acting resolves this paradox.*

Against this unitary casualness, the task of a scientific thought of the real – which would abandon the philosophical bricolage of "systems," a bricolage sublimated in *play* and in *games* – is to describe how ordinary man, "deprived" of philosophy, reaches the Other itself, which he has not yet encountered in his most intimate essential life, for the first time.

Even if the essence of man is defined for its part through its "exclusion" of all transcendence, he encounters, following the World, something like "transcendence" or the Other, but probably not in the same form in which Greco-Christian philosophy thought it had recognized this Other, onto which it projected its most delirious fantasies. We do not yet know if the Other is possible and above all in what form, and following what experience it is real for the individual who entrusts himself to its experience alone. The first knowledge we have of the Other, before we are able to make it useful for tasks of alteration, destruction, deconstruction, differentiation, etc., is its absolute knowledge, not its functional use or requisition – and it is in acting, in its inalienable immanence, that we acquire it. *Without the finite individual having to go out of himself, and precisely because he does not go out of himself*, he has an immediate experience of the Other and reaches even the *immediate givens of the Other*. This paradox, which embarrasses all unitary philosophy, is resolved by real acting.

The drive, too, though finite, is not empty of material or produced effect. Indeed, its finitude is not a withdrawal. Far from withdrawing from the World or the universal processes of production, this positivity that precedes them or this precedence does not prevent it – quite to the contrary – from being a drive on . . . and from revealing a specific sphere of reality. Paradoxically, it is its finitude that warrants it being "filled." Nothing, no unity, no mediation, unifies use and the Other (or Meaning), yet the drive that innervates use nevertheless possesses a "correlate" of transcendence. Here, as before, we must learn to think without the aid of mediation, without an intermediary, without representing and representation. Finite acting does not continue in its effect, but makes that effect arise *ex mundo* in an absolute emergence that does not therefore take the form of a continuous production.

Theorem 127. *The paradox of an immediate givenness of the Other is unintelligible from the unitary point of view, which straightaway moves in the mixture of the transcendent and transcendence.*

Generally speaking, we assume that to reach something as a Transcendent, a Transcendence, an Other, the subject must identify with it, at least partially, must go out of itself and alienate itself. Of course, this is a completely vicious and crude argument of the sort that is customary with unitary philosophy: it begins by surreptitiously presuming the existence of the Other, and then constructing access to this Other. Though supposedly originary or primitive, this access is obviously nothing of the sort. The unitary process, often denounced under this form but rarely expelled in a radical manner (phenomeno*logy*, by definition, cannot overcome it as it would like), consists of amphibologically doubling existence, admitted beforehand and thus already transcendent, through the knowledge of this in itself. The Other is thus a reflected, doubled, transcendence, a cut enclosed in a unitary horizon. The transcendent and its transcendence (that is, its cut, scission, or separation) form a mixture, and thus a sort of redoubling or duplication of the one by the other. If the criterion of finite phenomenality, that is, of immediate givenness, is not satisfied, then in fact we have to dogmatically assume a transcendence that is already given towards which the subject must surpass itself, in reality coming back to it, appropriating it, but also uselessly redoubling it. The alienation of the subject in the experience of the Other becomes inevitable unless we recognize that it entails imposing an external and always somewhat onto-theo-*logical* transcendence on the subject, and in so doing missing a rigorous transcendental "genesis" of the Other. Acquired in this circular and non-rigorous way, the Other enters into the mythology of philosophical marionettes in the role of the Malicious one [*du Méchant*], who so entertains the big Greek children we have remained, and with which we identify more and more extensively in the naive hope of disrupting the traditional game.

Unitary thought cannot escape the mixture of transcendent and transcendence in order to experience a givenness of the former that does not pass through the latter. It requires finite or ordinary acting: the Non-thetic Other is no more a cut deprived of horizon than a unity deprived of scission. Non-Thetic-Transcendence (NTT) is not taken from unitary structures, but is rather extracted from them as an autonomous material.

Theorem 128. *The finite drive reveals a Transcendent-without-Transcendence, a Transcendent that was never a thing or an object; it manifests the Other in a primitive and non-posing manner.*

In reality, there is no longer a paradox once the unitary amphibology of the Other and its tricks are dispelled by finitude, which is a simplification of this situation. The paradox of an immediate givenness of the Other is resolved in the transcendental condition of reality this givenness brings with it: the drive is givenness without – unreflective – transcendence of the Transcendent; here, the Other is given in an unreflective way, which is to say, as it is. It is the immediate experience of transcendence, but which is not reflected in itself and does not redouble itself so as to be able to give itself. The drive acts without passing through an identification, be it global, specific, or even partial. It reveals its effect (NTT) without surpassing itself towards it, without being indivisible *with* it or forming a difference with it.

Unitary acting, which only acts by surpassing itself, does not reach the Other unless it is its Other and unless it is identifiable with acting. When it is not the Idea, the mechanical cause, or the End – all universals – it is the difference between acting and the Other, its effect, which serves as the ultimate, though most immediate, mediation. Conceiving of an immediation of transcendence cannot but appear contradictory. It is nevertheless an experience that *must* be real if we want to no longer think theologically or post-theologically of the *gift*, the *offering* of Being, etc.; and that is real if we think rigorously while following the guiding thread of individual finitude, here that of the drive.

How can we give NTT yet another name? For their part, deconstructions of metaphysics seek a pure transcendence (scission, withdrawal, différance), without a transcendent thing, but thus in spite of everything relative to that thing. The essence of ordinary acting is the reversal and also something other than the reversal of this transcendence-without-transcendent. It is what must be called a transcendent-without-transcendence. Not a transcendent abstractly taken from a transcendence, that is, from a separation, presuming a separation to later deny it, but in fact a non-objectivated transcendent, thus an Other, positively devoid of separation or scission in relation to the drive that reveals it. The revelatory power of the drive, we know, is not of the order of the As Such or the horizon of objectivity; it is the Other, a transcendent that never was a thing, that never was conditioned by a scission or an objectivation. Without transcending, the drive is capable of manifesting or revealing a non-posed

Transcendent. It is, immediately, the announcement of the Other and the *non-posing manifestation* of the Other, revealed *as it is* in its abruptness and blunt brutality.

The examination of the content of the Non-thetic Other must still be carried out. But we already know that because acting is not on the order of a transformation of the World, which is only an occasional material, it likewise does not produce a "finite product" of the unitary sort. Reduced to its phenomenal content, the "effect" is not the synthesis of a matter and a new form, nor a condensation, an overdetermination of forces and determinations. It is first of all a sort of reality that is utterly distinct in its turn from the drive, as the World already is. No dimension of pragmatics is continuous: the product is indeed "finite," but in the sense that there is a difference in nature between it and acting, and in the sense that it is not – any more than the World – a part or a "limit" of acting. The Other or Meaning thus revealed is not a limit of a process that it restarts, but an absolute completion. Furthermore, it is the same immediacy-without-transcendence, the same lack of a gap between the drive and the Other as between the drive and the World. It reveals the Other immediately, without having to surpass itself towards it or persist in it. Acting does not continue or complete itself in the perfection of its product: it reveals it immediately through a sort of spontaneous extraction outside of mixtures, *ex mundo*.

We must return to the problem of the Other, but henceforth in its "relation" to the World and to Authorities, and define the reality of a minoritarian "resistance" with a pragmatic rather than an immediately political nature.

36. The Essence of Pragmatics: (3) The Other, The Signal, and The Pragmatic Foundation of Communication

Theorem 129. *A science of the relations of individuals to Authorities must elaborate an a priori concept of the Other and of "resistances" that is non-empirical and sufficiently determined in its essence – an individual concept.*

We cannot, as in contemporary deconstructions, settle for resorting to an insufficiently determined experience of the Other. The scraps, remainders, margins, symptoms, etc., all the unitary forms of the Other, are *presumed-resistances* whose essence-of-resistance has not yet been elucidated or evaluated. Such transcendent resistances, authoritarian in their own way, are all Difference in general and polito-logical Difference in particular manage to produce; and through them they confirm a bit more the illusion of an authoritarian hold over individuals.

The Other, Transcendence "in general," must be examined in its real essence and not only in its mere possibility. The dual rather than the unitary problematic can recognize the right and above all the reality of anti-authoritarian resistances in general. Only it can reduce them to their finite essence in ordinary subjects without trying to empirico-logically, that is, hypothetically and merely possibly, induce the continuities of resistance (lines, parties, political or other strategies, etc.) whose authentic – that is, non-worldly, non-authoritarian – reality is merely presumed but not proven. For minoritarian resistances are not only qualitatively different than the presumed-resistances tolerated by Authorities, to which they give rein and which are necessary to their nature, which is to "function" (what would Authorities be without possible or presumed resistances?). They are first of all real.

The immanent phenomenal givens of resistances, political or ecological for example, are enclosed and hidden by the Unitary Illusion. But they alone can rigorously ground – these are examples – a transcendental politics or ecology not understood from the outset by that against which they must "struggle," not taken from transcendent phenomena, but which would be the immediate correlates of acting itself or would find their sources directly in the immanent necessity of finite pragmatics. Here, the radical subjective point of view is the only rule: it grounds an *eco-pragmatics*, for example, more real, less phantasmatic than *ecology*. To reach real human resistances, we have to begin with the finite individual and his acting rather than from what Authorities tolerate. A *minoritarian* concept of minoritarian resistance requires that we are put back into the individual structures of use and that we acquire the concept of a strictly a priori resistance, at least in its essence and finite cause, and even that this be the resistance to the World of which the *transcendental or real apriori* is capable.

Theorem 130. *The Non-thetic Other is neither the continuity nor the unity of phenomena of resistance to the World or of the margin of Authorities. It is an a priori resistance and is immediately given to ordinary acting, of which it is the correlate.*

Here, the Other is not the continuity of phenomena that would wrongly return to the sphere of Authorities and break or fracture a putative authoritarian closure. It is not the collection of phenomena of alterity that Authorities allow to escape. Authorities do not allow anything to escape, because they have the infinity of time and history to re-appropriate it. What is required instead is an acting that is already really distinct from the World so as to tear from it an ungraspable Other, irreversible in its own way and not relative to that of which it is the Other. It is the originary correlate of pragmatics, not the recollection of local facts of resistance, catastrophe, failure, which could affect Authorities and out of which it would have to be constituted. The Other is produced a priori by ordinary acting; it is not *constituted* starting from the World, Sexuality, Language, Writing, Games of Power: it is no more an unconscious than finite operativity was. The Other is so little induced from the World, so little a remainder, a reject of Authorities, that it arises *ex abrupto* from ordinary acting without having been the object of a philosophical operation that would identify with it. In general, the World is not affected by a becoming-Other that would reverse its hierarchies, but an Other-without-becoming has always bordered the World as a specific sphere of reality that does not wait for a philosophical blessing to exist.

Here, therefore, we do not approach the Other as a motor of a symptom, as *really* enclosed in authoritarian appearances, an Other we would settle for re-marking upon, re-emphasizing, re-affirming, etc. A symptomological reading of Authorities would risk being a unitary gesture (returning, for example, to an "ecological" or "political" form of the Unitary Illusion), would neglect the content of real givens that the finite subject produces starting from Authorities, though not as their form, mode, or margin. A priori but real resistance assumes a dualism. The Other is the immediate "object" of acting, it does not resist it, but it resists the World because it conveys a part of the (non-)One itself or is its practical effect. It is originarily given to the subject without being opposed to it, without passing through a scission or a fracture. And even when the subject and the Other together are opposed to the World, it is not in the mode of transcendence. We remain in the dual, not in the unitary, which would make the World a scission of the One, an alienation of the subject, a cut affecting both the subject and the World.

Theorem 131. *The Non-thetic Other is not a limitation of the World or a border imposed on Authorities. It is yet another form of unilateralization whose effect is to transform the World into a mere "support" of the Other.*

The Other is not a limitation, at once internal and external, of the World. Just as the mystical in its finitude did not limit the World, but rather rendered it unilateral, so acting and its correlate, the finite Other, do not unitarily or relative-absolutely limit the World, but rather impress upon it a certain form of unilaterality that we will analyze under the title of *support* or of *signal*. The Other no doubt maintains a certain relation to the World, but it is not relative to it, at least not in its essence, which here is still individual finitude. Real critique does not consist of limiting the unlimited and thus reviving Authorities through an authoritarian limitation of their power. The transcendental or real finitude that we contrast to infinite authoritarian processes is completely different from a limitation from without, or even from within. Critique is only real if it proceeds by uni-lateralization rather than by limitation. It allows whatever has illimitation for its principle to develop, but it has already refused to enter into this game for its benefit, a precedence that is sufficient to irreversibly de-rive the infinite itself, which draws its *hybris* from unitary philosophy.

This has two consequences. If the Other no longer main-tains an ambiguous relation of interiority/exteriority to the World, then the World ceases to be a center or a point of view in order to become the mere support of the Other. And if critique no longer takes the form of a delimitation, border, or closure, of philo-centrism for example, if it is no longer an interface or a connection, this is because without being an exit out of . . ., it *is* immediately the exit as it is, the leap itself, the pure possible that is no longer relative to that towards which or from which it would spring. Pragmatics produces a specific order of reality, of *non-thetic possibles*, from effectivity as occasional material, which is as a result transcendentally reduced to the state of support or signal. Far from being a common border between Authorities and minorities, NTT is an absolute, non-thetic closure of the thetic sphere par excellence, the World. It is positive critique that does not pass through the process of a limit but rather of a dualysis, this time in the form of a duality (indeed, a dualism) of Meaning and Signal, which extends that of the dual and which is not moreover an analysis of the symptom, which is always unitary, as before.

Theorem 132. *When it is put in the service of a philosophical opera-tivity, the Other acts through Reversal and Displacement, which are its two principal unitary effects. When it is acquired originally from ordinary acting, it neither reverses nor displaces Unity: it uni-lateral-izes in its own way.*

213

The contemporary identification of the philosophical project with the Other presumed to be given comes back to affect the Other with a relativity in relation to a logos, a center, a closure, etc., and therefore to manipulate it, to put it in the service of a *unitary operation of reversal or displacement*. The Other is functionally required in unitary thought, serving a preliminary and above all transcendent philosophical operativity. Instead of being the correlate of an ordinary operativity, it is used *against* identity or the center and therefore *against itself* because it is first inscribed in this same center where it is presumed to be present in a latent state: from this comes its use as a motor for a Reversal or as a factor in a Displacement. The reversal is nothing other than the auto-positional continuity of the Other; displacement is its over-positional continuity. These are the two operations under which the Other is unitarily requisitioned and falsified, deprived of its finite non-thetic essence and blended with the World, forced to receive the form of the mixture.

In reality, Transcendence can be non-thetic, but then it only exists through acting, even if it needs the support of the World, because it is henceforth devoid of its *position* in Being or in mixtures. It does not continuously leave Being under its own powers, in reality the powers of Being, where it would still be caught. The Non-thetic Other, being no longer relative to the World or to Unity and no longer the object of a position, can thus no longer announce itself in the form of a Reversal of this Unity ("logocentric," for example), which would preserve positionality and remain a continuous unfolding from hierarchy or from already reversed Unity, the mixture auto/hetero-affecting itself and working on itself. To the contrary, if the finite subject cannot reverse mixtures, it can dualyze them, that is, extract the Other from these mixtures without remainder; for their part, such mixtures cease to be a position so as to become mere support. NTT does not transcend *in relation* to the World, it arises beside it, and this is already saying too much: no topology here. The Other is directly extracted from Authorities as a specific instance of reality that no longer maintains a relation of seats or positions in the World, but finds in the latter a mere support or signal. It leaves it absolutely without proceeding by a cut on Unity or a transcendence in relation to it: it *is* straightaway this non-redoubled transcendence . . . Dualysis is not an analysis; it is the dual absolution of the lysis, the only "operation" still possible on mixtures as they are.

The Other thus unilateralizes the World in a certain way, without reversing it in any way, and even, properly speaking, without displacing it.

And this is not an operating that assumes the co-operation of the philosophical will: it is the real itself. The finite Other is the way to measure the World against the real, by still taking as real the need the World has to be evaluated and measured.

Theorem 133. *Ordinary practice transforms the World into a mere support or signal for the Other, a remainder of Authorities necessary to the Other. It is a form of uni-lateralization, not an operation of natural or industrial transformation; it grounds the reality of human communication.*

Finite pragmatics does not concern nature or matter, but rather the World, its mixtures, and its Authorities. It is a "dualyzable" material whose final finite product is double: NTT or the possibles, on the one hand – what we will soon call meaning – and on the other, the signal or support function. NTT is produced simultaneously with the practical transformation of the World into signal or support on the basis of the affection of the subject by the World. It is this second aspect of pragmatics that must now be described, once it is substituted for the unitary operations of Reversal and Displacement: with the system of non-thetic signal/meaning, the individual possesses the real phenomenal givens of any possible communication.

The mixture thus becomes support or signal for NTT. It is what remains of the mixture for NTT and from the point of view of NTT; it is that by which the mixture is necessary for it. It is not, strictly speaking, broken or dissolved; the extraction of the Other – of meaning or its real experience – leaves it in some sense intact, at least in its intimate constitution. It is not broken up = analyzed as mixture, separated into two sides according to length. Instead, it becomes a signal *for . . .* meaning and *from* meaning, and from this angle it is no longer an auto-reflective mixture and self-mastery; its essence is also unreflective and devoid of positionality.

Individu-a-lity absolutely and everywhere suppresses – as (non-) One, *non* (of) the One – thetic or positional characteristics. It is the same thing as dualysis: it volatilizes the Unitary Illusion and restores the terms back to their solitude. It is not a natural and/or industrial transformation; the One projects its immediate (non-) on the World, stripping it, at least for the finite individual, of its form-as-mixture more than a merely presumed Other would do. This is also something different from a suspension, a nihiliation, or even an alteration, which remain unitary operations. It is also not a topological displacement, unless we understand that between the Other and its signal or support there is a transcendental remainder of any possible topological neighborhood.

The signal is the first appearance of the condition of reversibility in an experience of pure irreversibility, or at least in an experience that has its essence in pure irreversibility; for this reason, it is the first and minimal limitation of uni-lateralization – the possibility of communication. The transformation of the World into a support, a practical form of acting, is not as radical as its mystical form: less irreversible than that of the One itself. It is still a matter of a setting-aside, in the form of a reduction to the functions of signal-support that come to determine the already emplaced World. But that the World is finally recognized as occasional material of NTT indicates a "limitation" of its unilateralization: even across distance without return and de-distancing without proximity that affect it, it can nevertheless act as a signal and thereby give rise to the first communication.

Nevertheless, it does not serve as a signal for the determination of the finite subject itself in its essence, but only for its acting and the effect of that acting. Further, the functions of occasional material, and then of support-signal, still do not amount to a reciprocal determination of the Other, forever precluded by the finitude of the Other, but rather to a specific contingency of pragmatics, that is, of a mode of the (non-)One that is only activated according to the World and *for it*.

Finally, Authorities in general intervene in three ways and three times in a minoritarian thought: as affection of man in an authoritarian mode, simultaneously internal and external, immanent and transcendent; this is the irreducible given, without which unitary philosophy would not have been able to constitute itself and deploy its illusion. Then, as givens in the "chora," in the mode of uni-laterality of which ordinary mysticism is capable. And finally, as signal for ordinary pragmatics, a signal that develops out of the preceding state of "quasi-suspending" of Authorities, and that explains that Authorities induce a minoritarian action "against" themselves. But the reduction of Authorities as support or signal of NTT returns to recognize in them, for the finite individual himself, a real function and a necessary intervention.

Theorem 134. *The (non-thetic) Other and the World (support) no longer main-tain unitary relations, that is to say, relations. They are only terms or immediate givens devoid of the relations (in reality unintelligible) that we habitually set between them.*

What has happened? As if the mixture of the Other and the universal horizon had split or dissociated dually: on one side, an Other that no longer opens a horizon to be grasped once more by it; on the other, a support that is no longer the effect of an opening or a spread out horizon, but rather an inert place, without becoming and without life. Horizon-term, deprived of relation to the Other, become in-itself. The function-support is only the transcendental index of a necessary passage of all pragmatics through the affect of the World. And the Other is only a bare transcendence, without relation to support, save to *immediately* assume it without any relation, mediation, or continuity.

Finally, the Non-thetic Other is not an Other inserted into Being, a factor in reversal, nor is it an Other abstractly absolutized outside of all relation to position or to Being: it remains "relative," but only to a support. Here we break the ontological circle that imprisoned the Other, but without abstractly breaking all relation to Being. The Other is not that which cracks the I *or* renders it thoroughly responsible, denudes it, numbs it, etc. – two contemporary solutions that are opposed in a certain sense. It is indeed a cut, but without analysis, a way of numbing the World through and through but without rendering it responsible. It is that which transforms the World into a signal, and this signal function – communication in its most irreducible phenomenal givens – is the final remainder of responsibility, the effect of a special recurrence of the Other on mixtures which, nevertheless, themselves no longer transcend towards or even as the Non-thetic Other. The signal is the signal of acting only because it is the signal *for* acting. More precisely, it is a signal for-the-Other, but its signification, which is not empirical or mechanistic but rather transcendental, is fully constituted by acting alone. The dual was already transcendental straightaway, even while including affection by the World as it is: the individual can only reach the World through the individual conditions of the (non-)One that are at once mystical and pragmatic. The World no longer intervenes into the practical dualism except as a function-signal or a support: it is not – any more than the One alone – the guiding point of view. So much so that the Other, NTT, is what remains of both the One and authoritarian mixtures. It is not a mode of the World, even if it is necessary to pass through the World to reach it.

It is of course impossible to prevent the unitary illusion from endlessly reconstituting itself and drawing its forces from this resurgent abyss of the *non-(One)* that desires its autonomy. Authorities are an unfathomable evil, an infinite evil of circularity and Unity, of the unitary and specular undecidable wrong. It is against these that individuals struggle, transforming them into a mere signal of the possibles or of the meaning that they extract from them. In this way, individuals save from the necessity of the World what can be saved of it for them and by them. This struggle is the "pragmatic" foundation of all communication.

This clarifies the "relations" of Unity and the Other. The Other has no foothold in Being or in the World, which contest it, but their contestation of the Other makes a system with it from their point of view alone.

There are no longer these *unintelligible* relations contemporary thinkers place between Unity and the Other, unintelligible because the Other is not grounded in its essence but simply requisitioned. The finite individual acts on the World by producing the Other: this is how their duality is respected. The mere hetero-critique of Unity by the Other-in-Unity, their interminable games, are eliminated by the real or individual *Krisis*. The essence of real critique is not itself critique, it is practice, and it residualizes the World to the state of a mere signal.

Theorem 135. *Dualism is an experience of the autonomy of "terms" prior to their relation of Difference or Contradiction, and the condition of the genesis of any possible relation, in particular of the Unity-of-Contraries or the thwarted pairs of philosophy. This is the essence of the communication of which philosophy is a unitary mode.*

The elucidation of the unreflective essence of the Other renders useless any recourse to forms of the unity-of-contraries, to a neutral and transcendent element of synthesis. These are modes of the unitary solution; they proceed from exclusion to Difference and resolved Contradiction. The dual, then duality, and finally dualism, do not restore these types of unity, but rather allow "contraries," "sides," or "terms" to live freely, outside of any relation of analysis or synthesis. The final dualism is the resolution of the initial dual, its effect or its real content, the point of view that justifies the dual, that is, the resistance of the World – but a point of view that is transcendental or for the individual. The Other is the way in which the One admits the existence of the World and of the *non(-One)*.

From the subject to the Other, from the Other to the World, from the subject to the World, there is the same unreflective essence, but not the same relation. The subject and the Other practically refuse the World, which they resist, but the subject does not repel the Other, which is its correlate; as we saw, the subject gives it in an immediate way and without "resisting" it (the subject resists the World through it, which is completely different), since the One "inhabits" all these forms regardless. The (non-)One and the non(-One) are not forces in equilibrium in the Other; they do not share a single field of reality or even maintain

218

relations of difference: the dual definitively disallows these solutions. The signal and the Other, two terms that require each other, form a pure duality, but without returning through some sort of continuity from one *to* the other. No transcendence, here, either of the support towards the Other or of the Other towards the support: the signal is the transcendental remainder of the necessity of transcendence; the Other is the transcendental remainder of transcendence itself. This is duality insofar it has the One itself, and not some unity of the gap, as the essence of both terms. This is the recognition of what unitary thought has always left unelucidated in its essence or has sometimes denied in the Judaic forms of the Other: that the Other is never an autonomous reality, a sufficient and primary domain, but that it is "relative" nevertheless: not to the support, because the support or the fact that there is such a function is in itself already the recognition of this relativity.

The support or the signal is thus the residual transcendental function of relation as indivisible unity, the final trace of any possible relation – any communication. When we strip the relation of its ontological flesh, it does not remain Difference, at which contemporary thinkers stop, but rather the support-signal, purged by the One and the acting that ensues from it of all its metaphysical determinations, circular and unitary. Perhaps with the Other and the support it is a question of the real non-philosophical kernel of what Greco-contemporaries call *Difference* and even *Différance*, the non-unitary phenomenal content, an experience that is already or once more unitary. However positive it might be, Difference is in fact still a negative or quasi-negative interpretation of indivisible duality. It always proceeds from the one and the other term, aiming at their indivision only relatively (and negatively) to each of them or to their mixture. By contrast, here we witness the entirely positive genesis of this duality, in which the essence of the indivisible precedes the experience of terms, which are not thought from their unitary mixture and which there gain a non-thetic status.

Theorem 136. *The Unitary Illusion, in its meager reality, is legitimated by the Non-thetic Other or by pragmatics.*

There is a dualist history of the Unitary Illusion. Its mystical and then pragmatic dualysis push it from the state of a contingent fact to the state of (relative) necessity. The latter assumes the point of view of the Other, which allows forgetting to appear by unilateralizing it as it is.

The pragmatic point of view is the culmination of the critique of the Unitary Illusion. We must repeat about it what was said about its mystical critique: in a sense, the Illusion remains unassailable and resurgent, it combines with the World. But it is pragmatics that allows us to understand (in a unilateralizing and thus critical-real mode) that it is pegged to the World, is as indestructible as the World, and above all that it must continue because the World is required as a signal of the Other, and that this function is the ultimate real condition of the illusion. The forgetting of the Other by Authorities and the unitary repression of the non-thetic form of transcendence are certainly real in the sense that their cause will not be suppressed in the revelation of the Other as it is outside of its repression, because it will receive – this will be its own truth – this function as support. The World is not only the occasional material of ordinary practice, it is also *that for which* the latter acquires a necessity (even if its essence comes to it from elsewhere, that is, from the One), and therefore becomes a support of the Other. This was not the case in the first mode of the (non-)One, for which the World was a mere occasion and no more, and did not become a support of the finite place. If there is a reality of the non(-One) or of the authoritarian denial of the One, a reality different from that of the One, it is the reality that the Other makes comprehensible. It is NTT, which is *really* repressed by the non(-One) and which legitimates after the fact the Unitary Illusion, or at least the meager reality of this illusion.

Theorem 137. *Even partially legitimated by practice, the Unitary Illusion is not constituent of the Other in the sense of a unitary conditioning. The Non-thetic Other is not an unconscious and does not result in symptoms.*

However real the Unitary Illusion is here in relation to its hallucinatory vacuity that is denounced by the One, it is not yet and never will be the unitary reality of symptom. The pragmatic *as it is* – the signal function – appears to be somewhat similar to a *deferred action* because it assumes in its prior conditions the occasional material of the World, to which it retroactively gives meaning and truth; but it does not have its reality – it is not a symptom to be analyzed. Repression is not simply denounced as an empty misunderstanding of reality and of the object; it is indeed as repression and illusion that it is unilateralized, that is, recognized in its "positive" reality, but strictly insofar as a dualism allows. Instead, there is a reduction of the Unitary Illusion itself as regards the Other, both its destruction – insofar as it negates the non-thetic form of transcendence and ordinary acting in general, interpreting them as an unconscious – and its reduction to its core of truth, which is the mere support. The World does not acquire this reality when the Other is already produced and as extracted from it; rather, it is the practical production of the Other outside of the World, as of its material, that makes it clear in the "deferred action" to which practical unilateralization is susceptible that there was indeed an illusion that misrecognized itself "as such." The function of signal, elucidated in its truth, does not indicate a reconstitution of *unity*. The World is only the signal of the Other, what remains of the occasional material when transcendental acting is applied to the latter as a finite drive can do – and a *support* does not reciprocally determine, in a reversible manner, the Other with which it maintains this lesser relation.

Even if we can admit that there is indeed an originary repression of the Other, it no longer takes the same form as an unconscious. The Other is unreflective; it is a finite Transcendence and not a biological unconscious, nor even a logical or logico-linguistic one, as in certain contemporary thinkers in whose work it therefore remains reflected and gives way to a reversal, a displacement, etc. Accordingly, the worldly support of the Other cannot claim to co-constitute the Other in its essence as is necessarily the case, in spite of appearances, in the relations of consciousness and the bio-*logical* unconscious, a position of the problem, which, deployed in its real phenomenal content, still implies a unitary reciprocity and not the heterogeneity and irreversibility of the Other and the World-support.

37. Meaning and the Rigorous Science of the Unitary Structures of the World

Theorem 138. *The parallelism of meaning and logico-linguistic signification is broken by meaning as non-thetic correlate of use; the symbolic is grounded in the pragmatic rather than the inverse.*

Is meaning the use of a word or thing, their insertion within the calculation of determinate rules, their continuation, and their unity-of-slippage? But use is not only an immanent givenness of meaning: as immanent, it itself has a truth more foundational than meaning. Rather than grounding meaning in logic or extending it beyond logic towards language and everyday practice, it is instead a change of terrain that is needed to rigorously set out the problem of its production. Human activities are "signifying" and "understanding," but this performativity must be freed from its unitary conditions and the transcendent logico-linguistic model. The parallelism of meaning and logico-linguistic signification must be broken and meaning subordinated to truth. Meaning does not belong to the finite essence of truth, but rather en-sues irreversibly from it. Contemporary thought, believing that it is liberating itself from logical restrictions, surrenders to linguistic signification and carries out a nihilistic outburst of meaning (of use, of practice, etc.); it thinks it solves its problems by elevating meaning to the state of a solution, when it is an entirely terminal product. The unconditional primacy of truth over meaning does not indicate dogmatism, but rather – and this is a nuance that is barely accessible to contemporary thinkers – science. The reversal of the real order in favor of meaning only expresses the will to self-dissolution of unitary metaphysics.

It is not enough to say that meaning is not the fact or the reference that corresponds to the proposition, that it is the product of a logical calculation of diverse rules. This merely moves from one extreme to the other and misses an experience whose specificity is thus reduced to the mere overdetermined conditions of existence of a proposition, conditions of use that lose meaning as the immediate and specific correlate of "finite" use. This confuses meaning and signification, copies meaning from signification, reduces it to effects of totality, that is, to language, which nevertheless does not belong to the essence of man. It is obvious that language is the power and the element of ontology, that its use defines the ideal essences around empirical things, but this is still a mixture of meaning and signification. Once more the logico-linguistic game is raised to the condition of a final and unsurpassable apriori, as though the rules of use produced the real essence of things. These are external philosophical entities, thwarted by ordinary or finite use, which is already an apriori for the language game itself, a priori evidently real or non-thetic and not only ideal and possible like that of the philosophers.

More generally, the passage from the symbolic to the pragmatic, the rigorous transcendental foundation of the first in the second, requires an overhaul of the pragmatic and its radical distinction from the symbolic. The pragmatic is not copied from the symbolic any more than use is understood according to the privileged model of the use of language. It precedes it and determines it in its own way in the last instance. Neither the symbolic nor symbolico-pragmatic mixtures belong to the essence of the finite individual. Otherwise, the individual or the real would still be an effect of a "language game" and an avatar of logos. The refusal of a transcendent instance, anthropo-logical for example, in which symbolic power would be anchored, cannot hold for the One, which is not transcendent, though it certainly holds for the symbolic, which remains transcendent in relation to the One (ultimate transcendence of the "signifier," of the "sign," of "writing," etc.). Mixtures such as "language games" are determined in the last instance by finite individuals, which are no longer philosophical doubles of the real. Of course, nothing precedes the symbolic except for precedence itself or the real in its finitude, capable of "determining in the last instance." "Ordinary" pragmatics, in the rigorous and scientifically grounded meaning of the word, is that which decides the symbolic itself, the unitary veil par excellence.

Theorem 139. *Non-unitary meaning is the non-positional core of logos; from the point of view of effectivity, it is a manifold of unreflective and sterile possibles.*

We remember that pragmatics is not an effective inter-vention into the World, that it does not transform a raw material according to artisanal and industrial models of production. Instead, it produces a specific order of reality – the Other or Meaning – that leaves effectivity unaltered except for its transformation as "support." The laying out of the essence of *theoria* leads to the laying out of the essence of praxis and meaning. Reduced to its phenomenal content, not blended with theory, practice is not a positional transformation of matter, etc., but rather a production of non-thetic or unreflective communication. It is unsurprising that the possibles that form the manifold of meaning have a certain sterility, a sterility that does not bar all transformation but is discernible in relation to unitary modes of transformation. Just as the production of the Non-thetic Other in general was not at all a metaphysical or technological transformation, putting into play a causality other than that of the last instance, so also meaning is not a refined form of signification, continuous with it, the finite product of an idealizing linguistic operation. Ordinary man does indeed produce meaning and the possibles, but he is not a transformer of nature, a "worker" or a "producer" – *homo faber*, technician, engineer, inventor, consumer, etc. These are subjects of the four metaphysical causes and their combinations, already projects of the World, which are deployed in the veil of the Unitary Illusion, at least insofar as these figures claim to exhaust the essence of the individual.

If use does not produce meaning directly or continuously, and if meaning does not extend a transformation of raw material, then what is it? It is the result of the sort of contradiction that exists between the non(-One) and the (non-)One because the uncontrollable resistance

223

of the non(-One), despite the illusory character of this resistance as regards the One itself, ends in the emergence of pragmatics, then of the correlate of pragmatics, its "effect," which must retroactively legitimate both authoritarian resistance and the resistance of the finite subject to it. If it therefore nevertheless registers unitary logos, at least under the name of support-signal, then *"finite" meaning will be the non-thetic form of logos, logos in an unreflective or non-positional state, the non-objective correlate of pragmatics.* The performativity of unitary logos ("position" and its contemporary modes of critique) has its condition of real possibility in a non-thetic performativity that produces meaning outside-position, a "non-positional logos," as it were. Pragmatics straightaway dissolves the mixture of the "logic of meaning." Meaning is the Other of the World, and this non-thetic meaning forms a veritable *genetic code* for Authorities in general, for universal attributes, and for the World. Through it, all thought, beyond its essence however, is thought (of) the Other and is animated around non-thetic possibles devoid of effectivity.

Theorem 140. *Non-thetic meaning or the real apriori is the rigorous scientific – and not philosophical-circular – point of view on the World and Authorities. The unitary as it is is the object of a science when that science is no longer itself unitary, but rather "expanded" to non-positional or alogical apriories.*

We seek the scientific criterion of the *unitary* that allows us to say in a justified way what is mixed or authoritarian, etc. Is there such an invariant of Authorities or the World? And from where, on what foundation, will we reach such an invariant? And will we have the right to use it?

   The difficulty is that a rigorously scientific criterion *of* philosophy, *for* it, cannot itself be philosophical, just as a criterion of the World cannot be worldly. No philosophical process, precisely unitary, can help us identify this absolute invariant with certainty and preserve it as such. No doubt because it is unitary, philosophy cannot "pose" the unitary rigorously and without restriction, and a philosophy in particular cannot be declared unitary automatically and with certainty on the basis of philosophical arguments. *This is because these are circular and can never assure us of anything without immediately denying or limiting it, in particular without straightaway affirming that the unitary is also the multiple, etc., without falling into aporias and the unities-of-contraries.* The absolute knowledge of the unitary or the philosophical must be scientific rather than philosophical. This is why the true unitary is only the non-thetic meaning that gives it as an apriori for the unitary. After finite topics, non-positional meaning is the key to the rigorous science of Authorities.

Ordinary pragmatics is one part of the science of man. It bears upon the relations-of-meaning of finite man to the World or Authorities. The classical problem of pragmatics – what is the meaning of a word? how is a sign made to work? should it function or signify? what is it to understand? etc. – is defined too narrowly and links pragmatics to transcendent authoritarian conditions, including the conditions of language. An "expanded" pragmatics applies to all phenomena of existence as soon as they relate to the World *as it is*, which is not the correlate of use but its occasional material. It frees from it the real apriori as Non-thetic Other, that is to say, meaning. But the expansion of the World to language and to unitary philosophy (to Being, to Difference, etc.) entails that meaning be no longer an authoritarian universal, the internal relation to a totality, but rather *the non-universal, though a priori, relation of the finite individual to universals*. This relation is only possible if meaning itself ceases to be a unitary-universal so as to become what we call "expanded," which it becomes by being non-thetic or positively a-logical.

Meaning or the *expanded* point of view does not in its turn unify a manifold. It is meaning *for* the manifold-unity of the World (of philosophies, for example) and for all philosophical aporias, without for this reason being unitary in its turn and surveying a field of Authorities. *The expanded* is reduced from the universal to its singular or finite essence, anterior to that mixture of the universal-and-singular which is the unitary universal in person.

As soon as it is elucidated in its own condition of possibility, essence, rather than a language game, is an unreflective transcendental experience. It is no longer acquired as a mode of unity, a process of unification for a manifold. The condition of plurality as such is not a higher synthesis of plurality, but that which can let it be. The transeidetism or sureidetism of contemporary thinkers renews only the unitary experience of essence and meaning. But real thought does not go from ideal crystallized transcendences towards a more fluid eidos, it comes from the One; it does not reduce, it determines in the last instance. Real essence, the ingredient of the rigorous science of the World, is therefore not an additional level in universality, an Idea or a regularity even higher than those that are known to philosophy. Determination in the last instance, individual causality, is the sole content, modulated in various ways, of this science, and it is an absolutely singular content once and for all. Finitude is a causality that no longer proceeds along universal paths, precisely because it affects in an unreflective or individual way everything that appears as denying it, as non(-One), and then determines it at the same time as support, as a unitary or authoritarian universal. The science of man thus becomes, in its pragmatic aspect, a "universal" though non-unitary science of communication.

The "expanded" point of view is the point of view established by the One. Its non-ob-jective "object" is the *as it is* (meaning and no longer topics) of unitary forms, the special invariance of the circle, the only way an infinite circle can become an invariant and the only way a philosophy can, in a scientifically justified way, be declared "unitary." It is meaning and the transcendental aprioris that allow Authorities to be definitively totalized, the World to be gathered in a non-worldly way, for unitary philosophy to be extra-territorialized, to establish something other than a mere "perspective" on Totalities, to obtain knowledge from them without being included in them and without going around in their circle. Unitary structures in general cannot think themselves scientifically, but only reflect themselves circularly: only non-thetic, a-logical meaning is the scientific knowledge of unitary structures and of Authorities. It is *expanded* because, on the basis alone of its origin as the correlate of finite use, it is absolute non-circular knowledge, for example of metaphysics *and* of its deconstructions, of classical authoritarian invariants and unitary forms of the Other. The expanded point of view enables a unitary paradigm to be freed from the World and Philosophy and legitimated as it is. Left to itself, it dissolves, is constrained, and sinks into the nothingness of a bad empirical plurality as soon as it wants to think itself as unitary, because its reflection can only oscillate from its affirmation to its impossibility, from Unity to Multiplicity (of "Philosophy" or of the World). Only finite meaning is the science of the unitary *as it is*, whose expansion is enough to make it the condition of possibility. We cannot exceed the unitary while preserving it *as it is*, without dissolving it in its own inconsistency, its circles, its thetic operations, except through the *expanded* or meaning as real apriori. Only this allows us to speak in a justified and rigorous way about the unitary, and to discern in rational logos more than an event, even an ideal one, more than an a priori fact: a term in an irreducible duality. The World and Authorities (Language, Economy, Politics, Sexuality, etc.) are thus legitimated as objects of a rigorous science of man.

NOTES

1 For the distinction between individuel and individual, see the Translators' Introduction. [Translators' note]

2 *Arrière-monde* is the French translation of Nietzsche's *Hinterwelt*, which the Cambridge University Press translation of *Thus Spoke Zarathustra* renders as "hinterworld." See Friedrich Nietzsche, *Thus Spoke Zarathustra*, trans. Adrian Del Caro (Cambridge: Cambridge University Press, 2006), 20-2. [Translators' note]

3 Friedrich Nietzsche, *Beyond Good & Evil: Prelude to a Philosophy of the Future*, trans. Walter Kaufmann (New York: Vintage, 1989), 72. [Translators' note]

4 For the distinction between individuel and individual, see the translators' introduction. [Translators' note]

5 In French, this sentence revolves around the preposition *à* and its variants (*au, aux*, etc.). For example, "thrown-into-the-World" is *jetés-au-monde*, *à-l'Être* is "into Being," and so on. While all of these variations on the French preposition *à* are here rendered with the English preposition "into," the reader should be aware that *à* carries other meanings in French, many of which are in play here, including in, to, towards, and by. [Translators' note]

6 The French term *né-untralisent*, translated here as "nihil-utralize," is a portmanteau of two preceding words: *néantiser* (nihilate) and *neutralisent* (neutralize). [Translators' note]

7 What we have translated as "brushing aside with the back of the hand" is in French *écarter d'un revers de main*. While the latter phrase does indeed carry the meaning to "brush aside with the back of the hand," the French verb *écarter* on its own can mean "to brush aside," "to distance," "to move away," "to dismiss," "to rule out," and more. When the French verb *écarter* is repeated in the passages that follow, we have, whenever possible, translated it with variations on "to brush aside" in order to preserve the semantic cluster, but the reader is advised to keep in mind the additional French meanings of *écarter*. [Translators' note]

8 The phrase in French is "On écarte d'un *revers de main*." In what follows, we have translated *revers* simply as "back," but the reader should always hear

227

"back" with the full weight of the original "back of the hand" behind it. [Translators' note]

9 The phrase "the 'end of non-receiving'" in the original French is "la 'fin de non-recevoir,'" which has both colloquial and legal meanings. Colloquially, it means "refusal," but Laruelle here is drawing on its legal meaning, which corresponds roughly to a "plea in bar" in English law, that is, a plea that undermines the plaintiff's right to maintain his or her lawsuit, for example, a prior agreement. Because the phrase "the end of non-receiving" is relatively empty in English, the reader should keep in mind the weight of the French original. [Translators' note]

10 Obviously, it is from this rigorous experience of the (non-)One as unilateralizing sidelining rather than as negation that the *not* [ne...pas] we use to describe individuals and their relations to the World must be understood. It is a question of putting the unitary paradigm in its place, of rendering it unilateral or of determining it in the last instance. It would be absurd to claim to negate it. [Author's note]

11 The French for "It is a 'nihil-uniting' ... rather than a nihil-being" is "C'est un 'né-untir' ... plutôt qu'un né-entir." Both terms – *né-untir* and *né-entir* – play on the verb *néantir*, which we render into English as "nihilation." Cf. endnote 6. [Translators' note]

12 The general program of an absolute or transcendental science of man was outlined in the Introduction. This Section V resumes the part of this project constituted by Authorities, the World, the State, etc. [Author's note]

13 The French "*au*-Monde," which we have here translated into English as "*to*-the-World," is normally rendered in the text as "in-the-world," with an implied reference to Heidegger's famous phrase, *In-der-Welt-sein* or in English, "being-in-the-world." However, the French preposition *à* and its variants (*au, aux,* etc.) also carries the meaning of "to" – as in "a relation of the World to the One." [Translators' note]

14 Reading "le rapport transcendantal du logos au réel" for "le rapport transcendantal du logos réel." [Translators' note]

15 In the previous two sentences, the preposition *à* (or *au*) is rendered in several different ways – as "towards," "to," and "in." This is in part dictated by the fact that the expression *être-au-monde* is the traditional French translation of Heidegger's *In-der-Welt-sein*, which in English is "being-in-the-world." The original French reads "le rapport *à* ... (être-au-monde)." [Translators' note]

ANALYTICAL TABLE OF CONTENTS

philosophy's resentment against the World. Real critique has no
stakes: the real is not at stake.

foundation of communication. Meaning/Signal system: real
phenomenal givens of all possible communication. Dual and dualism:
genesis of duality. Finitude of terms or their "autonomy" before
the Unity-of-Contraries. The Other partially legitimates the Unitary
Illusion.

Breaking the parallelism of meaning and logico-linguistic signification.
The pragmatic and the symbolic. The scientific criteria of the unitary
and the philosophical cannot be unitary or philosophical. From the
unitary to the "expanded": non-thetic meaning as expanded criterion
of the unitary. Authorities, legitimated as object of rigorous science of
man.

INDEX

237

and ordinary pragmatics 164, 170, 191
of uni-laterality 124
transcendental unity 95
transversality, and uni-laterality 52, 119
truth
  and meaning 222
  see also transcendental truth

unary
  and the one 65–6
  unary/unitary distinction 61–3, 67–8
the unconscious
  and the finite drive 201–2
  and the individual 46–7
  and ordinary pragmatics 196
  and the other 220, 221
  and the unitary illusion 96, 102
uni-city 66
uni-laterality 47–55
  and absolute science 146, 149, 151–2
  and asymmetry 47–8, 49
  and authorities 86
  and bilaterality 48, 51
  and determination in the last instance 33, 34, 53–5, 128–9
  and the forgetting of the essence of the one 55–7
  and the individual 46–7
  and logocentrism 52–3
  and minoritarian thought 117–19
  minorities and authorities 69, 71, 73
  the (non-)one 93
  and the non-thetic other 212–16
  and nothing-but-minoritarian thought 35
  and the one 49, 50–1, 52, 54, 55–6, 79, 118
  and ordinary pragmatics 163, 192
  and the other 213–15
  phenomenal content of 117–24
  and the real 51–3
  and real critique 139
  and reversibility 47–8, 51, 55–6, 213–14, 215–16
  transcendental truth of 124

of the world 50, 51, 54, 110
  see also as it is
unitary ideal, and man as finite or ordinary individual 10
unitary illusion 29, 64–5, 78, 93–105, 124
  as hallucination 99–105, 134, 140–1
  and ordinary pragmatics 172, 179, 188–9
  essence of 211, 212, 215, 217–8, 219–21
  meaning 228
  possibility of 93–6
  and real critique 131, 132–3, 134–5, 137–8, 140–2, 144
  transcendental nature of 96–9
  and the unitary transcendental deduction 160
unitary paradigm
  and ordinary pragmatics 171–3
  and transcendental naiveté 17–20
unitary philosophy/thought
  and absolute science 147, 148–9, 155–7
  and authorities 85, 92
  critique of topology 112–13
  critique of the unitary transcendental deduction 159–62
  and the expanded point of view 226
  and the finite subject 107, 109
  and the individual 39, 77
  metaphysics 222
  and the (non-)one 124–6
  and non-thetic meaning 224–6
  and the one 44–5
  and ordinary pragmatics 190, 213
    the finite drive 200–2
  and the other 205–6
  and performativity 182–3
  and real critique 133, 135, 142–4
    pragmatics as 163–5, 167
  resistance of individuals to 121–2
  topology 112–14
  transcendental truth and the one 60–1
  and uni-laterality 52
  of use 173–5
  see also Greco-unitary philosophy
unitary resistance to the one 78–9

249